Dynamite Entertainment Presents

S0-BSJ-964

The BOYS ™

BUTCHER BAKER CANDLESTICKMAKER

It should not be assumed from the narration late in episode two that the battle for Mount Harriet was an easy affair for the British attackers; in fact it was anything but. Like the rest of the Falklands War it was a desperate struggle in wretched conditions against an often determined enemy, and it is to the soldiers, sailors and airmen of the Falklands Task Force- and in particular the Paratroopers and Royal Marines of 3 Commando Brigade- that this story is respectfully dedicated.

The BOYS™

volume ten:
BUTCHER, BAKER, CANDLESTICKMAKER

Written by:
GARTH ENNIS
Art and cover by:
DARICK ROBERTSON
Lettered by:
SIMON BOWLAND
Colored by:
TONY AVIÑA
Issue covers by:
DARICK ROBERTSON & TONY AVIÑA
The Boys created by:
GARTH ENNIS & DARICK ROBERTSON

Collects issues one through six of the mini-series,
The Boys: Butcher, Baker, Candlestickmaker, originally
published by Dynamite Entertainment.

Trade Design by: JASON ULLMEYER

DYNAMITE ENTERTAINMENT
NICK BARRUCCI   •   PRESIDENT
JUAN COLLADO   •   CHIEF OPERATING OFFICER
JOSEPH RYBANDT   •   EDITOR
JOSH JOHNSON   •   CREATIVE DIRECTOR
RICH YOUNG   •   BUSINESS DEVELOPMENT
JASON ULLMEYER   •   SENIOR DESIGNER
JOSH GREEN   •   TRAFFIC COORDINATOR
CHRIS CANIANO   •   PRODUCTION ASSISTANT

DYNAMITE®
ENTERTAINMENT
WWW.DYNAMITE.NET

ISBN-10: 1-60690-264-4   ISBN-13: 978-1-60690-264-6   First Printing   10 9 8 7 6 5 4 3 2 1

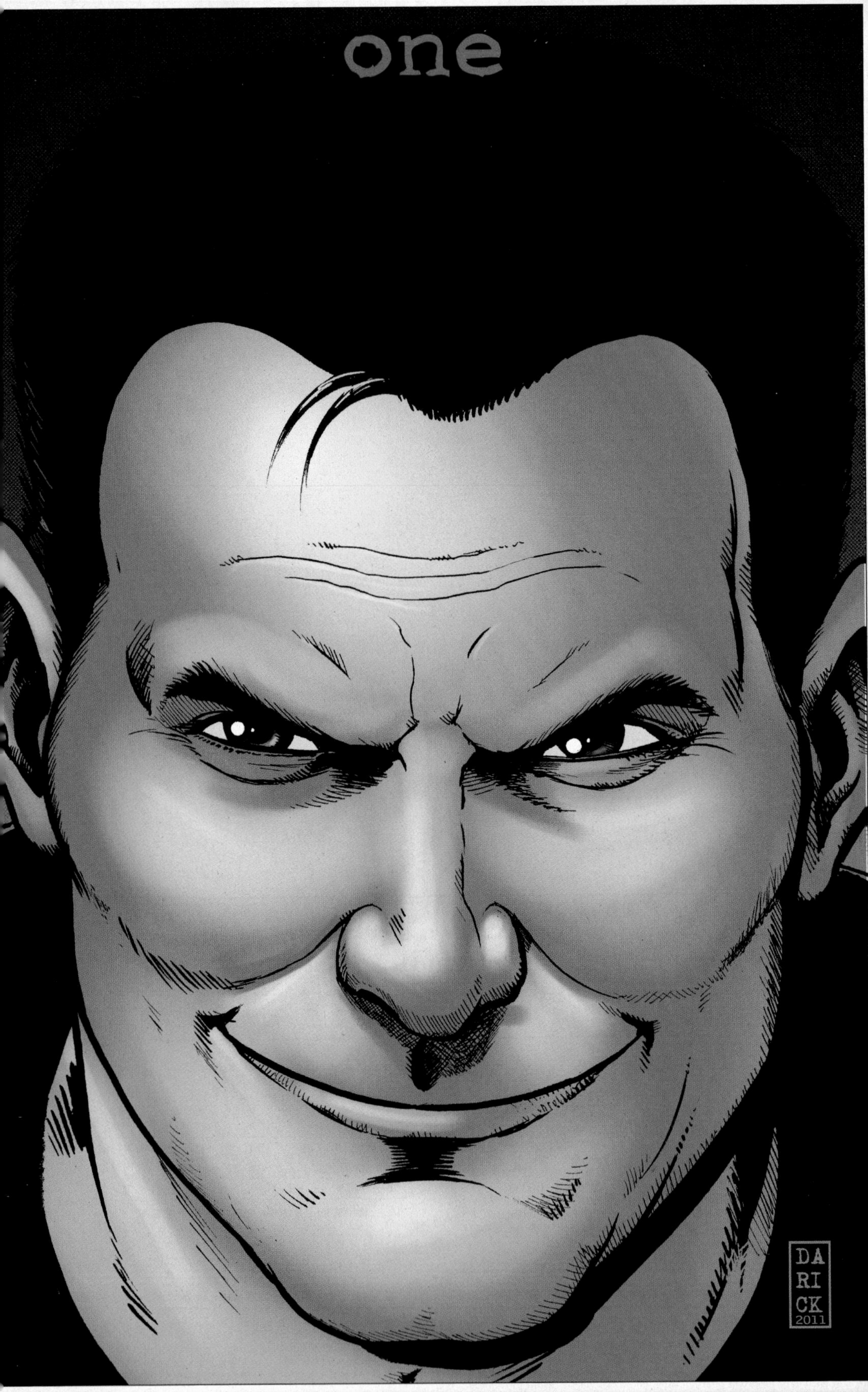
one
DA
RI
CK
2011

*It's time to demythologize an era and build
a new myth from the gutter to the stars.
It's time to embrace bad men and the price
they paid to secretly define their time.*

Here's to them.

- James Ellroy, *American Tabloid*

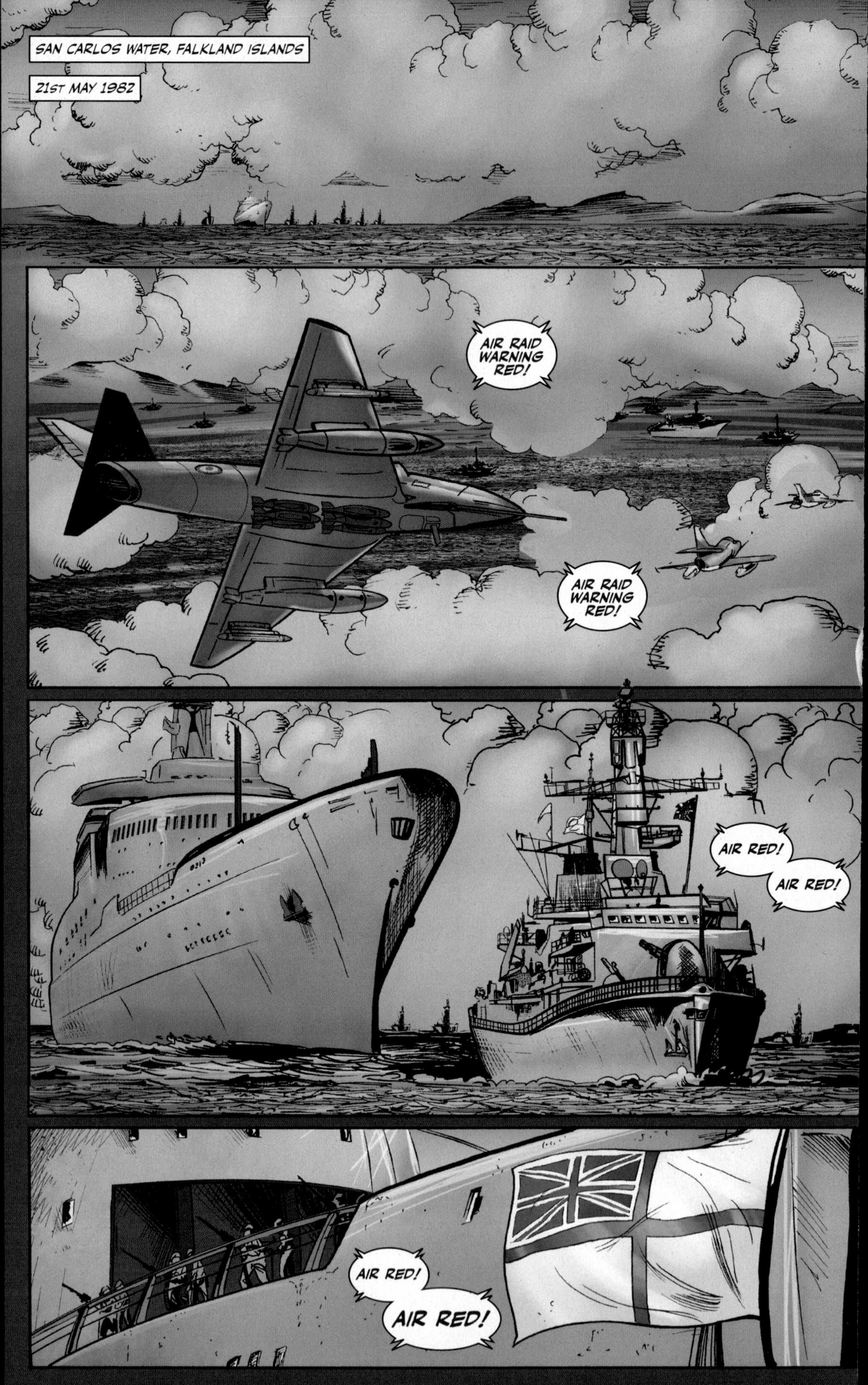
SAN CARLOS WATER, FALKLAND ISLANDS
21ST MAY 1982
AIR RAID WARNING RED!
AIR RAID WARNING RED!
AIR RED!
AIR RED!
AIR RED!
AIR RED!

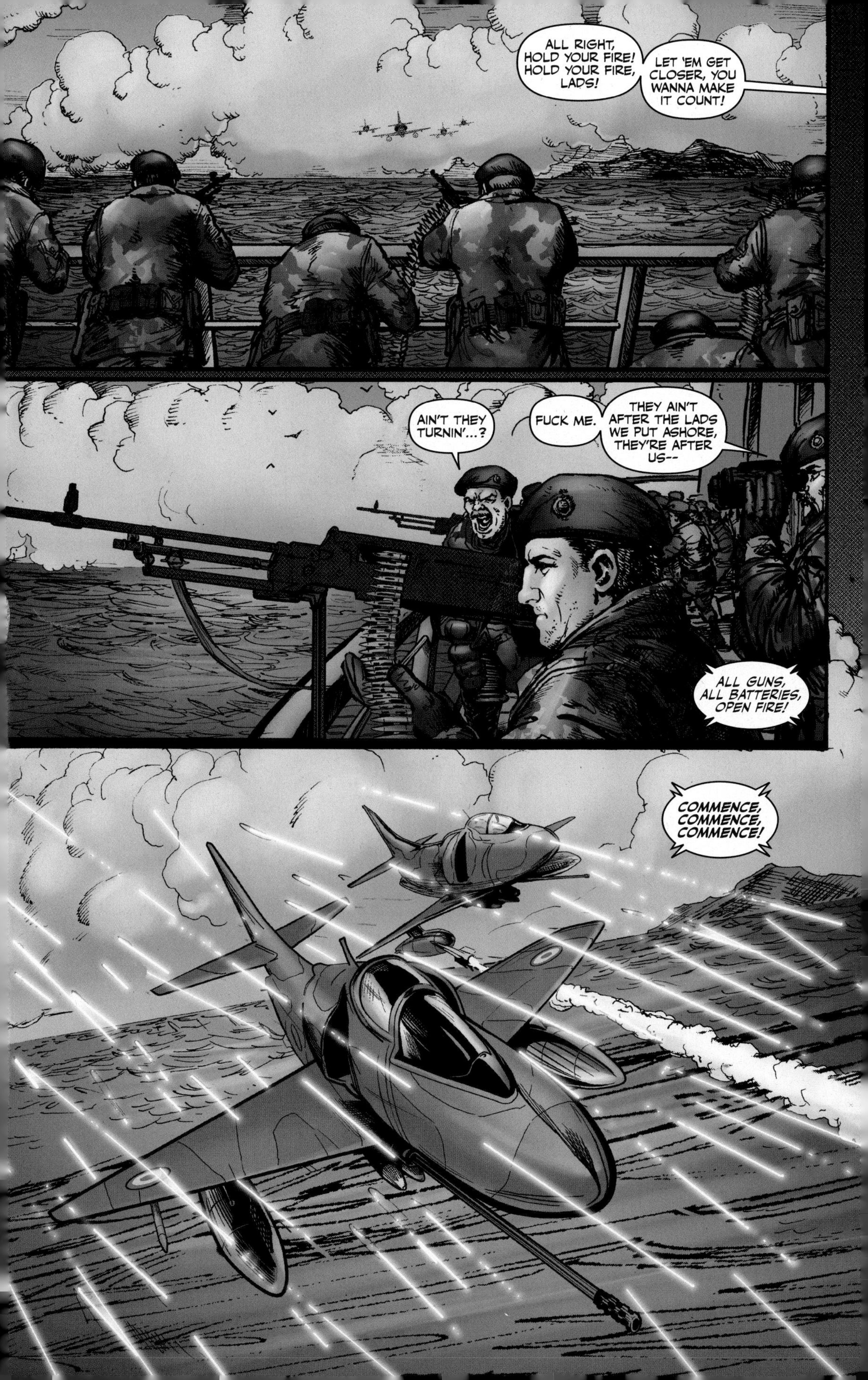

ALL RIGHT, HOLD YOUR FIRE! HOLD YOUR FIRE, LADS!
LET 'EM GET CLOSER, YOU WANNA MAKE IT COUNT!
AIN'T THEY TURNIN'...?
FUCK ME.
THEY AIN'T AFTER THE LADS WE PUT ASHORE, THEY'RE AFTER US--
ALL GUNS, ALL BATTERIES, OPEN FIRE!
COMMENCE, COMMENCE, COMMENCE!

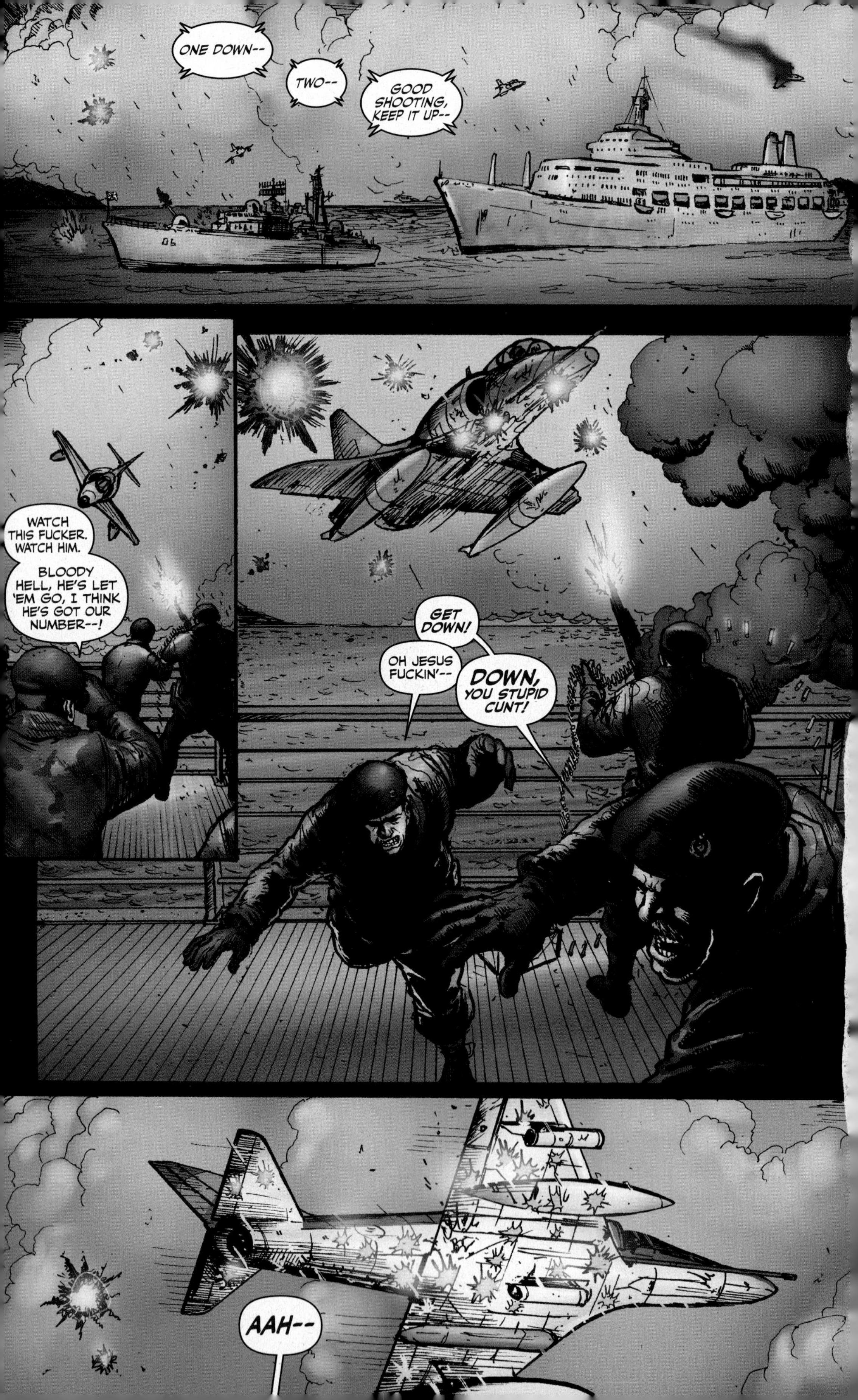
ONE DOWN--
TWO--
GOOD SHOOTING, KEEP IT UP--
WATCH THIS FUCKER. WATCH HIM.
BLOODY HELL, HE'S LET 'EM GO, I THINK HE'S GOT OUR NUMBER--!
GET DOWN!
OH JESUS FUCKIN'--
DOWN, YOU STUPID CUNT!
AAH--

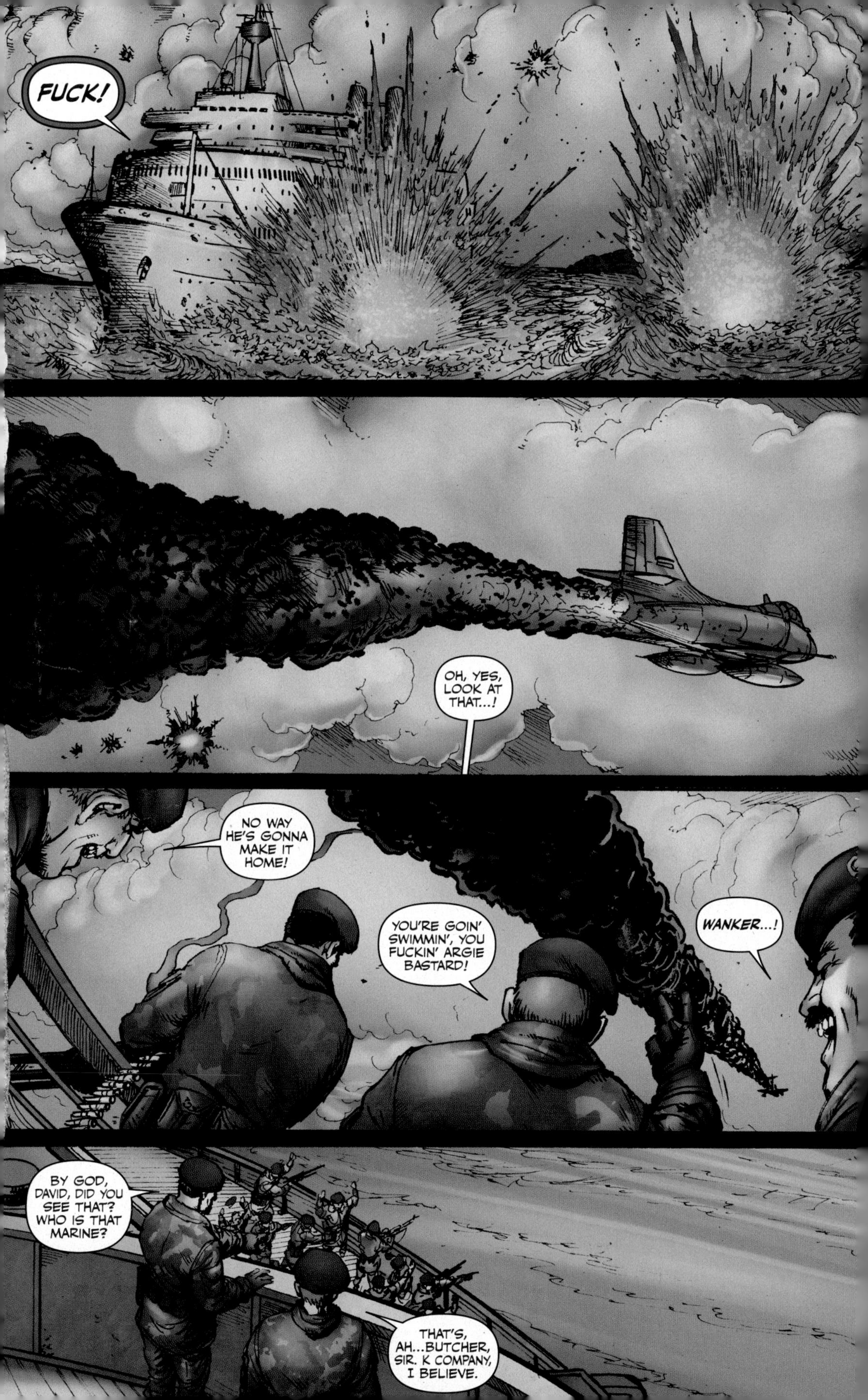
FUCK!
OH, YES, LOOK AT THAT...!
NO WAY HE'S GONNA MAKE IT HOME!
YOU'RE GOIN' SWIMMIN', YOU FUCKIN' ARGIE BASTARD!
WANKER...!
BY GOD, DAVID, DID YOU SEE THAT? WHO IS THAT MARINE?
THAT'S, AH...BUTCHER, SIR. K COMPANY, I BELIEVE.

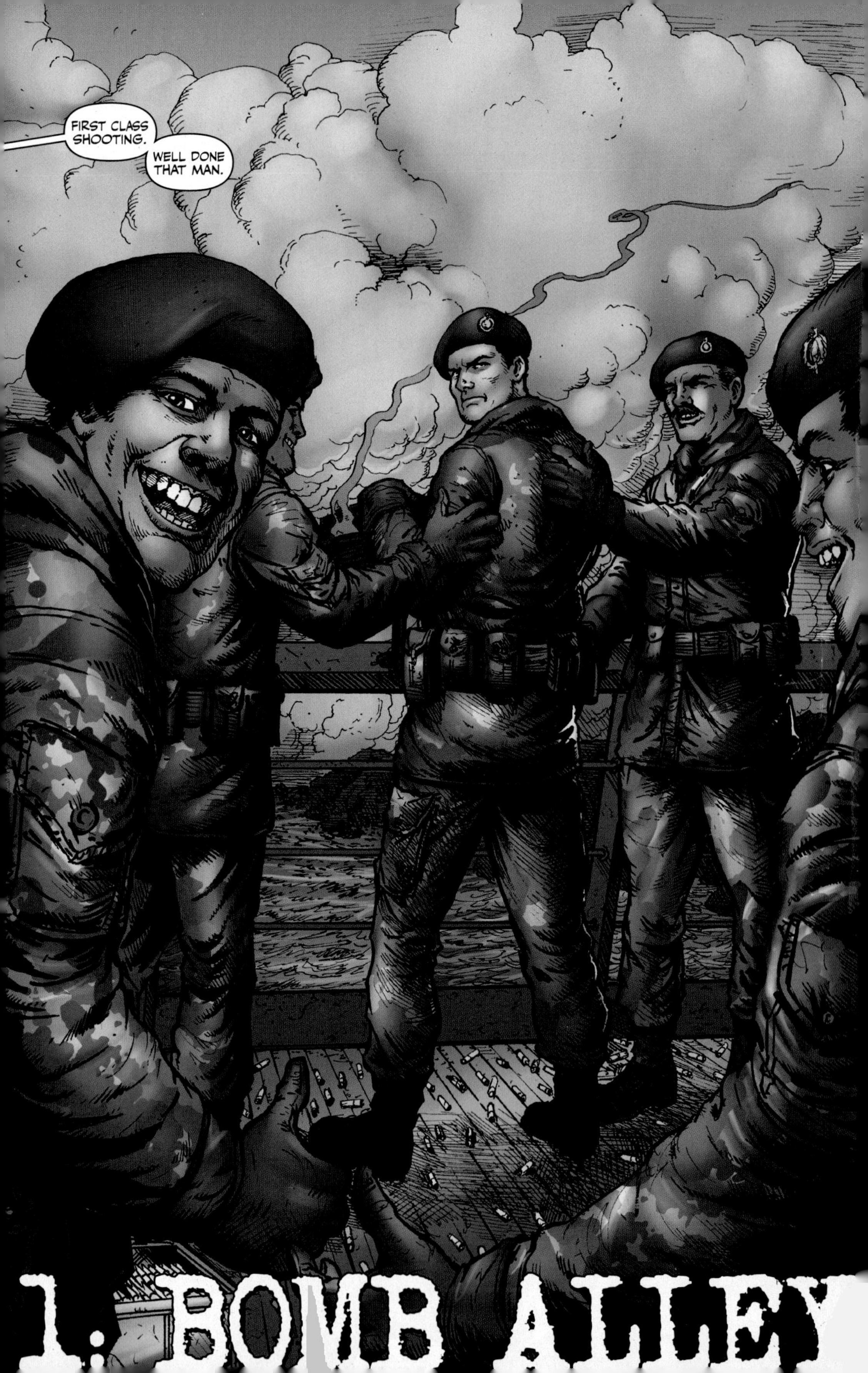
FIRST CLASS SHOOTING.
WELL DONE THAT MAN.
1. BOMB ALLEY

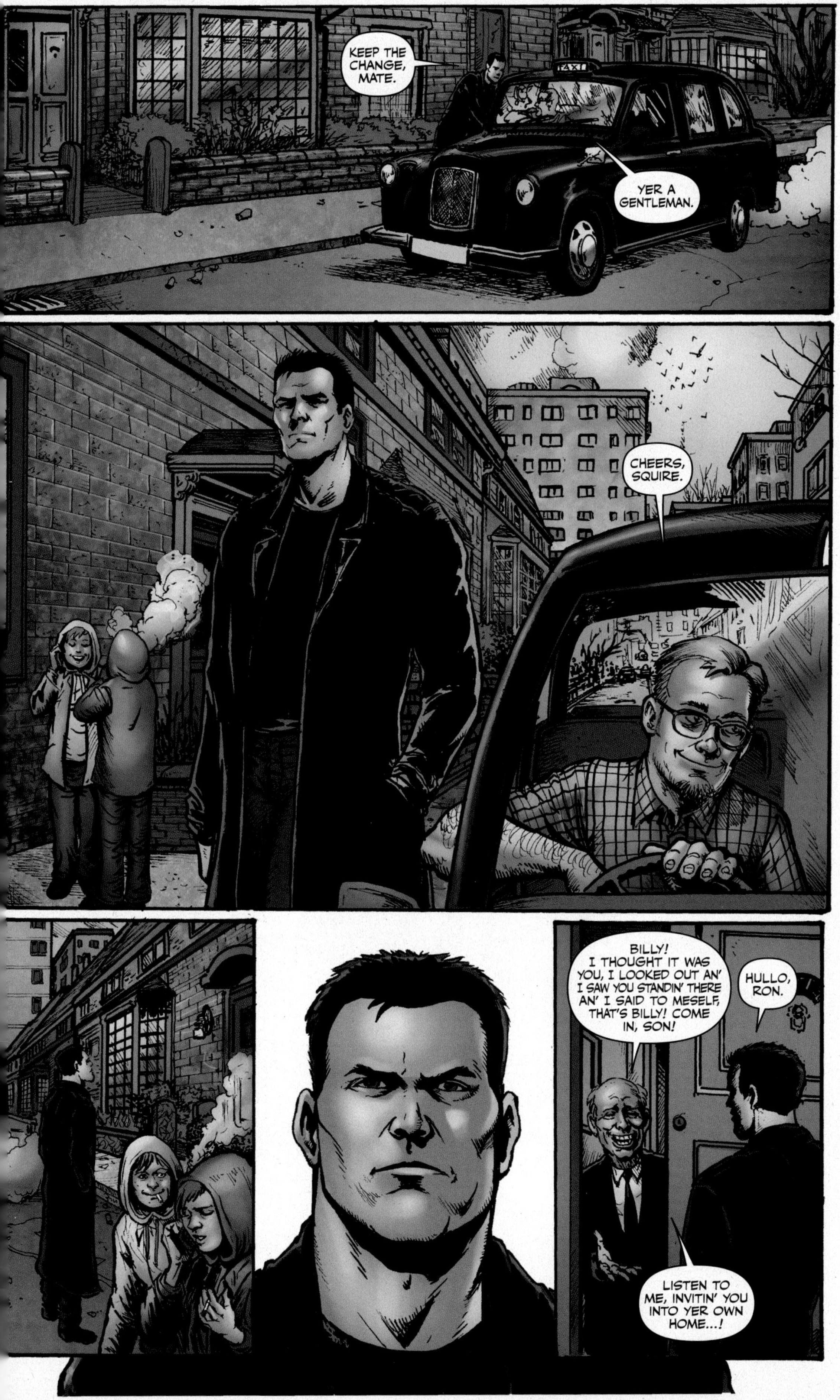
KEEP THE CHANGE, MATE.
YER A GENTLEMAN.
CHEERS, SQUIRE.
BILLY! I THOUGHT IT WAS YOU, I LOOKED OUT AN' I SAW YOU STANDIN' THERE AN' I SAID TO MESELF, THAT'S BILLY! COME IN, SON!
HULLO, RON.
LISTEN TO ME, INVITIN' YOU INTO YER OWN HOME...!

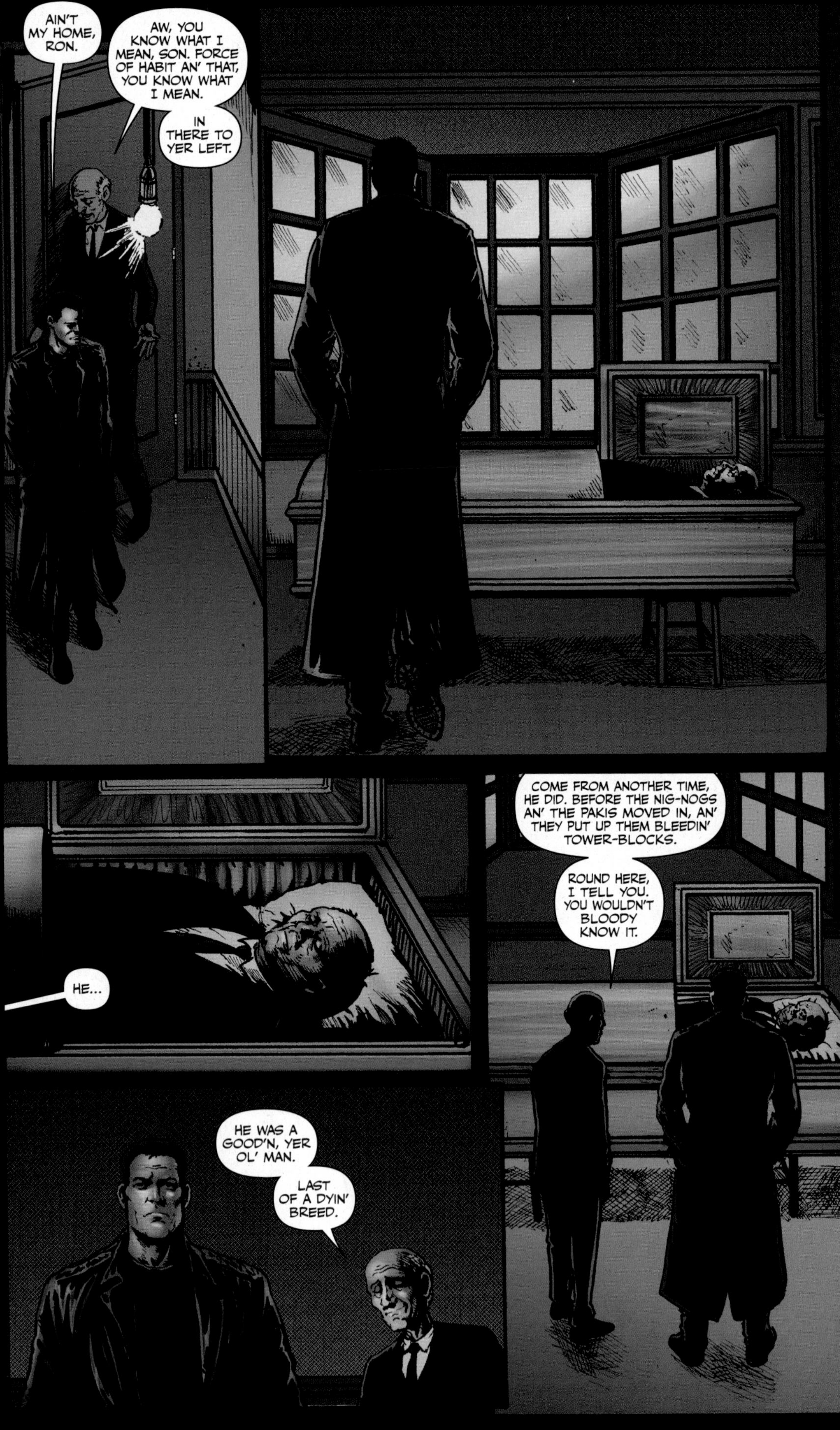
AIN'T MY HOME, RON.
AW, YOU KNOW WHAT I MEAN, SON. FORCE OF HABIT AN' THAT, YOU KNOW WHAT I MEAN.
IN THERE TO YER LEFT.
HE...
COME FROM ANOTHER TIME, HE DID. BEFORE THE NIG-NOGS AN' THE PAKIS MOVED IN, AN' THEY PUT UP THEM BLEEDIN' TOWER-BLOCKS.
ROUND HERE, I TELL YOU. YOU WOULDN'T BLOODY KNOW IT.
HE WAS A GOOD'N, YER OL' MAN.
LAST OF A DYIN' BREED.

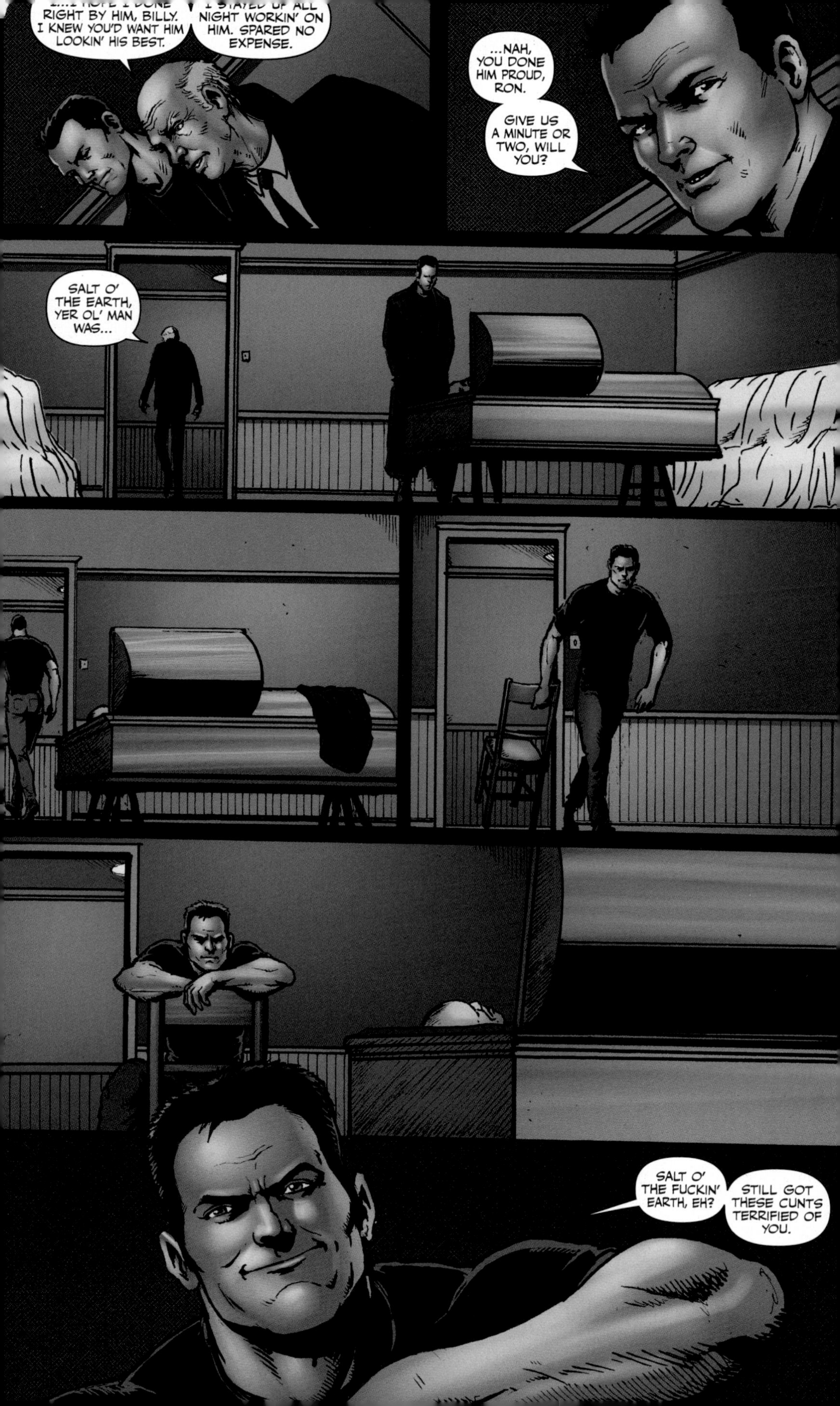
RIGHT BY HIM, BILLY. I KNEW YOU'D WANT HIM LOOKIN' HIS BEST.
NIGHT WORKIN' ON HIM. SPARED NO EXPENSE.
...NAH, YOU DONE HIM PROUD, RON.
GIVE US A MINUTE OR TWO, WILL YOU?
SALT O' THE EARTH, YER OL' MAN WAS...
SALT O' THE FUCKIN' EARTH, EH?
STILL GOT THESE CUNTS TERRIFIED OF YOU.

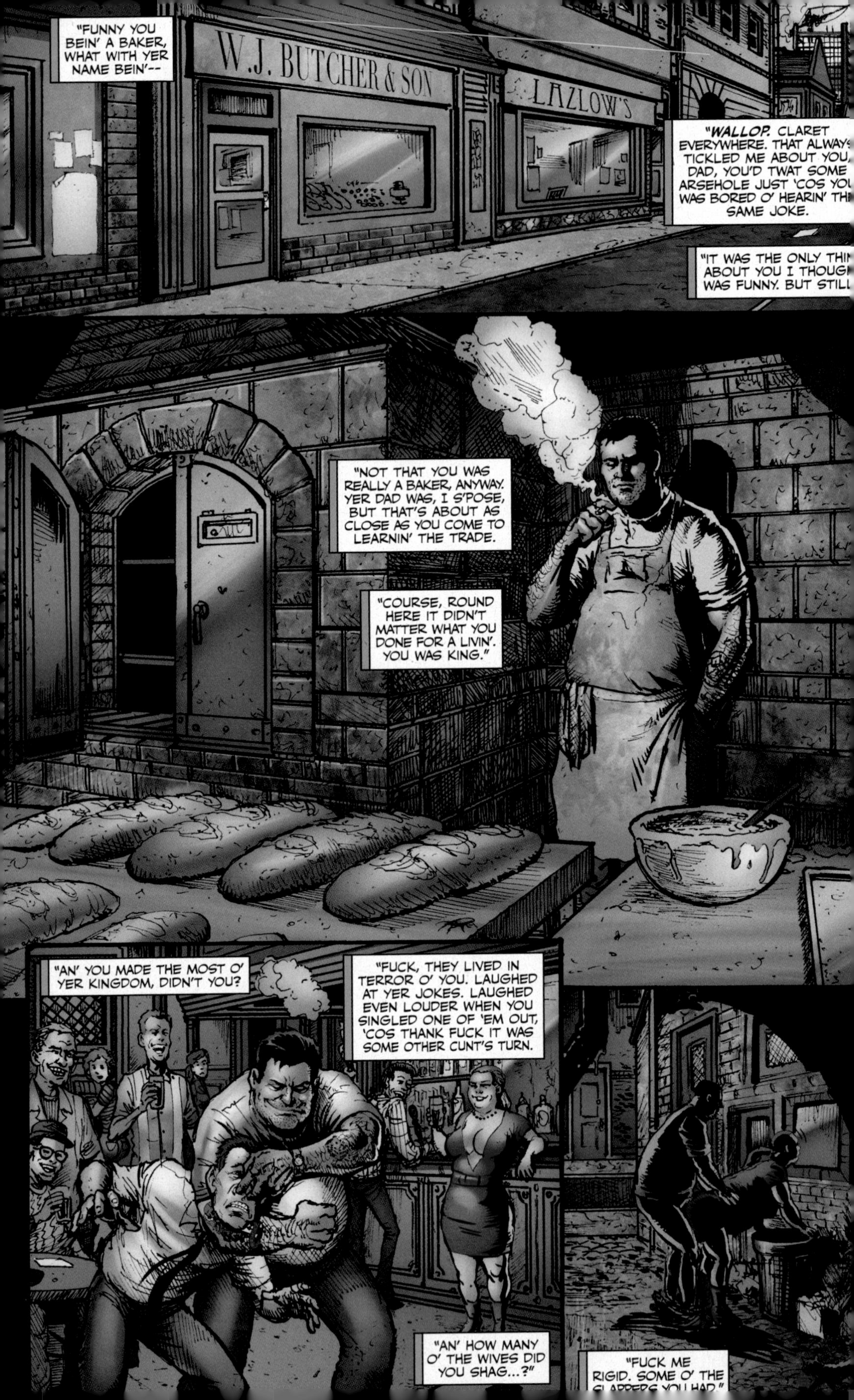
"FUNNY YOU BEIN' A BAKER, WHAT WITH YER NAME BEIN'--
W.J. BUTCHER & SON
LAZLOW'S
"WALLOP. CLARET EVERYWHERE. THAT ALWAYS TICKLED ME ABOUT YOU, DAD, YOU'D TWAT SOME ARSEHOLE JUST 'COS YOU WAS BORED O' HEARIN' THE SAME JOKE.
"IT WAS THE ONLY THIN ABOUT YOU I THOUGH WAS FUNNY. BUT STILL
"NOT THAT YOU WAS REALLY A BAKER, ANYWAY. YER DAD WAS, I S'POSE, BUT THAT'S ABOUT AS CLOSE AS YOU COME TO LEARNIN' THE TRADE.
"COURSE, ROUND HERE IT DIDN'T MATTER WHAT YOU DONE FOR A LIVIN'. YOU WAS KING."
"AN' YOU MADE THE MOST O' YER KINGDOM, DIDN'T YOU?
"FUCK, THEY LIVED IN TERROR O' YOU. LAUGHED AT YER JOKES. LAUGHED EVEN LOUDER WHEN YOU SINGLED ONE OF 'EM OUT, 'COS THANK FUCK IT WAS SOME OTHER CUNT'S TURN.
"AN' HOW MANY O' THE WIVES DID YOU SHAG...?"
"FUCK ME RIGID. SOME O' THE

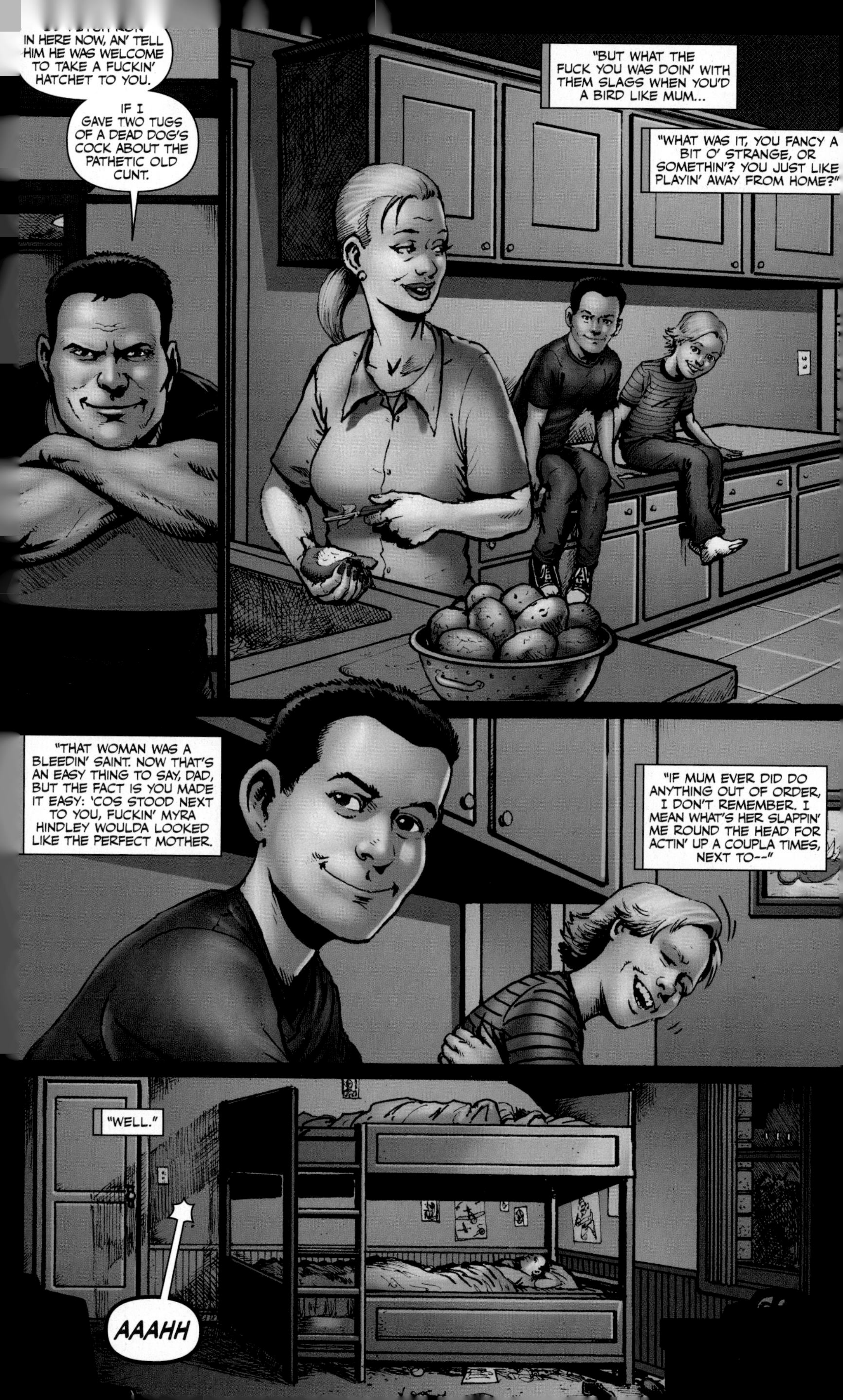
IN HERE NOW, AN' TELL HIM HE WAS WELCOME TO TAKE A FUCKIN' HATCHET TO YOU.
IF I GAVE TWO TUGS OF A DEAD DOG'S COCK ABOUT THE PATHETIC OLD CUNT.
"BUT WHAT THE FUCK YOU WAS DOIN' WITH THEM SLAGS WHEN YOU'D A BIRD LIKE MUM...
"WHAT WAS IT, YOU FANCY A BIT O' STRANGE, OR SOMETHIN'? YOU JUST LIKE PLAYIN' AWAY FROM HOME?"
"THAT WOMAN WAS A BLEEDIN' SAINT. NOW THAT'S AN EASY THING TO SAY, DAD, BUT THE FACT IS YOU MADE IT EASY: 'COS STOOD NEXT TO YOU, FUCKIN' MYRA HINDLEY WOULDA LOOKED LIKE THE PERFECT MOTHER.
"IF MUM EVER DID DO ANYTHING OUT OF ORDER, I DON'T REMEMBER. I MEAN WHAT'S HER SLAPPIN' ME ROUND THE HEAD FOR ACTIN' UP A COUPLA TIMES, NEXT TO--"
"WELL."
AAAHH

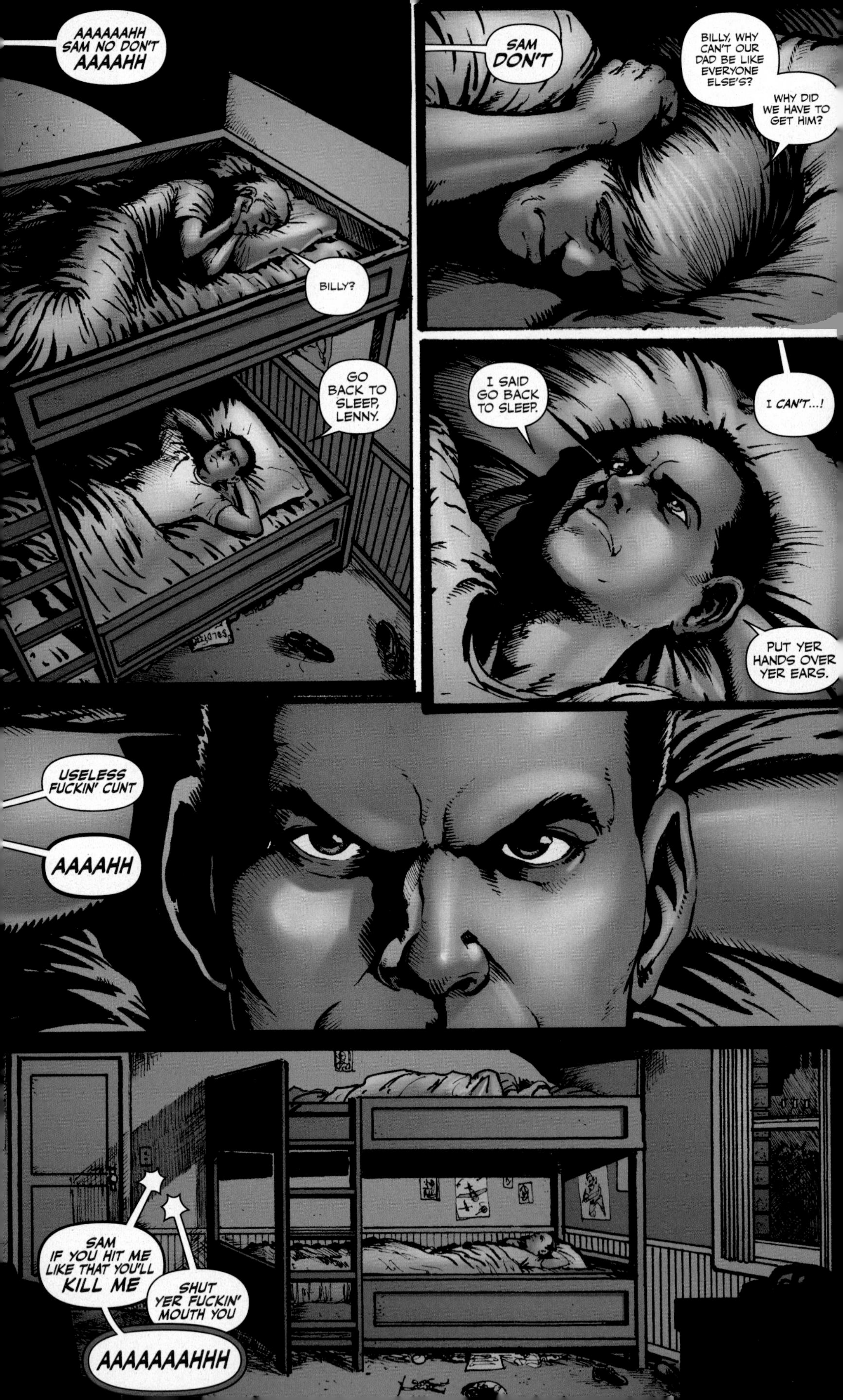
AAAAAAAHH SAM NO DON'T AAAAHH
BILLY?
GO BACK TO SLEEP, LENNY.
SAM DON'T
BILLY, WHY CAN'T OUR DAD BE LIKE EVERYONE ELSE'S?
WHY DID WE HAVE TO GET HIM?
I SAID GO BACK TO SLEEP.
I CAN'T...!
PUT YER HANDS OVER YER EARS.
USELESS FUCKIN' CUNT
AAAAHH
SAM IF YOU HIT ME LIKE THAT YOU'LL KILL ME
SHUT YER FUCKIN' MOUTH YOU
AAAAAAAHHH

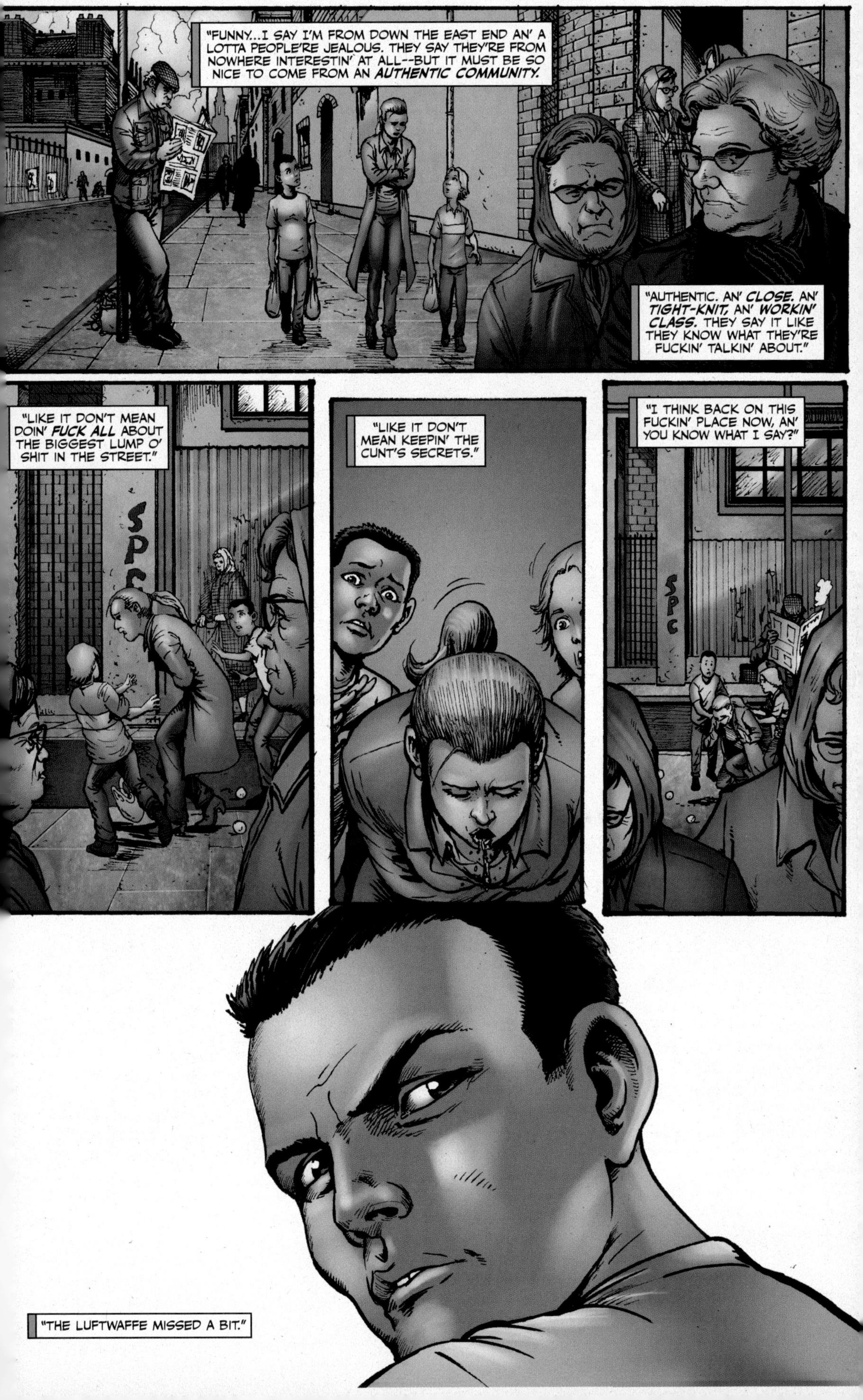
"FUNNY...I SAY I'M FROM DOWN THE EAST END AN' A LOTTA PEOPLE'RE JEALOUS. THEY SAY THEY'RE FROM NOWHERE INTERESTIN' AT ALL--BUT IT MUST BE SO NICE TO COME FROM AN *AUTHENTIC COMMUNITY.*
"AUTHENTIC. AN' *CLOSE.* AN' *TIGHT-KNIT,* AN' *WORKIN' CLASS.* THEY SAY IT LIKE THEY KNOW WHAT THEY'RE FUCKIN' TALKIN' ABOUT."
"LIKE IT DON'T MEAN DOIN' *FUCK ALL* ABOUT THE BIGGEST LUMP O' SHIT IN THE STREET."
"LIKE IT DON'T MEAN KEEPIN' THE CUNT'S SECRETS."
"I THINK BACK ON THIS FUCKIN' PLACE NOW, AN' YOU KNOW WHAT I SAY?"
"THE LUFTWAFFE MISSED A BIT."

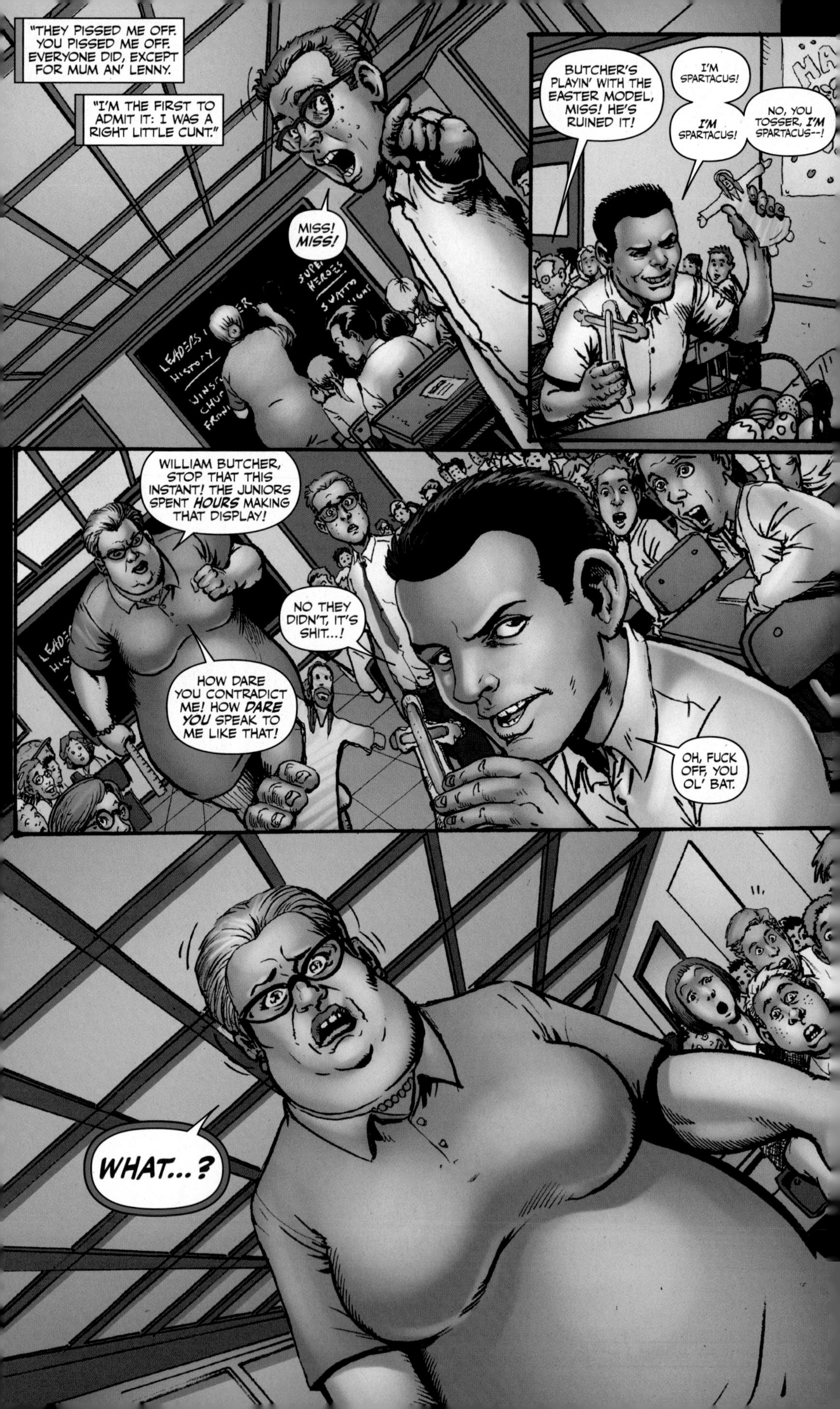
"THEY PISSED ME OFF. YOU PISSED ME OFF. EVERYONE DID, EXCEPT FOR MUM AN' LENNY.
"I'M THE FIRST TO ADMIT IT: I WAS A RIGHT LITTLE CUNT."
MISS! MISS!
BUTCHER'S PLAYIN' WITH THE EASTER MODEL, MISS! HE'S RUINED IT!
I'M SPARTACUS!
I'M SPARTACUS!
NO, YOU TOSSER, I'M SPARTACUS--!
WILLIAM BUTCHER, STOP THAT THIS INSTANT! THE JUNIORS SPENT HOURS MAKING THAT DISPLAY!
NO THEY DIDN'T, IT'S SHIT...!
HOW DARE YOU CONTRADICT ME! HOW DARE YOU SPEAK TO ME LIKE THAT!
OH, FUCK OFF, YOU OL' BAT.
WHAT...?

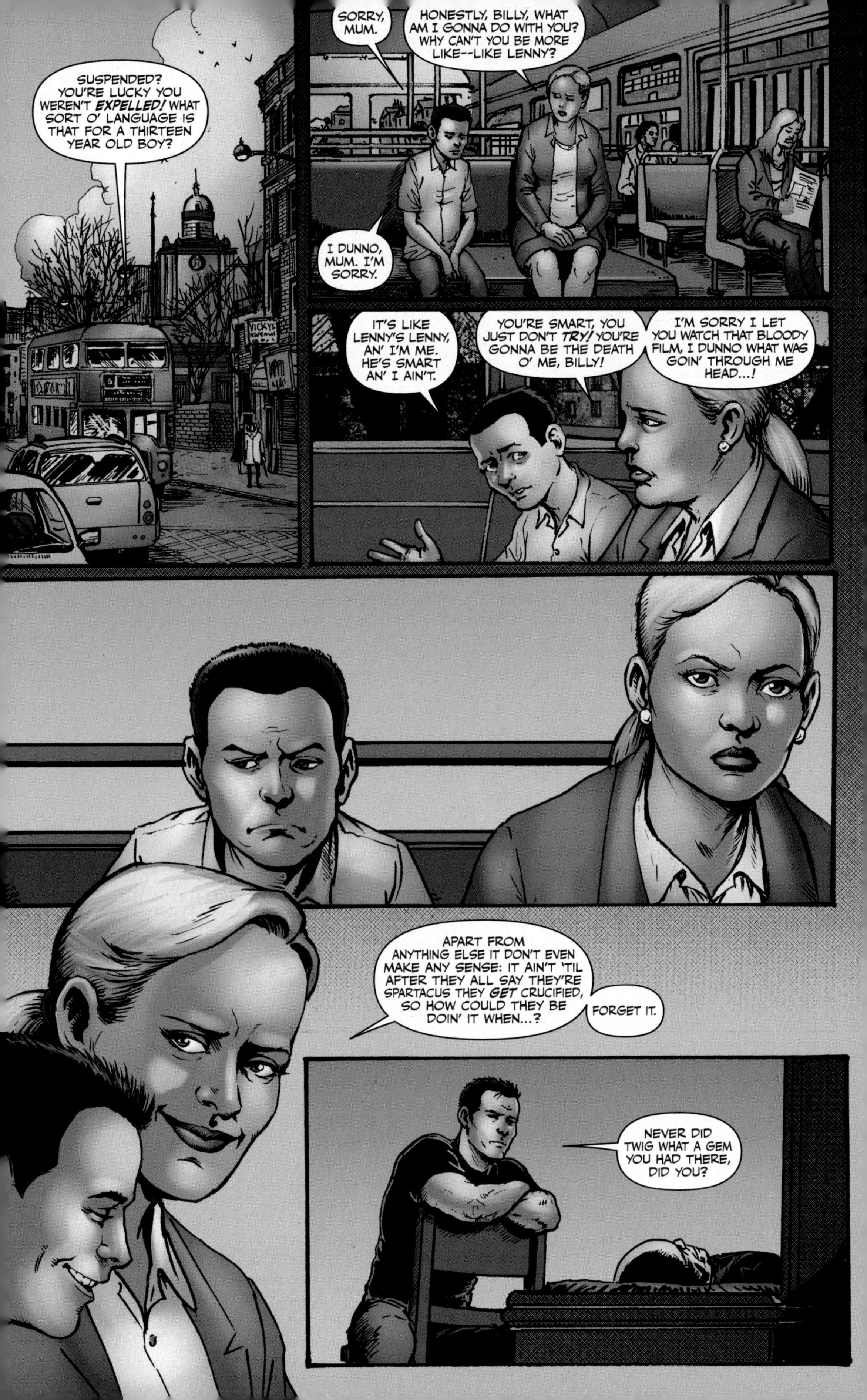
SUSPENDED? YOU'RE LUCKY YOU WEREN'T EXPELLED! WHAT SORT O' LANGUAGE IS THAT FOR A THIRTEEN YEAR OLD BOY?
SORRY, MUM.
HONESTLY, BILLY, WHAT AM I GONNA DO WITH YOU? WHY CAN'T YOU BE MORE LIKE--LIKE LENNY?
I DUNNO, MUM. I'M SORRY.
IT'S LIKE LENNY'S LENNY, AN' I'M ME. HE'S SMART AN' I AIN'T.
YOU'RE SMART, YOU JUST DON'T TRY! YOU'RE GONNA BE THE DEATH O' ME, BILLY!
I'M SORRY I LET YOU WATCH THAT BLOODY FILM, I DUNNO WHAT WAS GOIN' THROUGH ME HEAD...!
APART FROM ANYTHING ELSE IT DON'T EVEN MAKE ANY SENSE: IT AIN'T 'TIL AFTER THEY ALL SAY THEY'RE SPARTACUS THEY GET CRUCIFIED, SO HOW COULD THEY BE DOIN' IT WHEN...?
FORGET IT.
NEVER DID TWIG WHAT A GEM YOU HAD THERE, DID YOU?

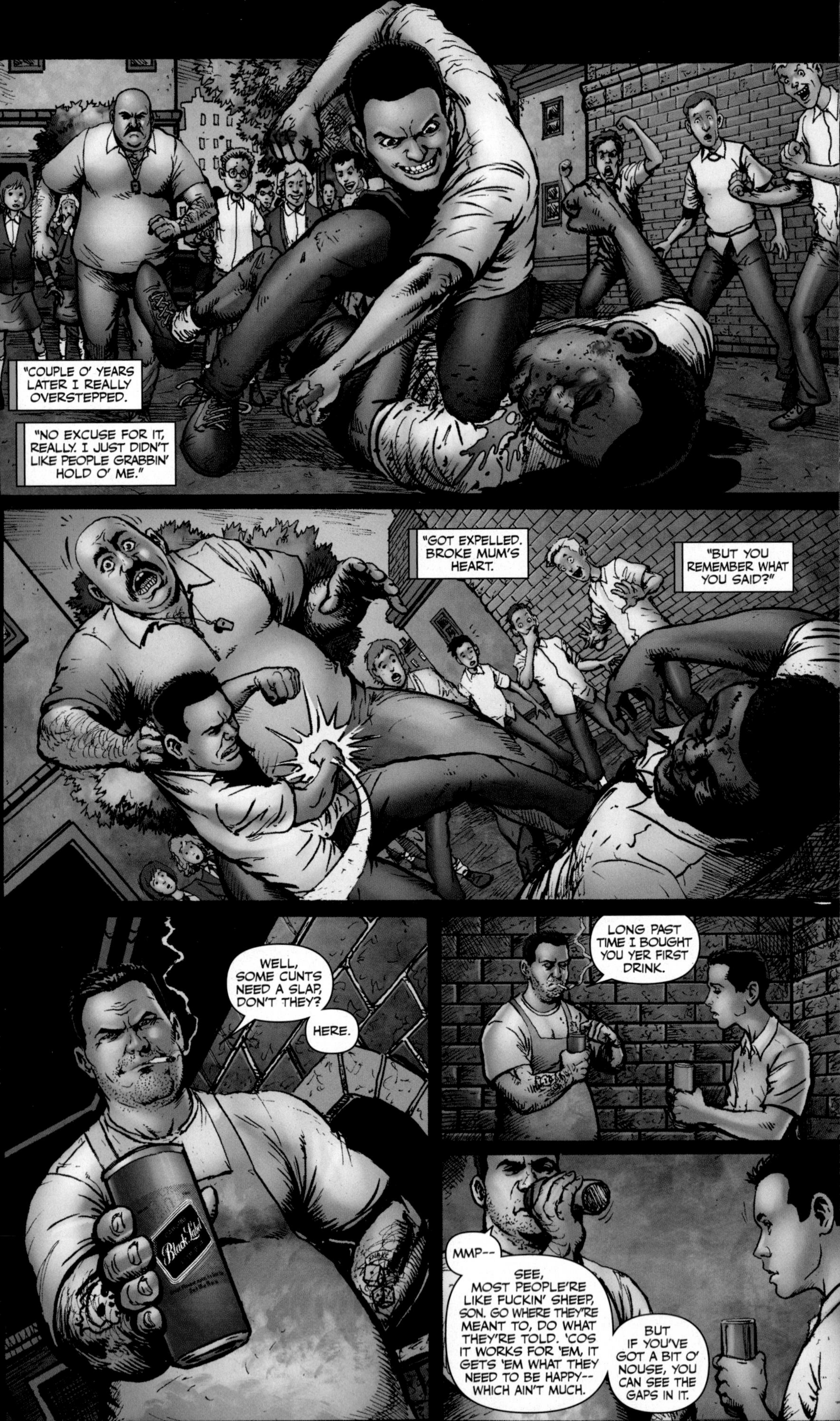
"COUPLE O' YEARS LATER I REALLY OVERSTEPPED.
"NO EXCUSE FOR IT, REALLY. I JUST DIDN'T LIKE PEOPLE GRABBIN' HOLD O' ME."
"GOT EXPELLED. BROKE MUM'S HEART.
"BUT YOU REMEMBER WHAT YOU SAID?"
WELL, SOME CUNTS NEED A SLAP, DON'T THEY?
HERE.
Black Label
LONG PAST TIME I BOUGHT YOU YER FIRST DRINK.
MMP--
SEE, MOST PEOPLE'RE LIKE FUCKIN' SHEEP, SON. GO WHERE THEY'RE MEANT TO, DO WHAT THEY'RE TOLD. 'COS IT WORKS FOR 'EM, IT GETS 'EM WHAT THEY NEED TO BE HAPPY-- WHICH AIN'T MUCH.
BUT IF YOU'VE GOT A BIT O' NOUSE, YOU CAN SEE THE GAPS IN IT.

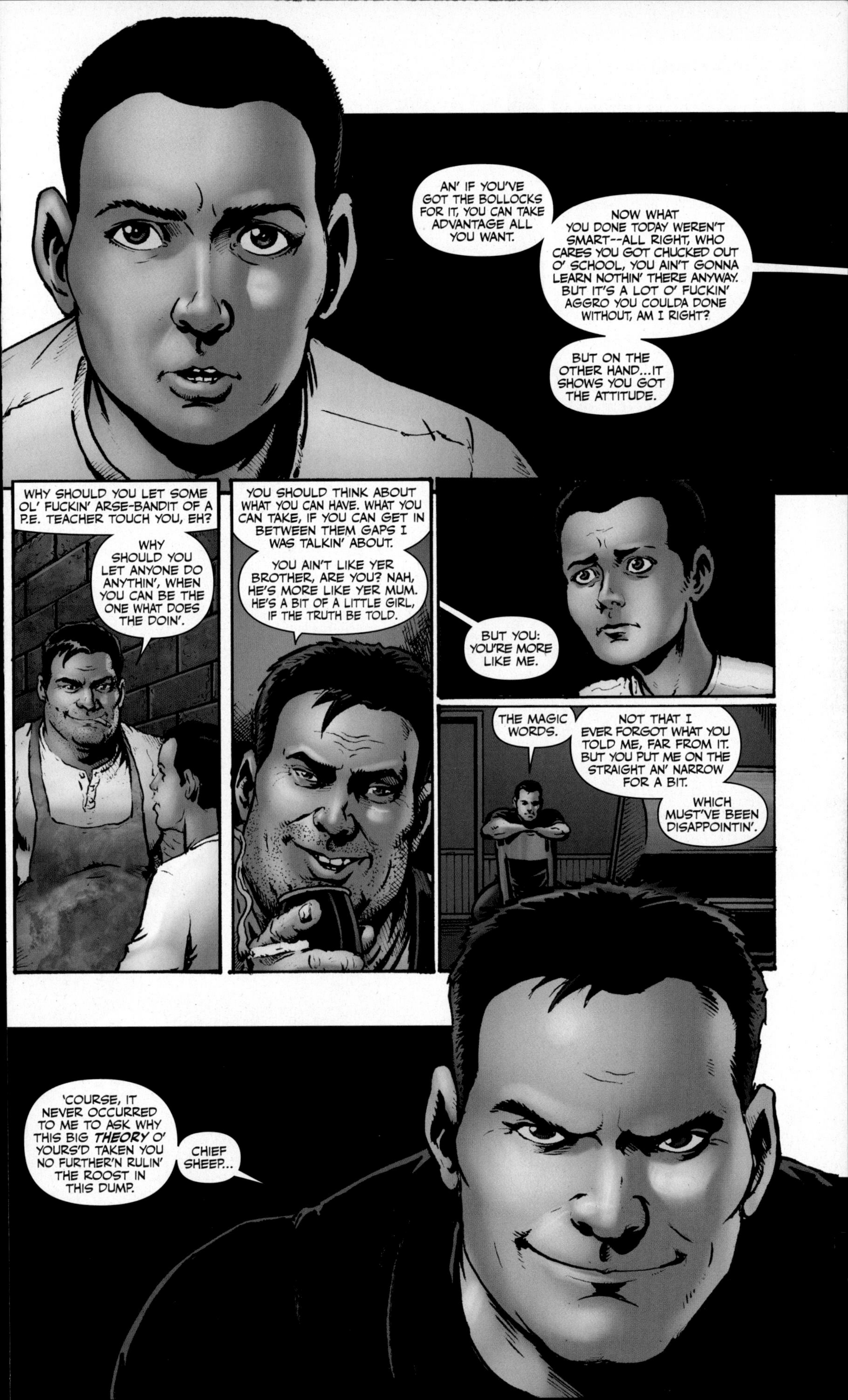
AN' IF YOU'VE GOT THE BOLLOCKS FOR IT, YOU CAN TAKE ADVANTAGE ALL YOU WANT.
NOW WHAT YOU DONE TODAY WEREN'T SMART--ALL RIGHT, WHO CARES YOU GOT CHUCKED OUT O' SCHOOL, YOU AIN'T GONNA LEARN NOTHIN' THERE ANYWAY. BUT IT'S A LOT O' FUCKIN' AGGRO YOU COULDA DONE WITHOUT, AM I RIGHT?
BUT ON THE OTHER HAND...IT SHOWS YOU GOT THE ATTITUDE.
WHY SHOULD YOU LET SOME OL' FUCKIN' ARSE-BANDIT OF A P.E. TEACHER TOUCH YOU, EH?
WHY SHOULD YOU LET ANYONE DO ANYTHIN', WHEN YOU CAN BE THE ONE WHAT DOES THE DOIN'.
YOU SHOULD THINK ABOUT WHAT YOU CAN HAVE. WHAT YOU CAN TAKE, IF YOU CAN GET IN BETWEEN THEM GAPS I WAS TALKIN' ABOUT.
YOU AIN'T LIKE YER BROTHER, ARE YOU? NAH, HE'S MORE LIKE YER MUM. HE'S A BIT OF A LITTLE GIRL, IF THE TRUTH BE TOLD.
BUT YOU: YOU'RE MORE LIKE ME.
THE MAGIC WORDS.
NOT THAT I EVER FORGOT WHAT YOU TOLD ME, FAR FROM IT. BUT YOU PUT ME ON THE STRAIGHT AN' NARROW FOR A BIT.
WHICH MUST'VE BEEN DISAPPOINTIN'.
'COURSE, IT NEVER OCCURRED TO ME TO ASK WHY THIS BIG THEORY O' YOURS'D TAKEN YOU NO FURTHER'N RULIN' THE ROOST IN THIS DUMP.
CHIEF SHEEP...

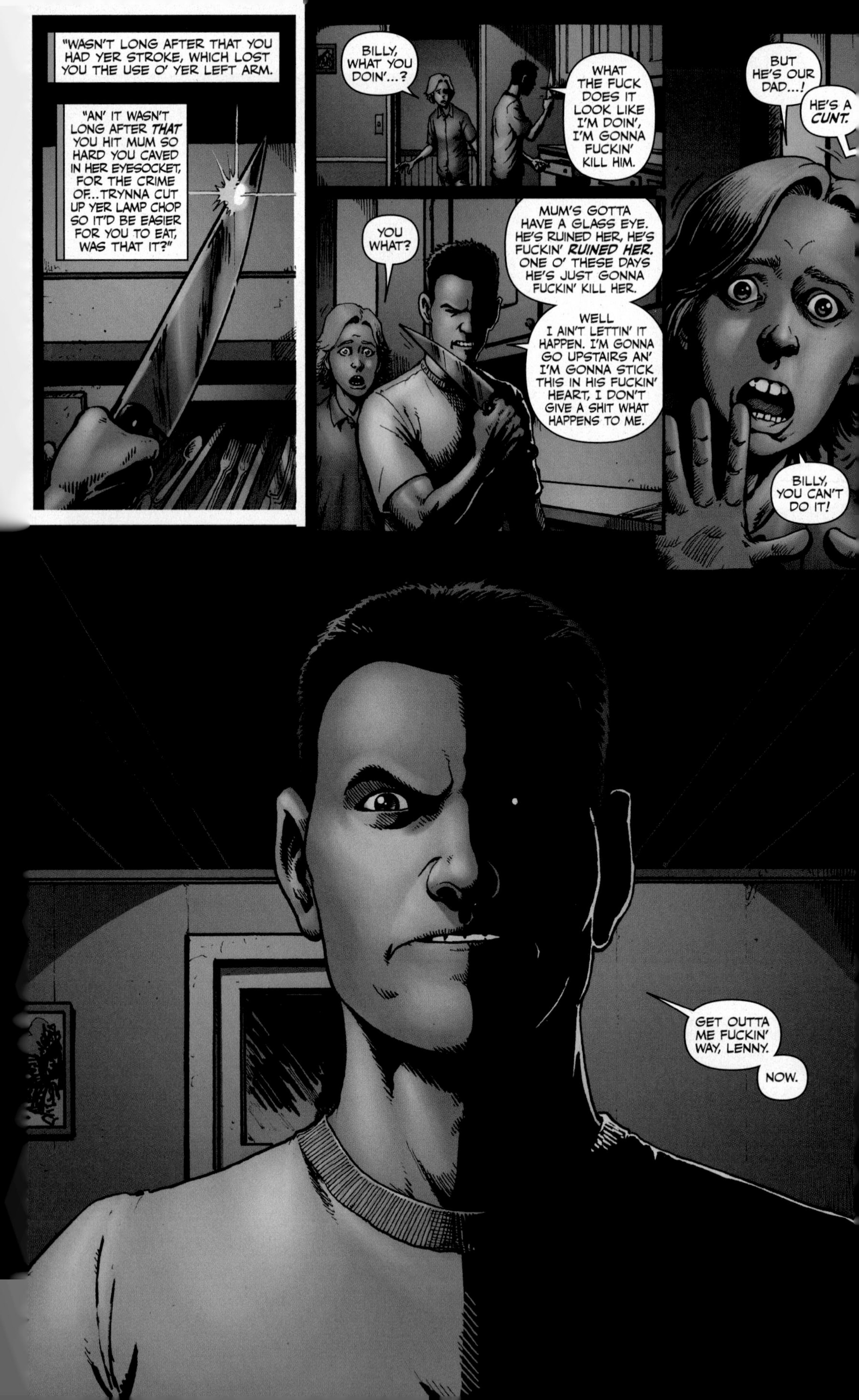

"WASN'T LONG AFTER THAT YOU HAD YER STROKE, WHICH LOST YOU THE USE O' YER LEFT ARM.
"AN' IT WASN'T LONG AFTER THAT YOU HIT MUM SO HARD YOU CAVED IN HER EYESOCKET, FOR THE CRIME OF...TRYNNA CUT UP YER LAMP CHOP SO IT'D BE EASIER FOR YOU TO EAT, WAS THAT IT?"
BILLY, WHAT YOU DOIN'...?
WHAT THE FUCK DOES IT LOOK LIKE I'M DOIN', I'M GONNA FUCKIN' KILL HIM.
YOU WHAT?
MUM'S GOTTA HAVE A GLASS EYE. HE'S RUINED HER, HE'S FUCKIN' RUINED HER. ONE O' THESE DAYS HE'S JUST GONNA FUCKIN' KILL HER.
WELL I AIN'T LETTIN' IT HAPPEN. I'M GONNA GO UPSTAIRS AN' I'M GONNA STICK THIS IN HIS FUCKIN' HEART, I DON'T GIVE A SHIT WHAT HAPPENS TO ME.
BUT HE'S OUR DAD...!
HE'S A CUNT.
BILLY, YOU CAN'T DO IT!
GET OUTTA ME FUCKIN' WAY, LENNY.
NOW.

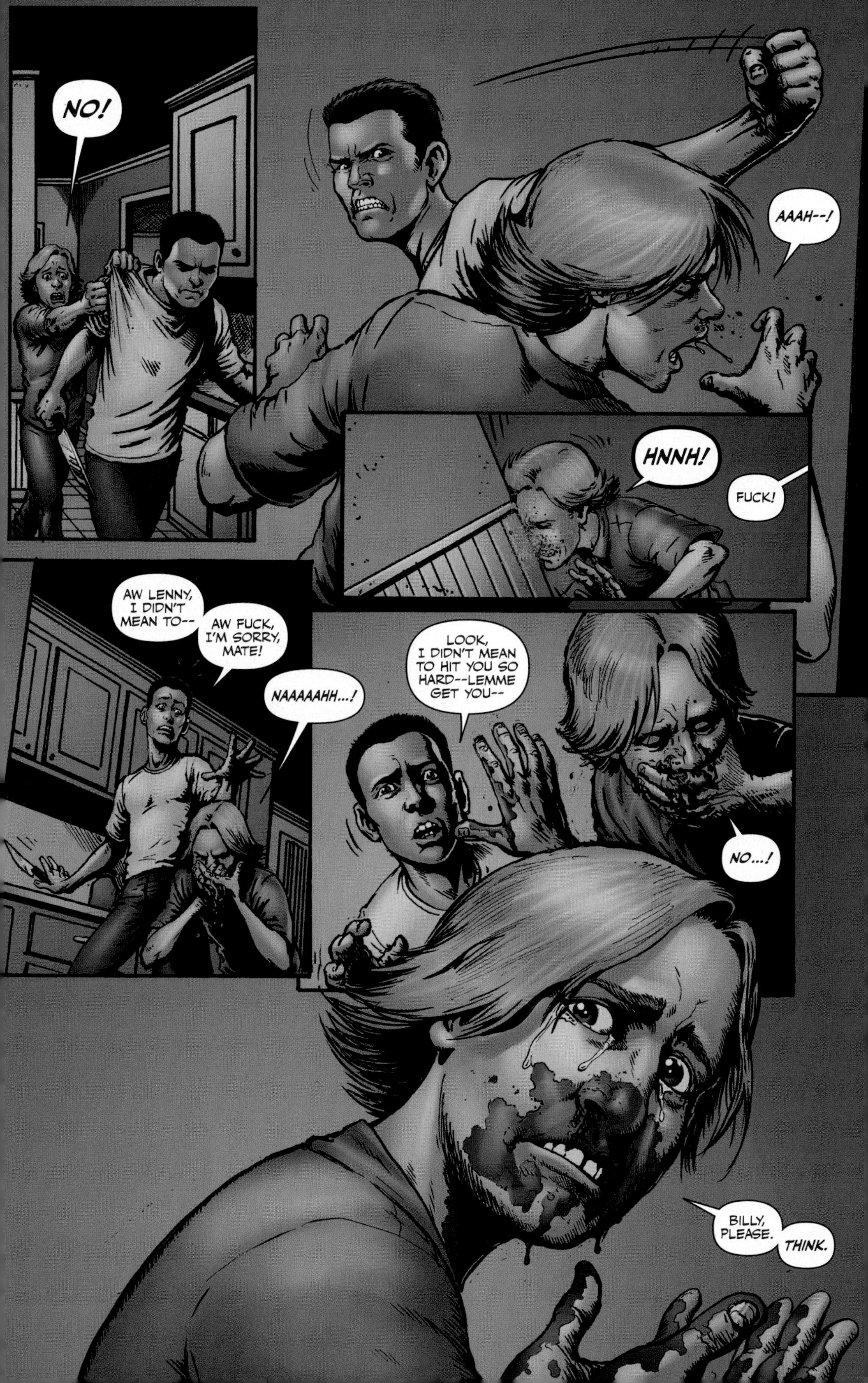
NO!
AAAH--!
HNNH!
FUCK!
AW LENNY, I DIDN'T MEAN TO--
AW FUCK, I'M SORRY, MATE!
NAAAAAHH...!
LOOK, I DIDN'T MEAN TO HIT YOU SO HARD--LEMME GET YOU--
NO...!
BILLY, PLEASE.
THINK.

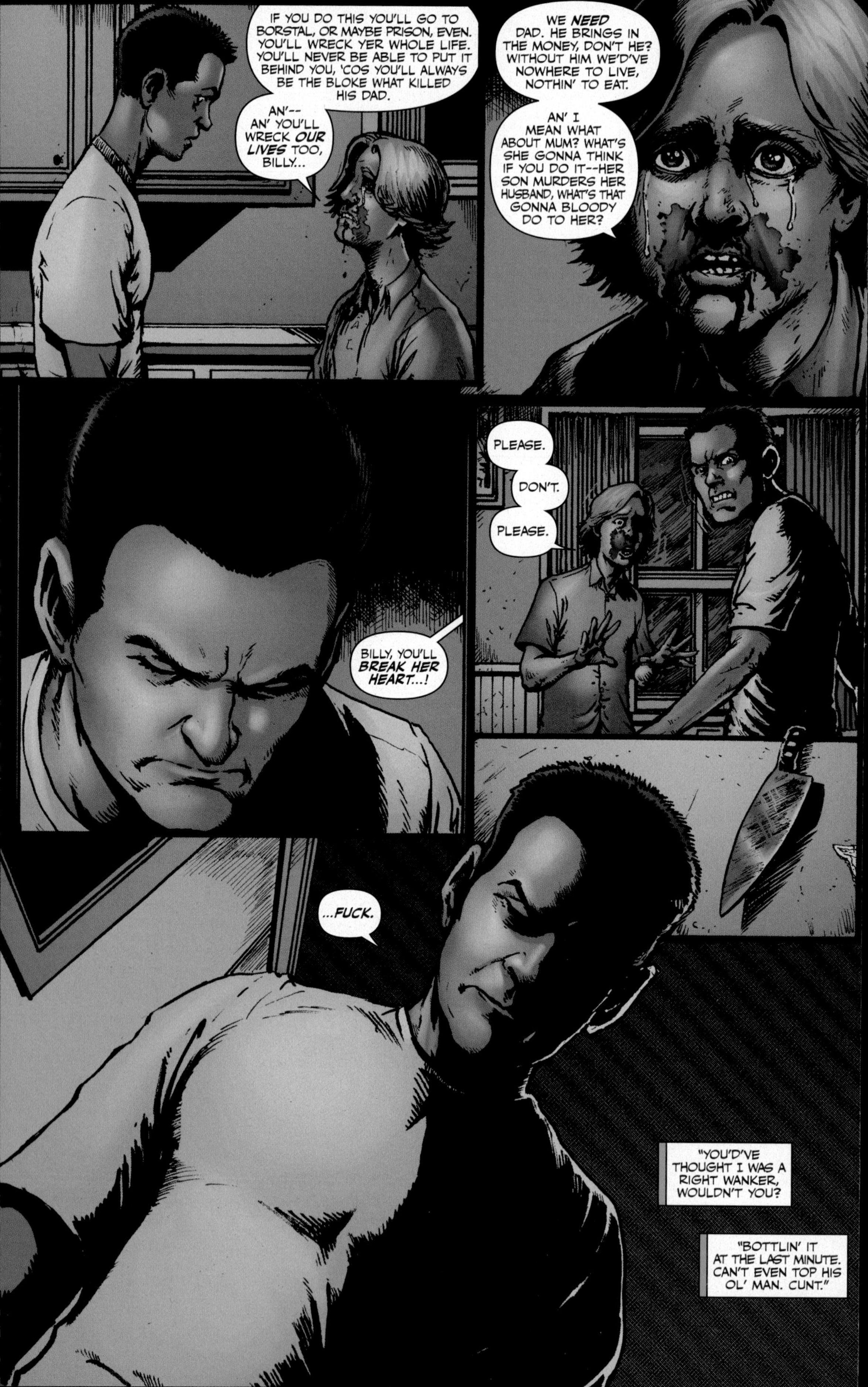
IF YOU DO THIS YOU'LL GO TO BORSTAL, OR MAYBE PRISON, EVEN. YOU'LL WRECK YER WHOLE LIFE. YOU'LL NEVER BE ABLE TO PUT IT BEHIND YOU, 'COS YOU'LL ALWAYS BE THE BLOKE WHAT KILLED HIS DAD.
AN'-- AN' YOU'LL WRECK *OUR LIVES* TOO, BILLY...
WE *NEED* DAD. HE BRINGS IN THE MONEY, DON'T HE? WITHOUT HIM WE'D'VE NOWHERE TO LIVE, NOTHIN' TO EAT.
AN' I MEAN WHAT ABOUT MUM? WHAT'S SHE GONNA THINK IF YOU DO IT--HER SON MURDERS HER HUSBAND, WHAT'S THAT GONNA BLOODY DO TO HER?
BILLY, YOU'LL *BREAK HER HEART*...!
PLEASE.
DON'T.
PLEASE.
...*FUCK*.
"YOU'D'VE THOUGHT I WAS A RIGHT WANKER, WOULDN'T YOU?
"BOTTLIN' IT AT THE LAST MINUTE. CAN'T EVEN TOP HIS OL' MAN. CUNT."

"IT WAS LENNY, DAD. HE WAS SUCH A GOOD KID. HE NEVER STOOD IN JUDGMENT ON ME, BUT HE HAD A WAY O' BEIN' SORTA *SAD* ABOUT THE WAY I COULD BE SOMETIMES..."

"HE COULD MAKE ME...NOT BE ME FOR A BIT."

"SEEIN' HIM STANDIN' THERE, BLOOD PISSIN' DOWN HIS FACE AN' CRYIN' HIS EYES OUT, AN' JUST THE THOUGHT THAT I DONE IT..."

"ALL I COULD THINK WAS--LEAVE IT OUT, YOU ARSEHOLE, THIS KID FUCKIN' *LOVES YOU*...!"

HE CAN'T COPE AS WELL AS HE USED TO. WITH THE STROKE AN' THAT.

ONE OF US IS GONNA HAVE TO HELP HIM.

NOT ME.

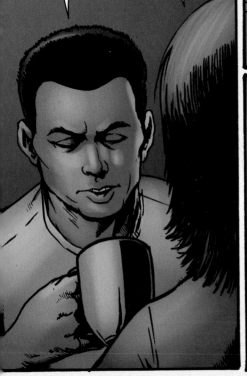

I CAN'T FUCKIN' WORK IN THE SHOP WITH HIM. ONE DAY HE'LL TURN HIS BACK AN' I'LL SMACK HIM OVER THE HEAD WITH A ROLLIN' PIN, AN' THEN I'LL BUNG HIM IN THE OVEN--I WON'T BE ABLE TO STOP MESELF...

I KNOW.

BUT WE GOTTA KEEP HIM EARNIN' SOMEHOW, BILLY. WE GOTTA MAKE ENDS MEET.

YEAH, WELL, THE FUNNY THING IS I WAS THINKIN' ABOUT THAT MESELF LAST WEEK. BEFORE ALL THIS KICKED OFF.

I CAN'T STAND BEIN' AROUND HIM, LENNY. IT DOES ME FUCKIN' HEAD IN. BUT, THERE IS YOU AN' MUM TO THINK ABOUT...

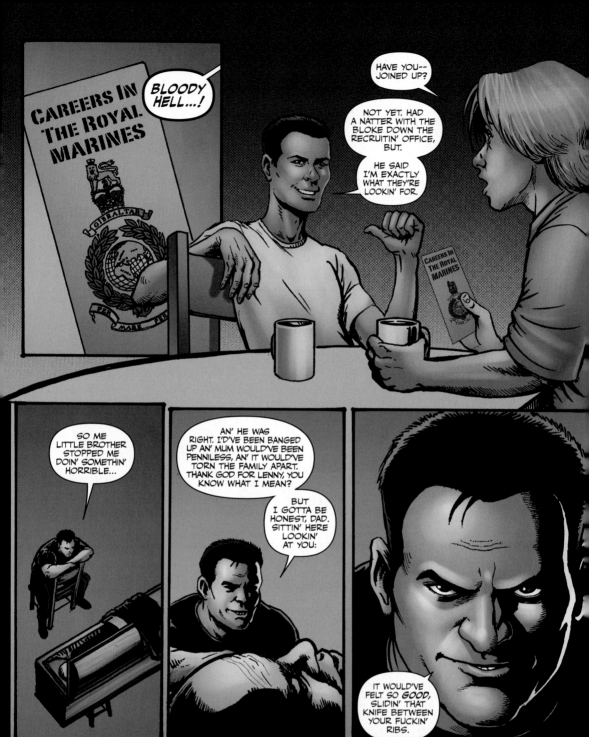

CAREERS IN THE ROYAL MARINES

BLOODY HELL....!

HAVE YOU-- JOINED UP?

NOT YET. HAD A NATTER WITH THE BLOKE DOWN THE RECRUITIN' OFFICE, BUT.

HE SAID I'M EXACTLY WHAT THEY'RE LOOKIN' FOR.

CAREERS IN THE ROYAL MARINES

SO ME LITTLE BROTHER STOPPED ME DOIN' SOMETHIN' HORRIBLE...

AN' HE WAS RIGHT. I'D'VE BEEN BANGED UP AN' MUM WOULD'VE BEEN PENNILESS, AN' IT WOULD'VE TORN THE FAMILY APART. THANK GOD FOR LENNY, YOU KNOW WHAT I MEAN?

BUT I GOTTA BE HONEST, DAD. SITTIN' HERE LOOKIN' AT YOU:

IT WOULD'VE FELT SO *GOOD*, SLIDIN' THAT KNIFE BETWEEN YOUR FUCKIN' RIBS.

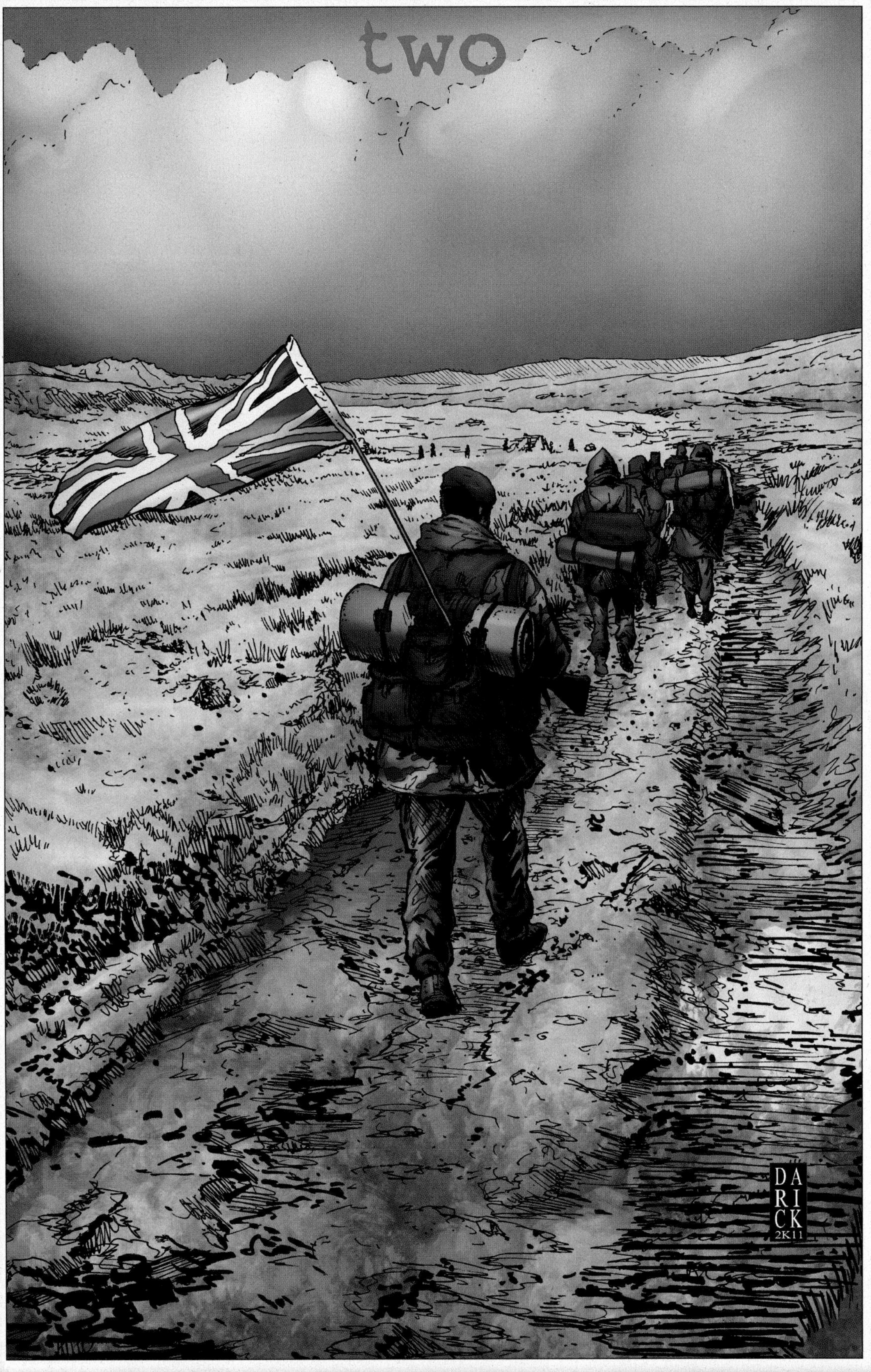
two
DA
RI
CK
2K11

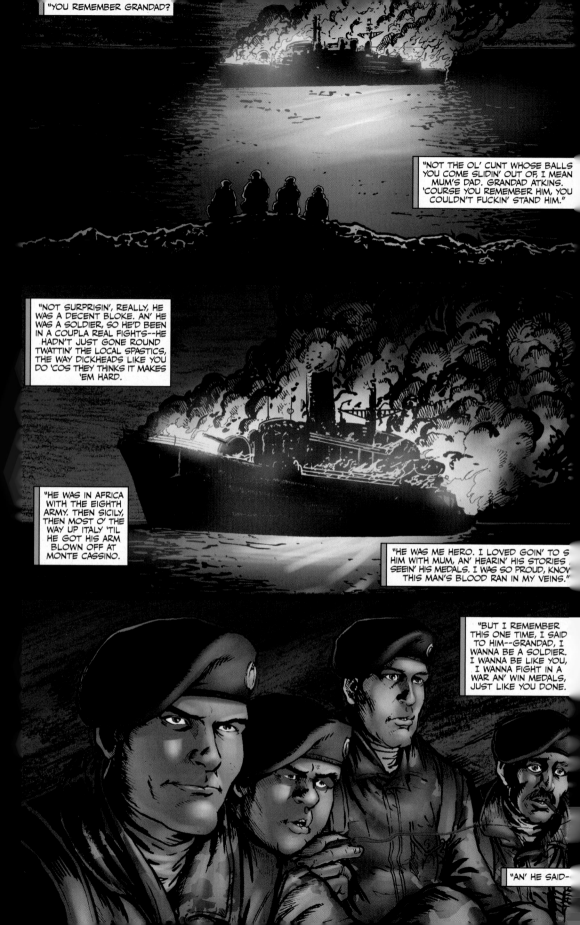

"YOU REMEMBER GRANDAD?

"NOT THE OL' CUNT WHOSE BALLS YOU COME SLIDIN' OUT OF, I MEAN MUM'S DAD. GRANDAD ATKINS. 'COURSE YOU REMEMBER HIM, YOU COULDN'T FUCKIN' STAND HIM."

"NOT SURPRISIN', REALLY, HE WAS A DECENT BLOKE. AN' HE WAS A SOLDIER, SO HE'D BEEN IN A COUPLA REAL FIGHTS--HE HADN'T JUST GONE ROUND TWATTIN' THE LOCAL SPASTICS, THE WAY DICKHEADS LIKE YOU DO 'COS THEY THINKS IT MAKES 'EM HARD.

"HE WAS IN AFRICA WITH THE EIGHTH ARMY. THEN SICILY, THEN MOST O' THE WAY UP ITALY 'TIL HE GOT HIS ARM BLOWN OFF AT MONTE CASSINO.

"HE WAS ME HERO. I LOVED GOIN' TO S HIM WITH MUM, AN' HEARIN' HIS STORIES SEEIN' HIS MEDALS. I WAS SO PROUD, KNOV THIS MAN'S BLOOD RAN IN MY VEINS."

"BUT I REMEMBER THIS ONE TIME, I SAID TO HIM--GRANDAD, I WANNA BE A SOLDIER. I WANNA BE LIKE YOU, I WANNA FIGHT IN A WAR AN' WIN MEDALS, JUST LIKE YOU DONE.

"AN' HE SAID--

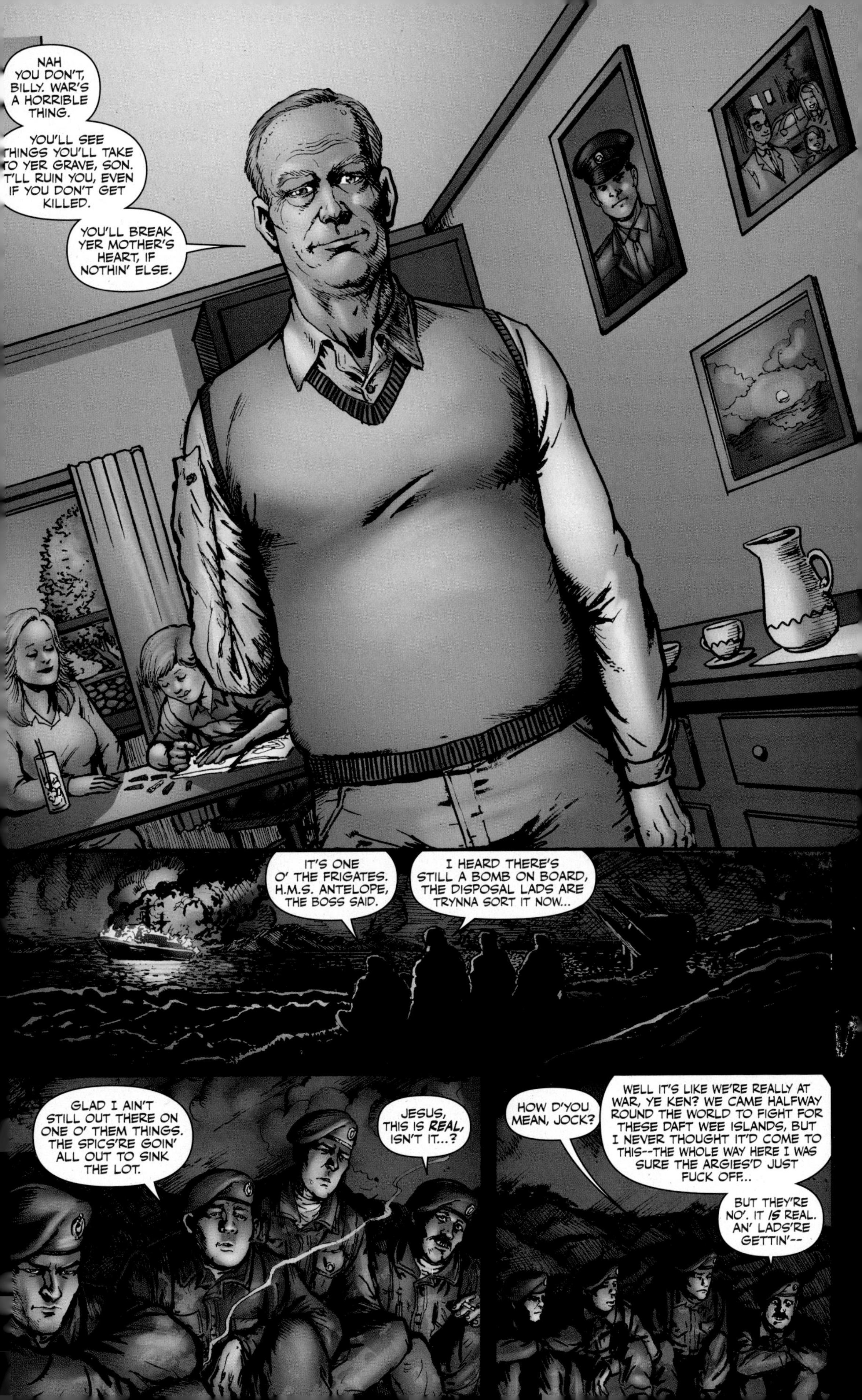
NAH YOU DON'T, BILLY. WAR'S A HORRIBLE THING.
YOU'LL SEE THINGS YOU'LL TAKE O YER GRAVE, SON. T'LL RUIN YOU, EVEN IF YOU DON'T GET KILLED.
YOU'LL BREAK YER MOTHER'S HEART, IF NOTHIN' ELSE.
IT'S ONE O' THE FRIGATES. H.M.S. ANTELOPE, THE BOSS SAID.
I HEARD THERE'S STILL A BOMB ON BOARD, THE DISPOSAL LADS ARE TRYNNA SORT IT NOW...
GLAD I AIN'T STILL OUT THERE ON ONE O' THEM THINGS. THE SPICS'RE GOIN' ALL OUT TO SINK THE LOT.
JESUS, THIS IS *REAL,* ISN'T IT...?
HOW D'YOU MEAN, JOCK?
WELL IT'S LIKE WE'RE REALLY AT WAR, YE KEN? WE CAME HALFWAY ROUND THE WORLD TO FIGHT FOR THESE DAFT WEE ISLANDS, BUT I NEVER THOUGHT IT'D COME TO THIS--THE WHOLE WAY HERE I WAS SURE THE ARGIES'D JUST FUCK OFF...
BUT THEY'RE NO'. IT *IS* REAL. AN' LADS'RE GETTIN'--

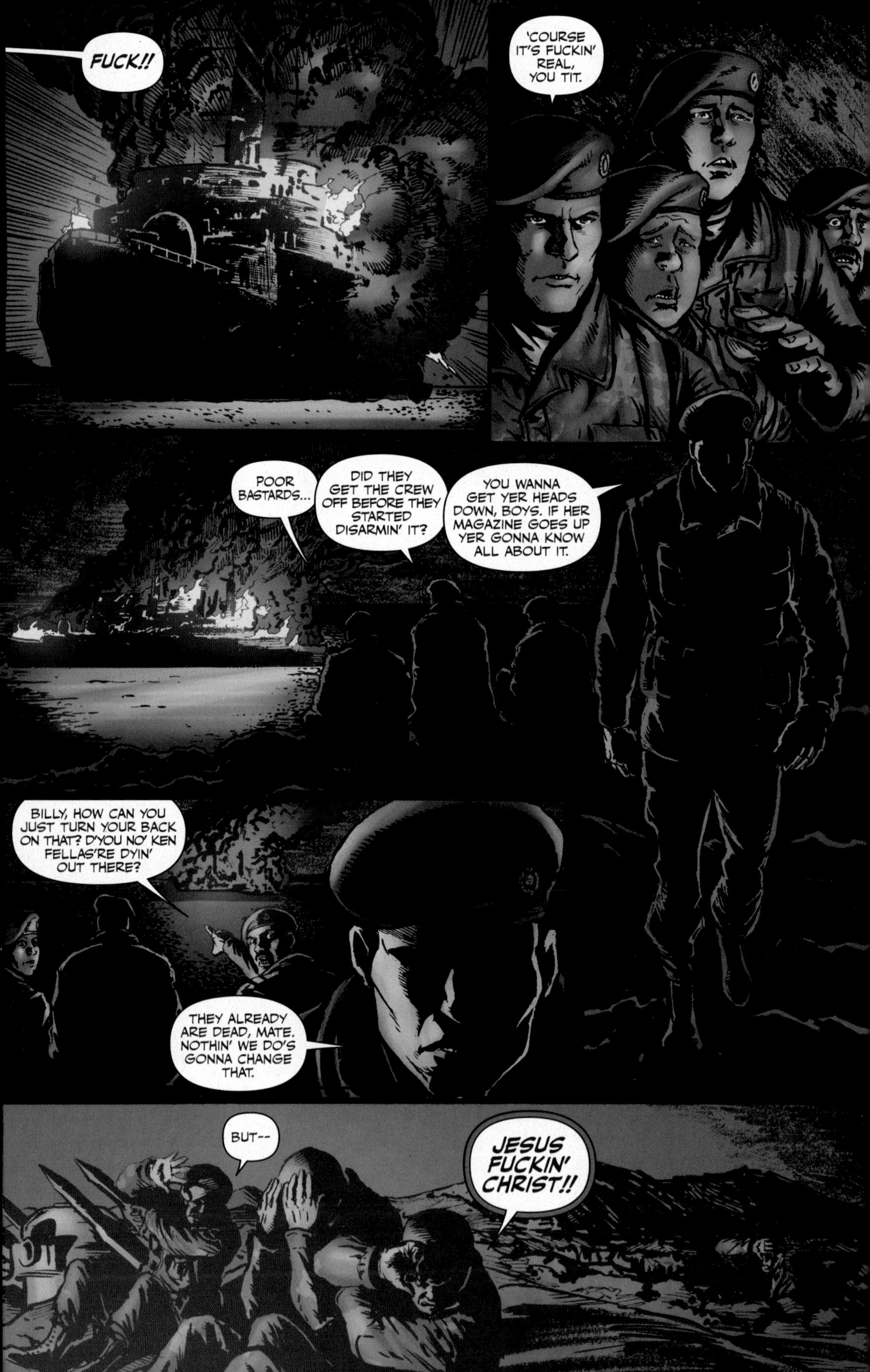

FUCK!!
'COURSE IT'S FUCKIN' REAL, YOU TIT.
POOR BASTARDS...
DID THEY GET THE CREW OFF BEFORE THEY STARTED DISARMIN' IT?
YOU WANNA GET YER HEADS DOWN, BOYS. IF HER MAGAZINE GOES UP YER GONNA KNOW ALL ABOUT IT.
BILLY, HOW CAN YOU JUST TURN YOUR BACK ON THAT? D'YOU NO' KEN FELLAS'RE DYIN' OUT THERE?
THEY ALREADY ARE DEAD, MATE. NOTHIN' WE DO'S GONNA CHANGE THAT.
BUT--
JESUS FUCKIN' CHRIST!!

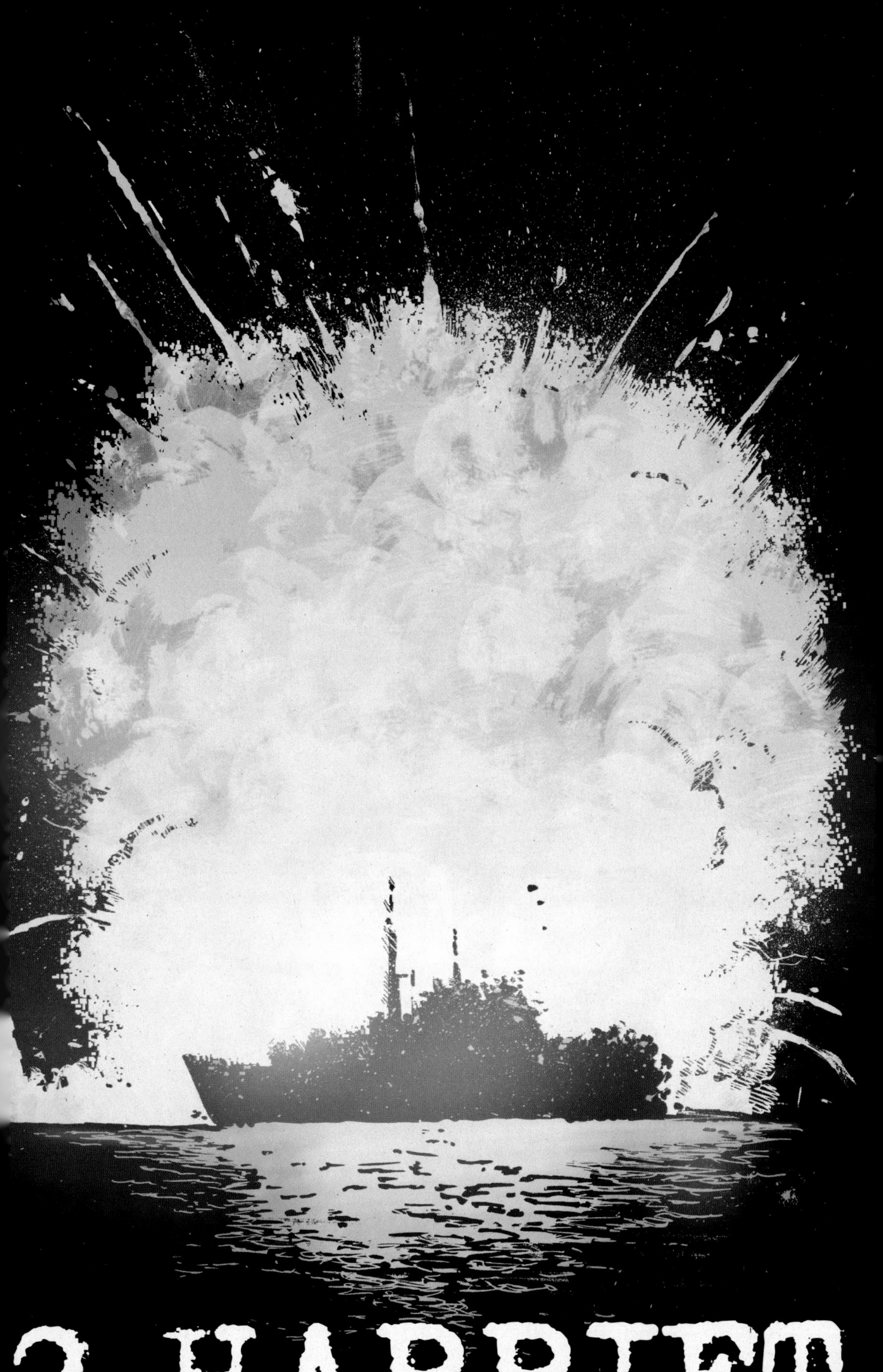

2: HARRIET

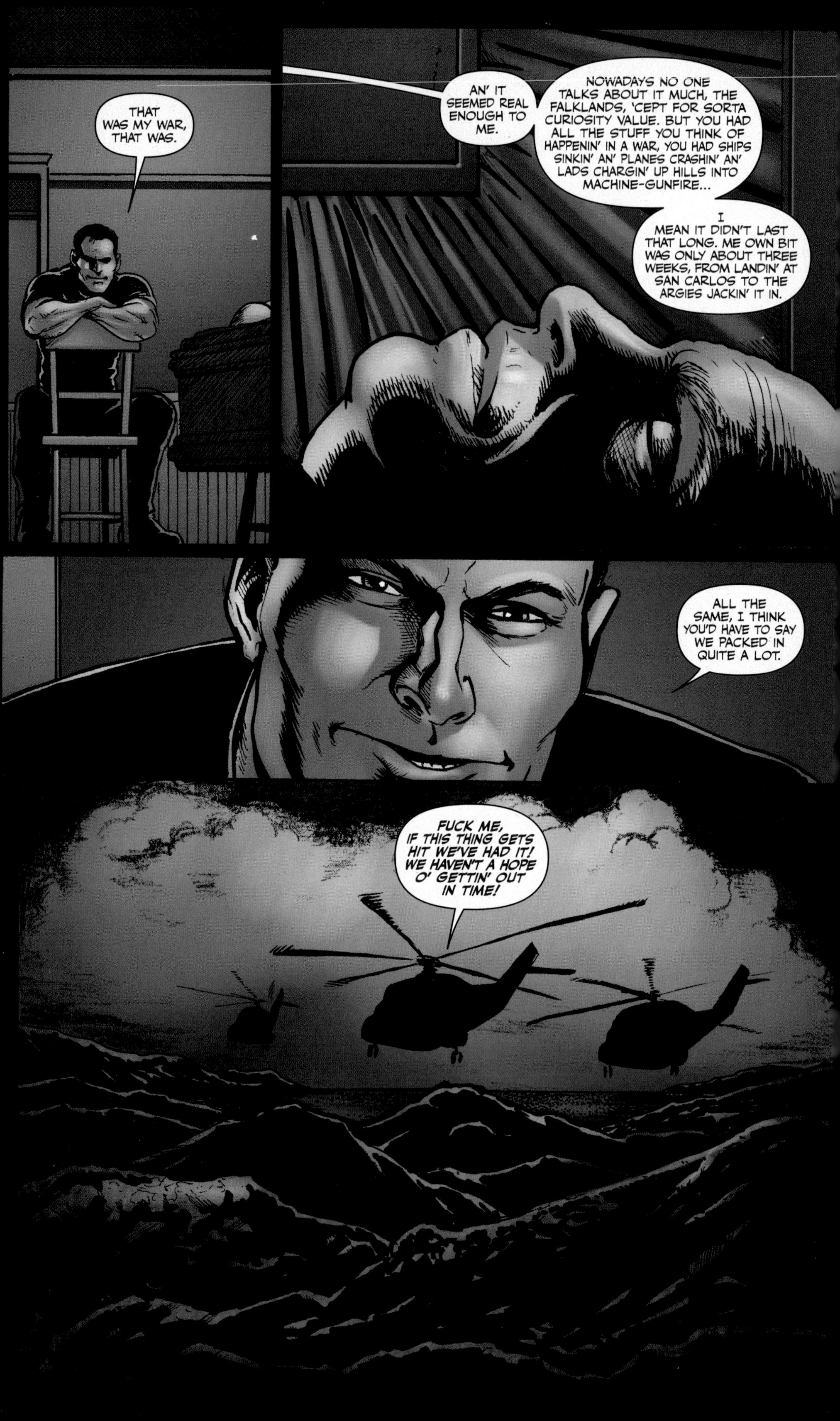
THAT WAS MY WAR, THAT WAS.
AN' IT SEEMED REAL ENOUGH TO ME.
NOWADAYS NO ONE TALKS ABOUT IT MUCH, THE FALKLANDS, 'CEPT FOR SORTA CURIOSITY VALUE. BUT YOU HAD ALL THE STUFF YOU THINK OF HAPPENIN' IN A WAR, YOU HAD SHIPS SINKIN' AN' PLANES CRASHIN' AN' LADS CHARGIN' UP HILLS INTO MACHINE-GUNFIRE...
I MEAN IT DIDN'T LAST THAT LONG. ME OWN BIT WAS ONLY ABOUT THREE WEEKS, FROM LANDIN' AT SAN CARLOS TO THE ARGIES JACKIN' IT IN.
ALL THE SAME, I THINK YOU'D HAVE TO SAY WE PACKED IN QUITE A LOT.
FUCK ME, IF THIS THING GETS HIT WE'VE HAD IT! WE HAVEN'T A HOPE O' GETTIN' OUT IN TIME!

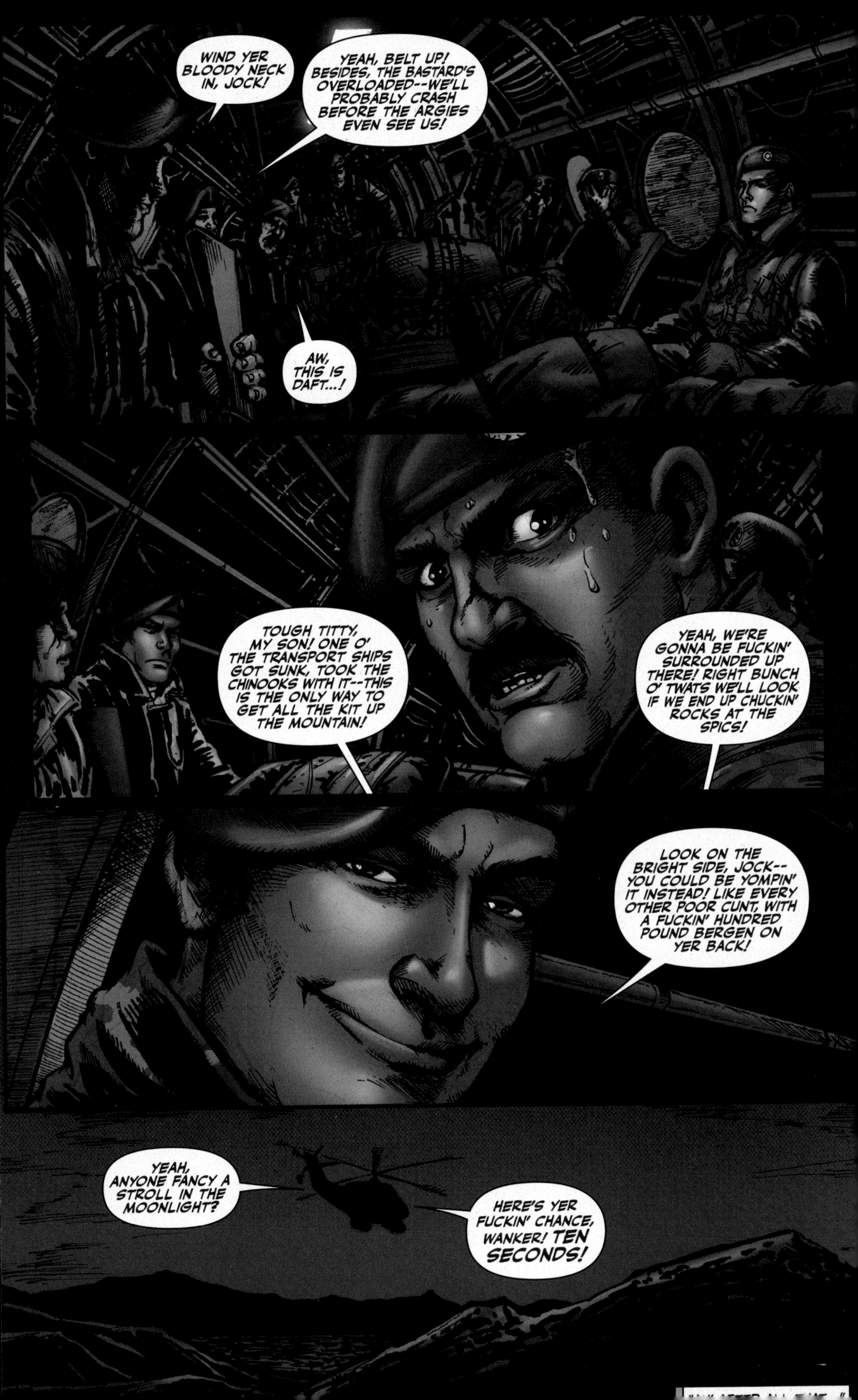
WIND YER BLOODY NECK IN, JOCK!
YEAH, BELT UP! BESIDES, THE BASTARD'S OVERLOADED--WE'LL PROBABLY CRASH BEFORE THE ARGIES EVEN SEE US!
AW, THIS IS DAFT...!
TOUGH TITTY, MY SON! ONE O' THE TRANSPORT SHIPS GOT SUNK, TOOK THE CHINOOKS WITH IT--THIS IS THE ONLY WAY TO GET ALL THE KIT UP THE MOUNTAIN!
YEAH, WE'RE GONNA BE FUCKIN' SURROUNDED UP THERE! RIGHT BUNCH O' TWATS WE'LL LOOK IF WE END UP CHUCKIN' ROCKS AT THE SPICS!
LOOK ON THE BRIGHT SIDE, JOCK--YOU COULD BE YOMPIN' IT INSTEAD! LIKE EVERY OTHER POOR CUNT, WITH A FUCKIN' HUNDRED POUND BERGEN ON YER BACK!
YEAH, ANYONE FANCY A STROLL IN THE MOONLIGHT?
HERE'S YER FUCKIN' CHANCE, WANKER! TEN SECONDS!

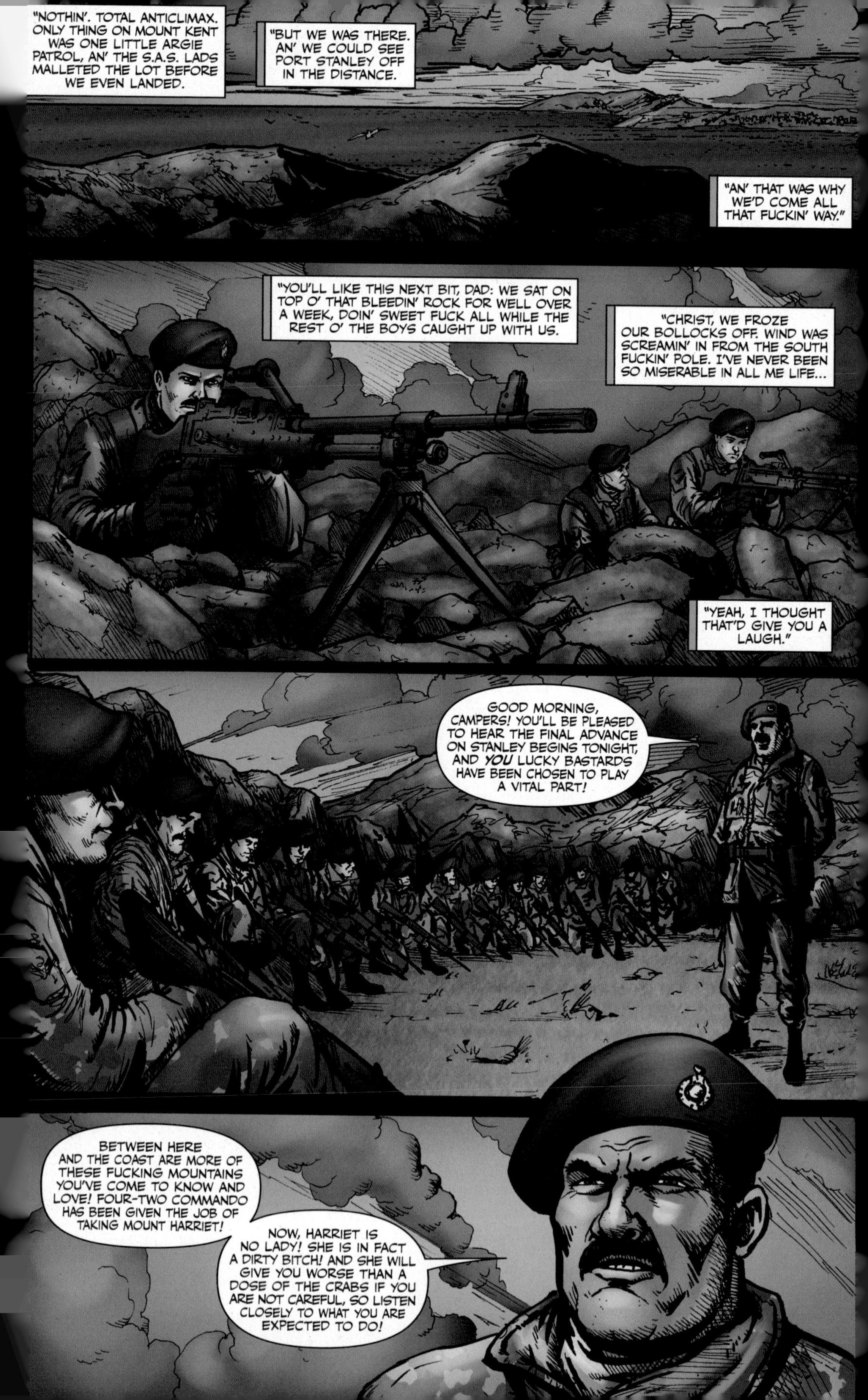
"NOTHIN'. TOTAL ANTICLIMAX. ONLY THING ON MOUNT KENT WAS ONE LITTLE ARGIE PATROL, AN' THE S.A.S. LADS MALLETED THE LOT BEFORE WE EVEN LANDED.
"BUT WE WAS THERE. AN' WE COULD SEE PORT STANLEY OFF IN THE DISTANCE.
"AN' THAT WAS WHY WE'D COME ALL THAT FUCKIN' WAY."
"YOU'LL LIKE THIS NEXT BIT, DAD: WE SAT ON TOP O' THAT BLEEDIN' ROCK FOR WELL OVER A WEEK, DOIN' SWEET FUCK ALL WHILE THE REST O' THE BOYS CAUGHT UP WITH US.
"CHRIST, WE FROZE OUR BOLLOCKS OFF. WIND WAS SCREAMIN' IN FROM THE SOUTH FUCKIN' POLE. I'VE NEVER BEEN SO MISERABLE IN ALL ME LIFE...
"YEAH, I THOUGHT THAT'D GIVE YOU A LAUGH."
GOOD MORNING, CAMPERS! YOU'LL BE PLEASED TO HEAR THE FINAL ADVANCE ON STANLEY BEGINS TONIGHT, AND *YOU* LUCKY BASTARDS HAVE BEEN CHOSEN TO PLAY A VITAL PART!
BETWEEN HERE AND THE COAST ARE MORE OF THESE FUCKING MOUNTAINS YOU'VE COME TO KNOW AND LOVE! FOUR-TWO COMMANDO HAS BEEN GIVEN THE JOB OF TAKING MOUNT HARRIET!
NOW, HARRIET IS NO LADY! SHE IS IN FACT A DIRTY BITCH! AND SHE WILL GIVE YOU WORSE THAN A DOSE OF THE CRABS IF YOU ARE NOT CAREFUL, SO LISTEN CLOSELY TO WHAT YOU ARE EXPECTED TO DO!

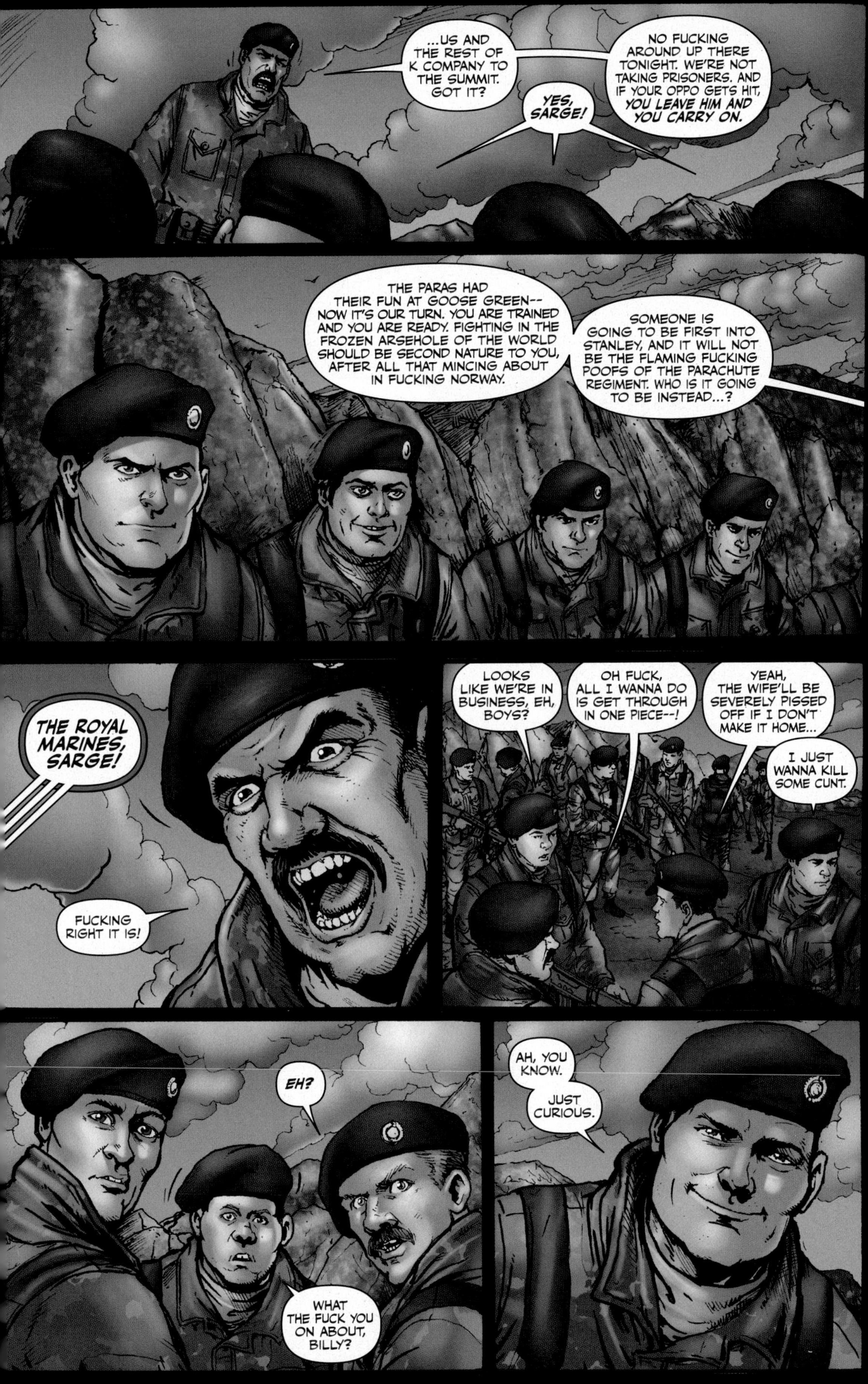
...US AND THE REST OF K COMPANY TO THE SUMMIT. GOT IT?
NO FUCKING AROUND UP THERE TONIGHT. WE'RE NOT TAKING PRISONERS. AND IF YOUR OPPO GETS HIT, YOU LEAVE HIM AND YOU CARRY ON.
YES, SARGE!
THE PARAS HAD THEIR FUN AT GOOSE GREEN-- NOW IT'S OUR TURN. YOU ARE TRAINED AND YOU ARE READY. FIGHTING IN THE FROZEN ARSEHOLE OF THE WORLD SHOULD BE SECOND NATURE TO YOU, AFTER ALL THAT MINCING ABOUT IN FUCKING NORWAY.
SOMEONE IS GOING TO BE FIRST INTO STANLEY, AND IT WILL NOT BE THE FLAMING FUCKING POOFS OF THE PARACHUTE REGIMENT. WHO IS IT GOING TO BE INSTEAD...?
THE ROYAL MARINES, SARGE!
FUCKING RIGHT IT IS!
LOOKS LIKE WE'RE IN BUSINESS, EH, BOYS?
OH FUCK, ALL I WANNA DO IS GET THROUGH IN ONE PIECE--!
YEAH, THE WIFE'LL BE SEVERELY PISSED OFF IF I DON'T MAKE IT HOME...
I JUST WANNA KILL SOME CUNT.
EH?
WHAT THE FUCK YOU ON ABOUT, BILLY?
AH, YOU KNOW.
JUST CURIOUS.

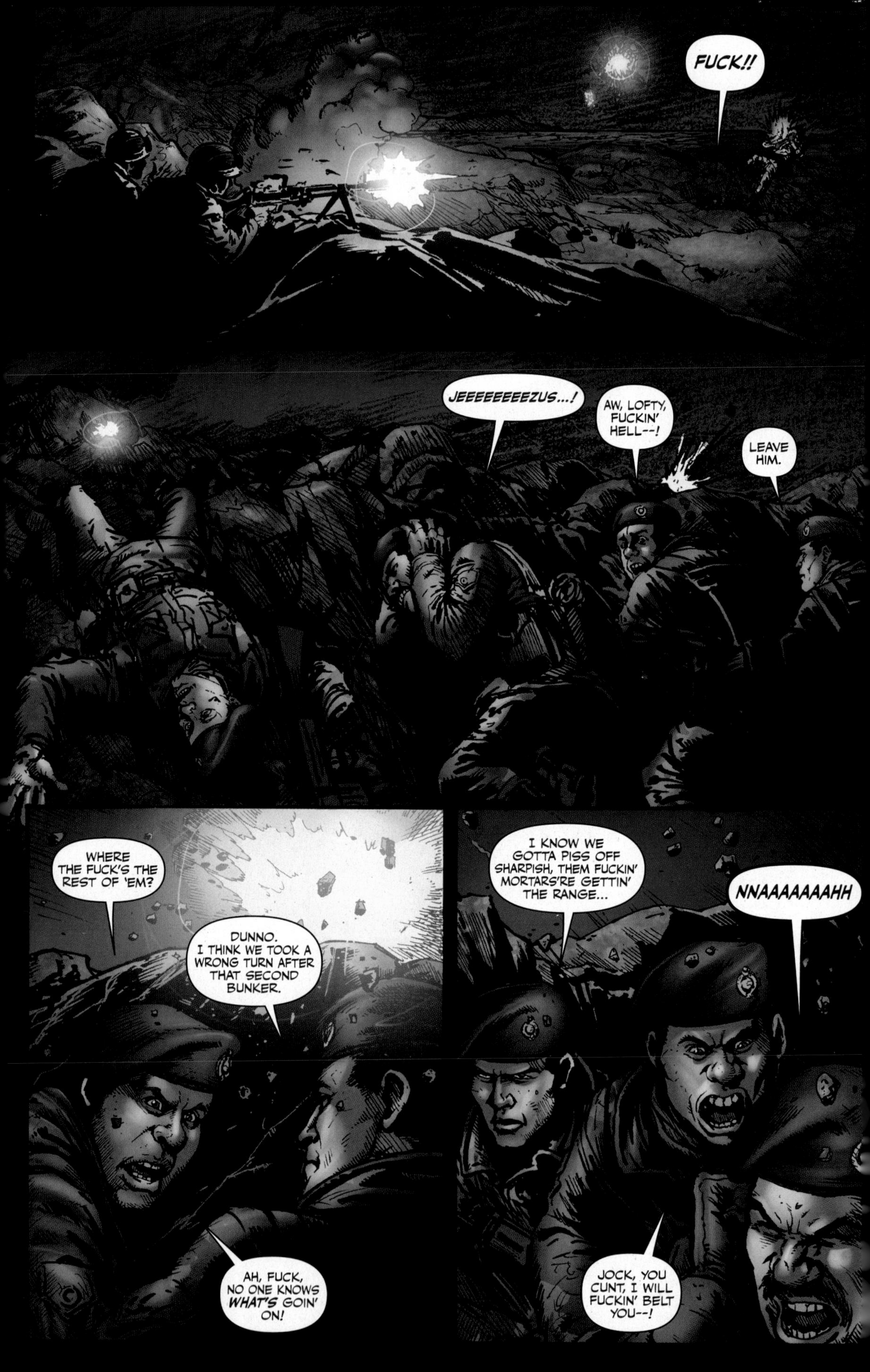
FUCK!!
JEEEEEEEEZUS...!
AW, LOFTY, FUCKIN' HELL--!
LEAVE HIM.
WHERE THE FUCK'S THE REST OF 'EM?
DUNNO. I THINK WE TOOK A WRONG TURN AFTER THAT SECOND BUNKER.
AH, FUCK, NO ONE KNOWS WHAT'S GOIN' ON!
I KNOW WE GOTTA PISS OFF SHARPISH, THEM FUCKIN' MORTARS'RE GETTIN' THE RANGE...
NNAAAAAAAAHH
JOCK, YOU CUNT, I WILL FUCKIN' BELT YOU--!

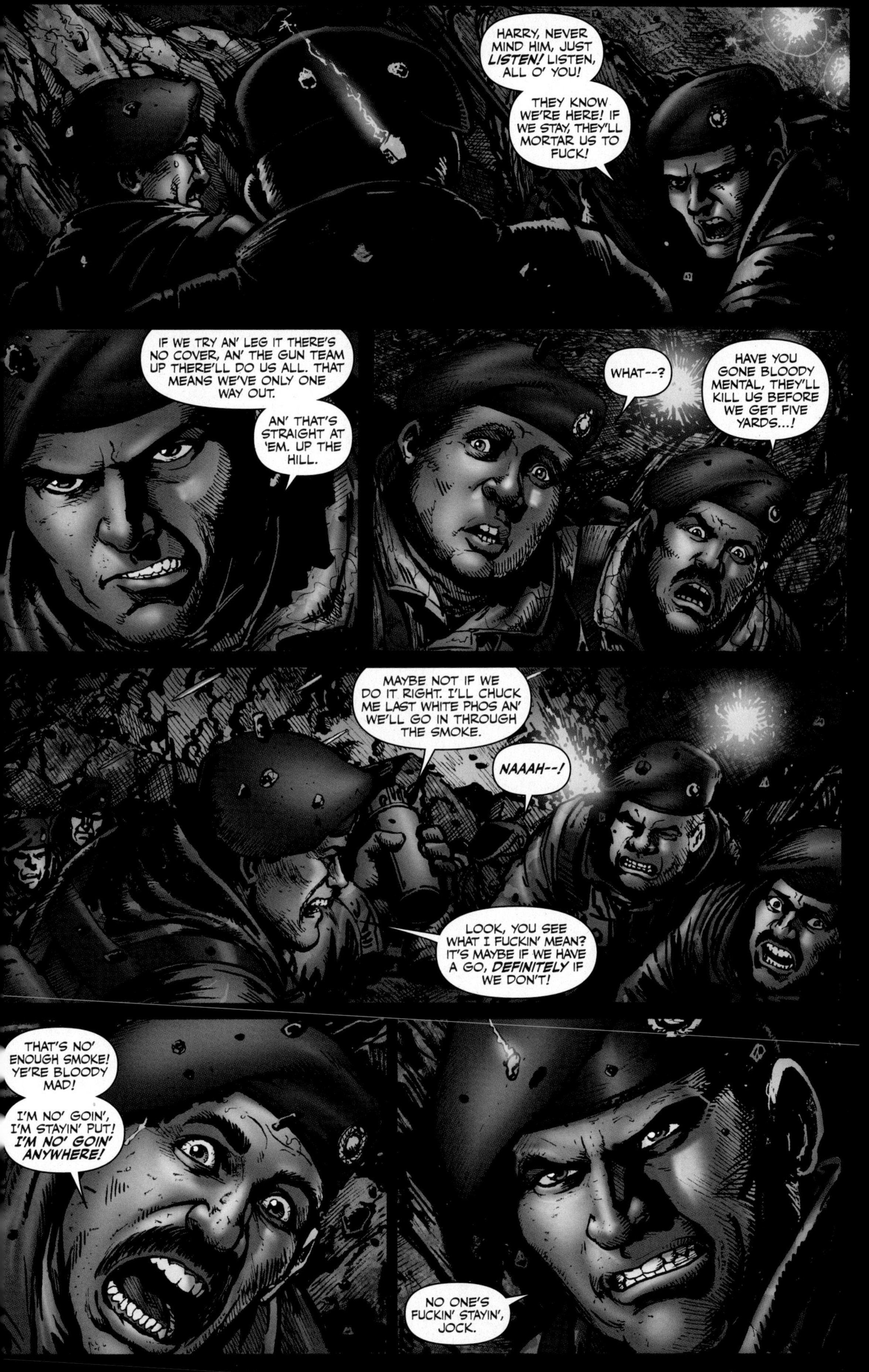
HARRY, NEVER MIND HIM, JUST *LISTEN!* LISTEN, ALL O' YOU!
THEY KNOW WE'RE HERE! IF WE STAY, THEY'LL MORTAR US TO FUCK!
IF WE TRY AN' LEG IT THERE'S NO COVER, AN' THE GUN TEAM UP THERE'LL DO US ALL. THAT MEANS WE'VE ONLY ONE WAY OUT.
AN' THAT'S STRAIGHT AT 'EM. UP THE HILL.
WHAT--?
HAVE YOU GONE BLOODY MENTAL, THEY'LL KILL US BEFORE WE GET FIVE YARDS...!
MAYBE NOT IF WE DO IT RIGHT. I'LL CHUCK ME LAST WHITE PHOS AN' WE'LL GO IN THROUGH THE SMOKE.
NAAAH--!
LOOK, YOU SEE WHAT I FUCKIN' MEAN? IT'S MAYBE IF WE HAVE A GO, *DEFINITELY* IF WE DON'T!
THAT'S NO' ENOUGH SMOKE! YE'RE BLOODY MAD!
I'M NO' GOIN', I'M STAYIN' PUT! ***I'M NO' GOIN' ANYWHERE!***
NO ONE'S FUCKIN' STAYIN', JOCK.

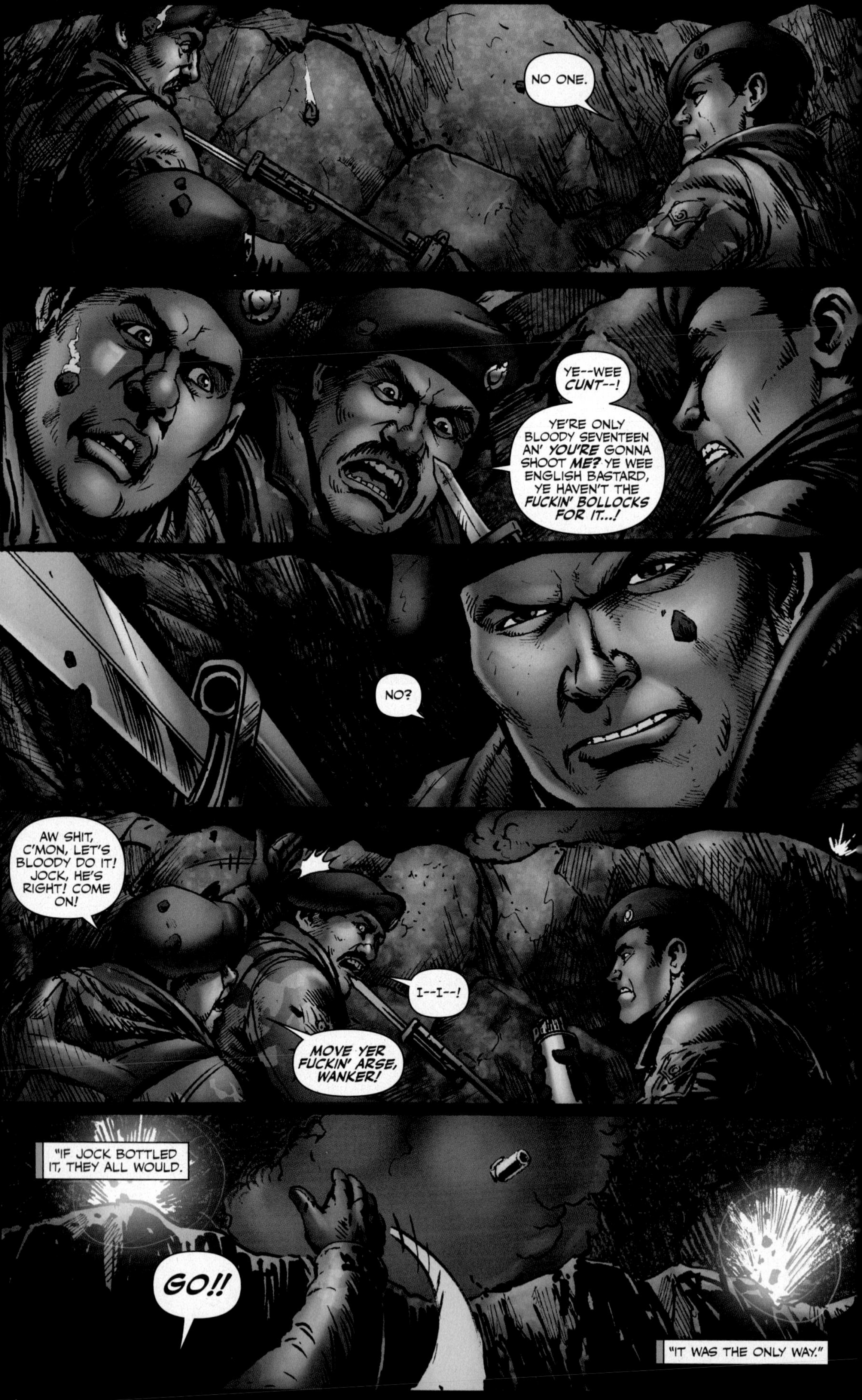
NO ONE.
YE--WEE CUNT--!
YE'RE ONLY BLOODY SEVENTEEN AN' YOU'RE GONNA SHOOT ME? YE WEE ENGLISH BASTARD, YE HAVEN'T THE FUCKIN' BOLLOCKS FOR IT...!
NO?
AW SHIT, C'MON, LET'S BLOODY DO IT! JOCK, HE'S RIGHT! COME ON!
I--I--!
MOVE YER FUCKIN' ARSE, WANKER!
"IF JOCK BOTTLED IT, THEY ALL WOULD.
GO!!
"IT WAS THE ONLY WAY."

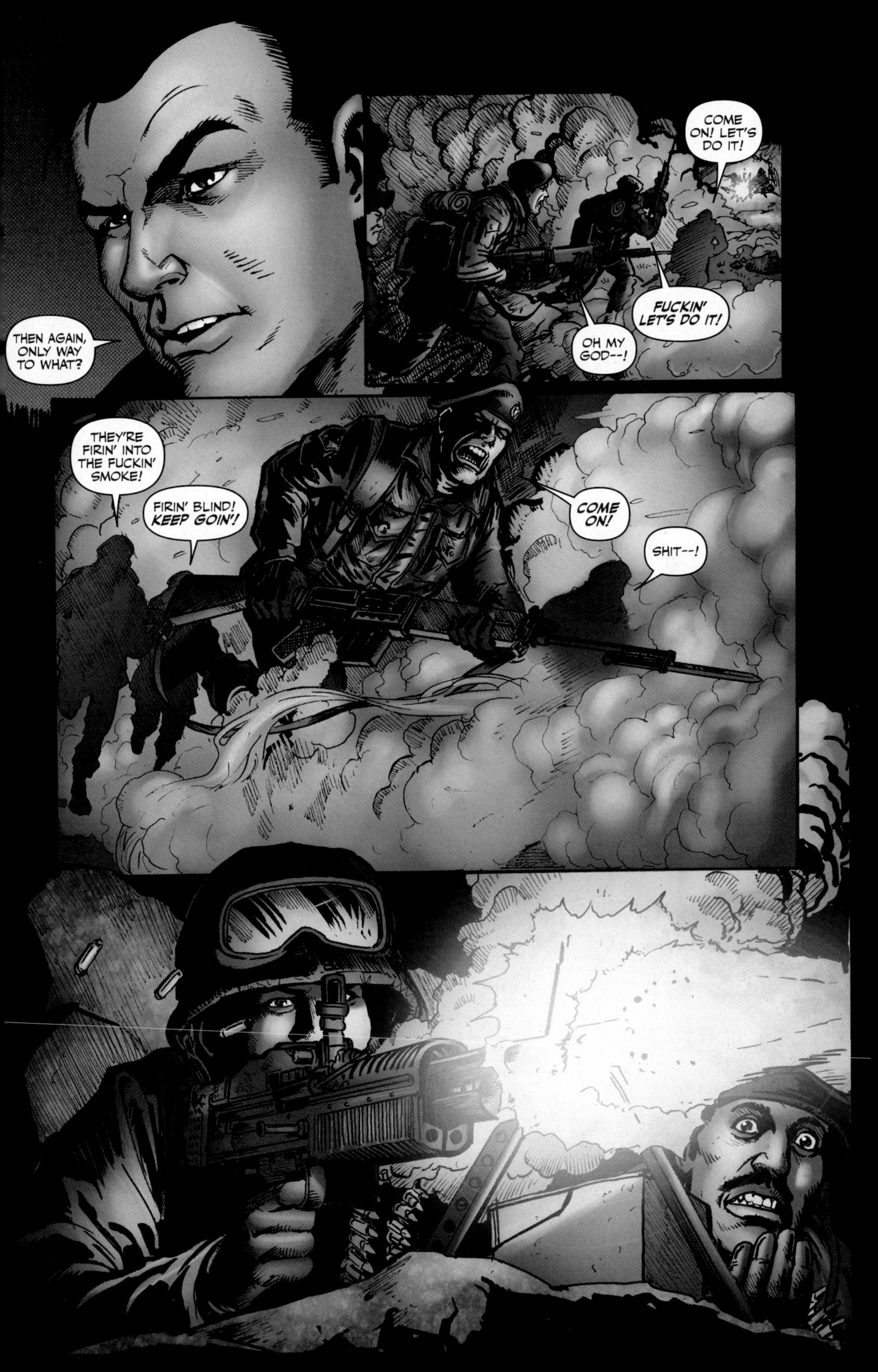

THEN AGAIN, ONLY WAY TO WHAT?
COME ON! LET'S DO IT!
FUCKIN' LET'S DO IT!
OH MY GOD--!
THEY'RE FIRIN' INTO THE FUCKIN' SMOKE!
FIRIN' BLIND! KEEP GOIN'!
COME ON!
SHIT--!

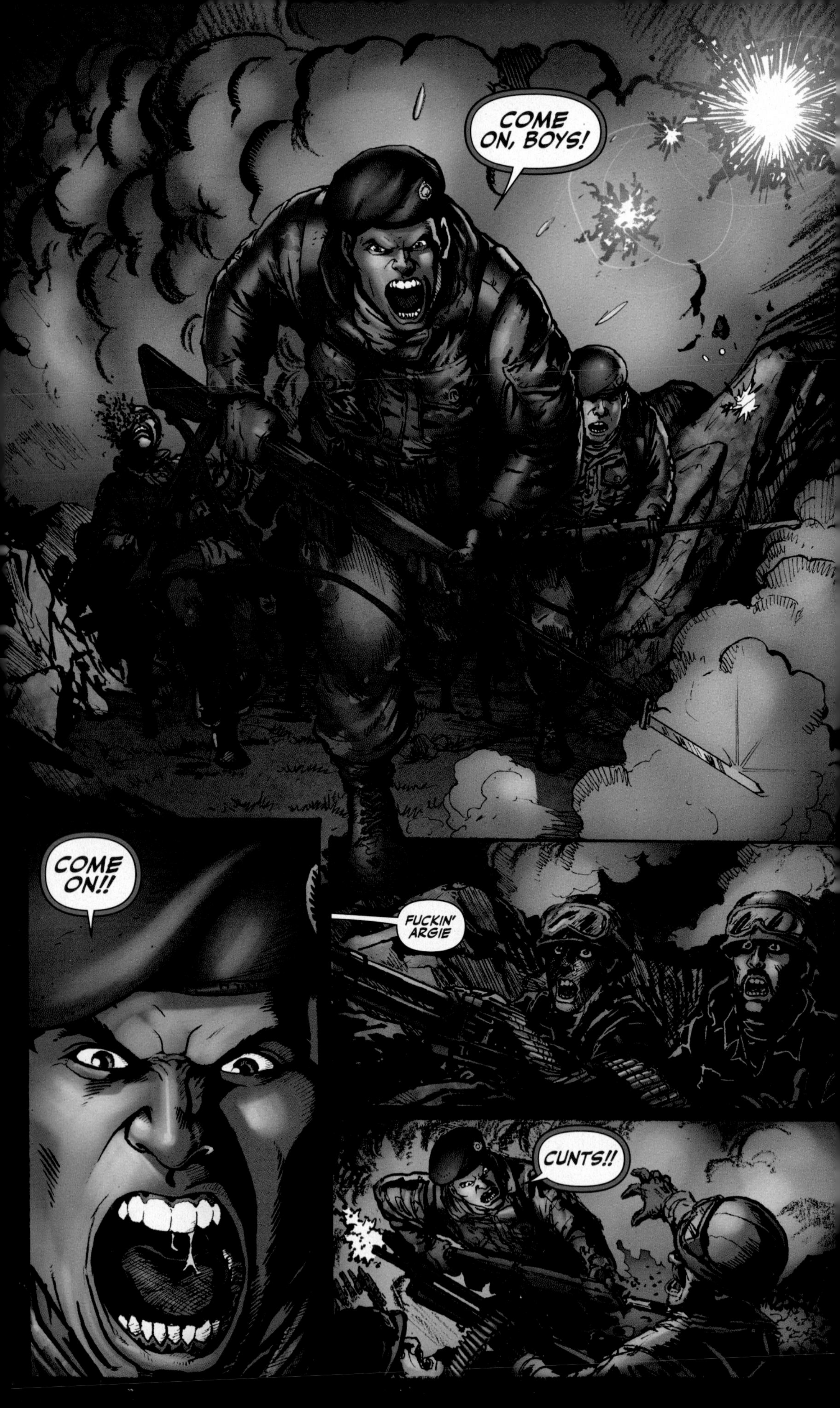

COME ON, BOYS!
COME ON!!
FUCKIN' ARGIE
CUNTS!!

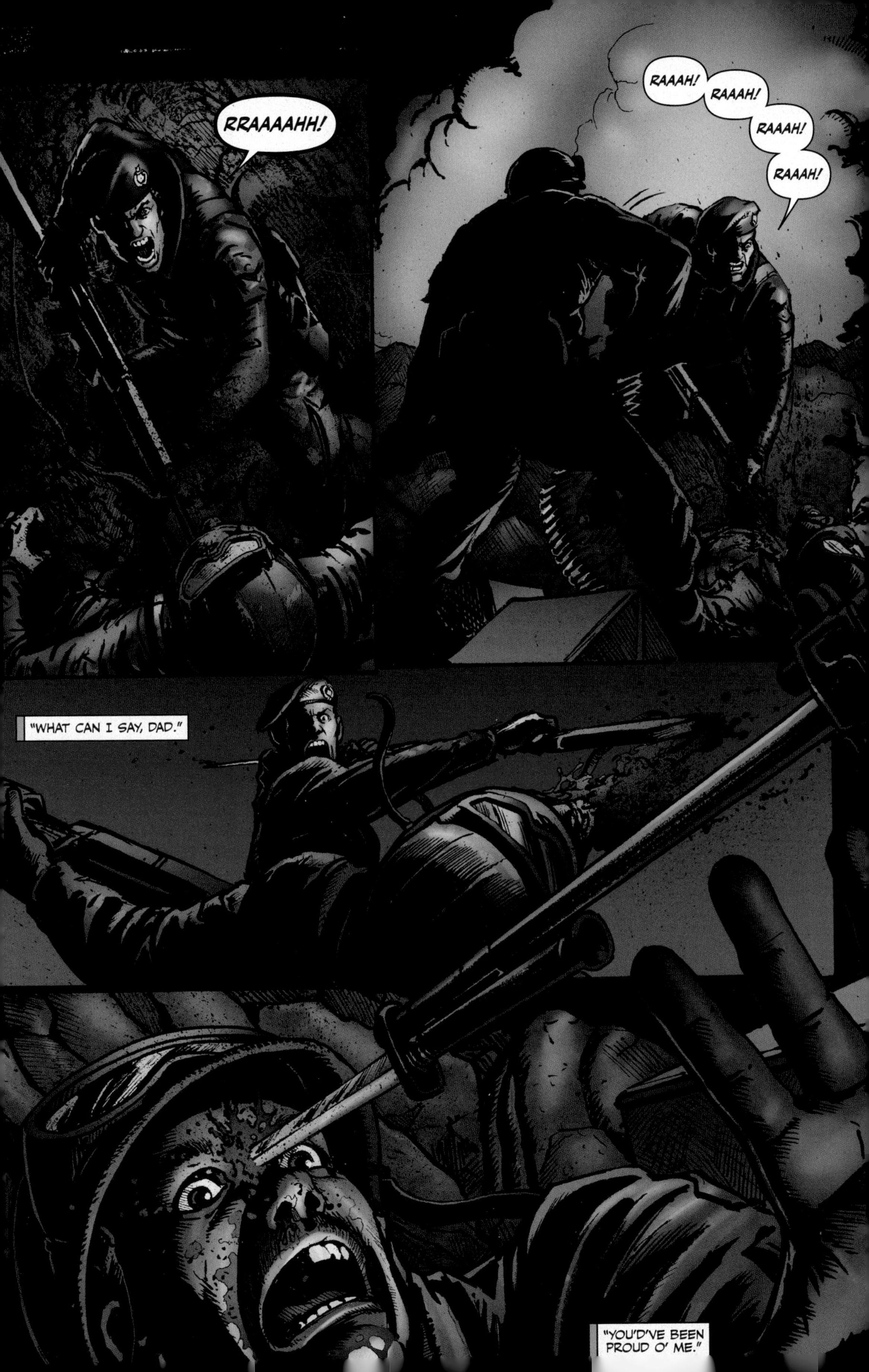
RRAAAAHH!
RAAAH!
RAAAH!
RAAAH!
RAAAH!
"WHAT CAN I SAY, DAD."
"YOU'D'VE BEEN PROUD O' ME."

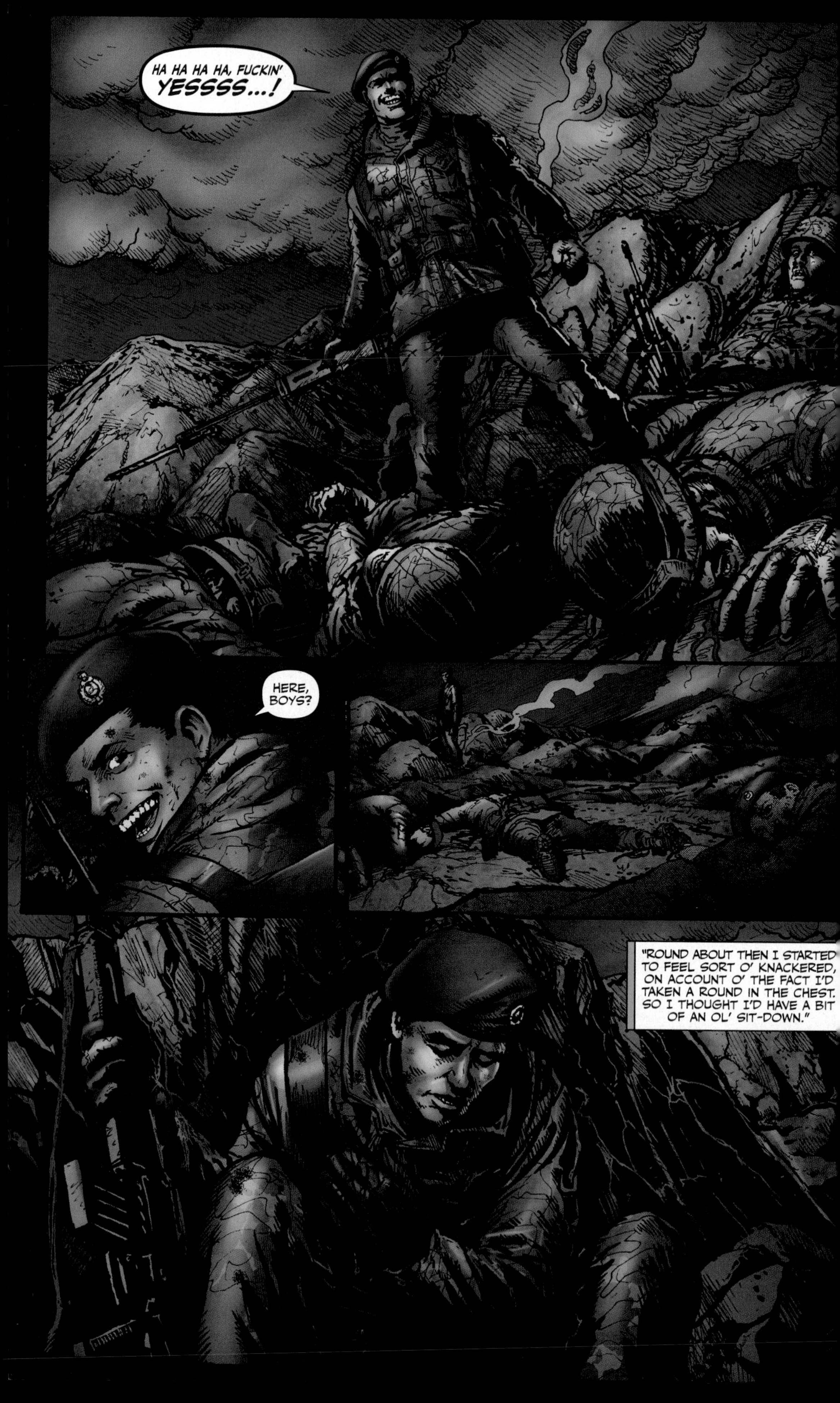
HA HA HA HA, FUCKIN' YESSSS...!
HERE, BOYS?
"ROUND ABOUT THEN I STARTED TO FEEL SORT O' KNACKERED, ON ACCOUNT O' THE FACT I'D TAKEN A ROUND IN THE CHEST. SO I THOUGHT I'D HAVE A BIT OF AN OL' SIT-DOWN."

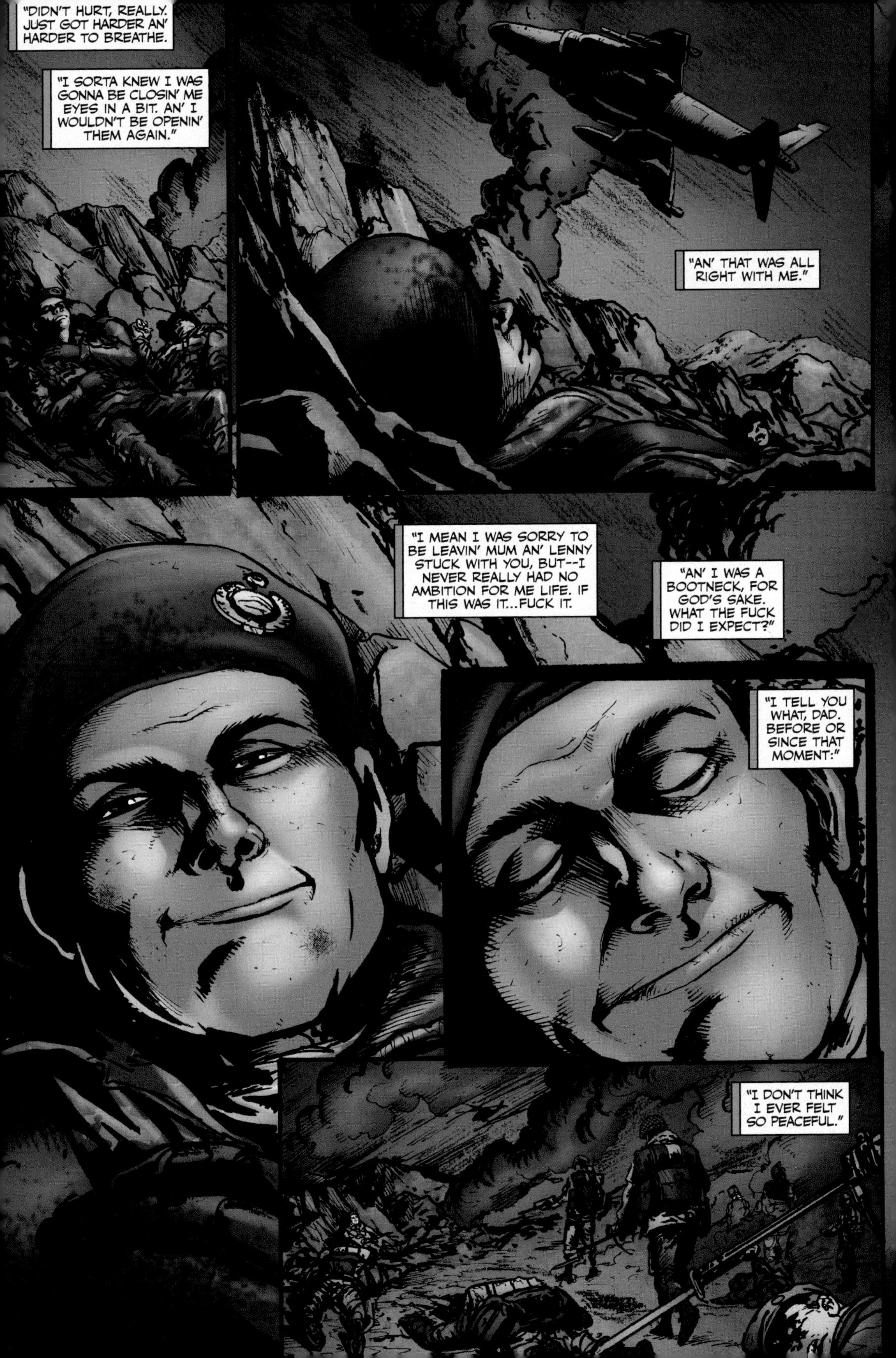
"DIDN'T HURT, REALLY. JUST GOT HARDER AN' HARDER TO BREATHE.
"I SORTA KNEW I WAS GONNA BE CLOSIN' ME EYES IN A BIT. AN' I WOULDN'T BE OPENIN' THEM AGAIN."
"AN' THAT WAS ALL RIGHT WITH ME."
"I MEAN I WAS SORRY TO BE LEAVIN' MUM AN' LENNY STUCK WITH YOU, BUT--I NEVER REALLY HAD NO AMBITION FOR ME LIFE. IF THIS WAS IT...FUCK IT.
"AN' I WAS A BOOTNECK, FOR GOD'S SAKE. WHAT THE FUCK DID I EXPECT?"
"I TELL YOU WHAT, DAD. BEFORE OR SINCE THAT MOMENT:"
"I DON'T THINK I EVER FELT SO PEACEFUL."

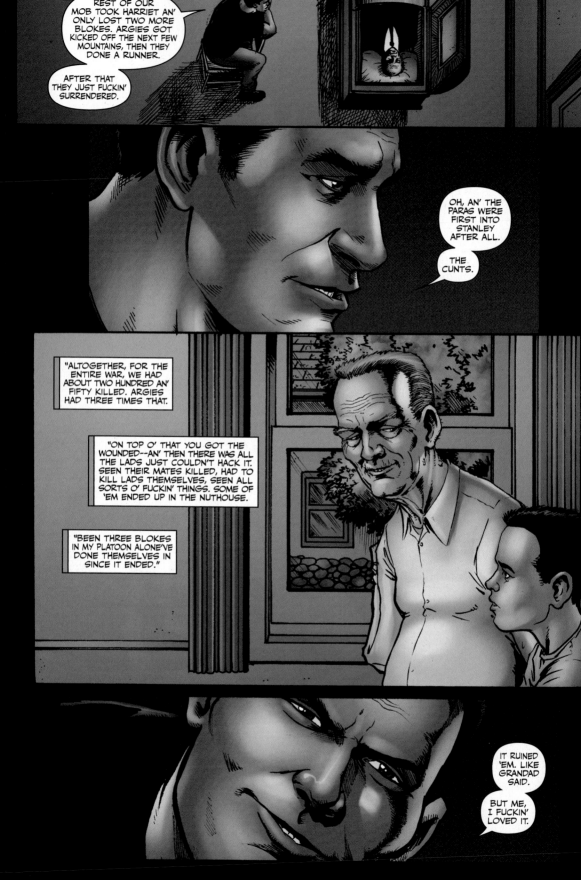

REST OF OUR MOB TOOK HARRIET AN' ONLY LOST TWO MORE BLOKES. ARGIES GOT KICKED OFF THE NEXT FEW MOUNTAINS, THEN THEY DONE A RUNNER.

AFTER THAT THEY JUST FUCKIN' SURRENDERED.

OH, AN' THE PARAS WERE FIRST INTO STANLEY AFTER ALL.

THE CUNTS.

"ALTOGETHER, FOR THE ENTIRE WAR, WE HAD ABOUT TWO HUNDRED AN' FIFTY KILLED. ARGIES HAD THREE TIMES THAT.

"ON TOP O' THAT YOU GOT THE WOUNDED--AN' THEN THERE WAS ALL THE LADS JUST COULDN'T HACK IT. SEEN THEIR MATES KILLED, HAD TO KILL LADS THEMSELVES, SEEN ALL SORTS O' FUCKIN' THINGS. SOME OF 'EM ENDED UP IN THE NUTHOUSE.

"BEEN THREE BLOKES IN MY PLATOON ALONE'VE DONE THEMSELVES IN SINCE IT ENDED."

IT RUINED 'EM. LIKE GRANDAD SAID.

BUT ME, I FUCKIN' LOVED IT.

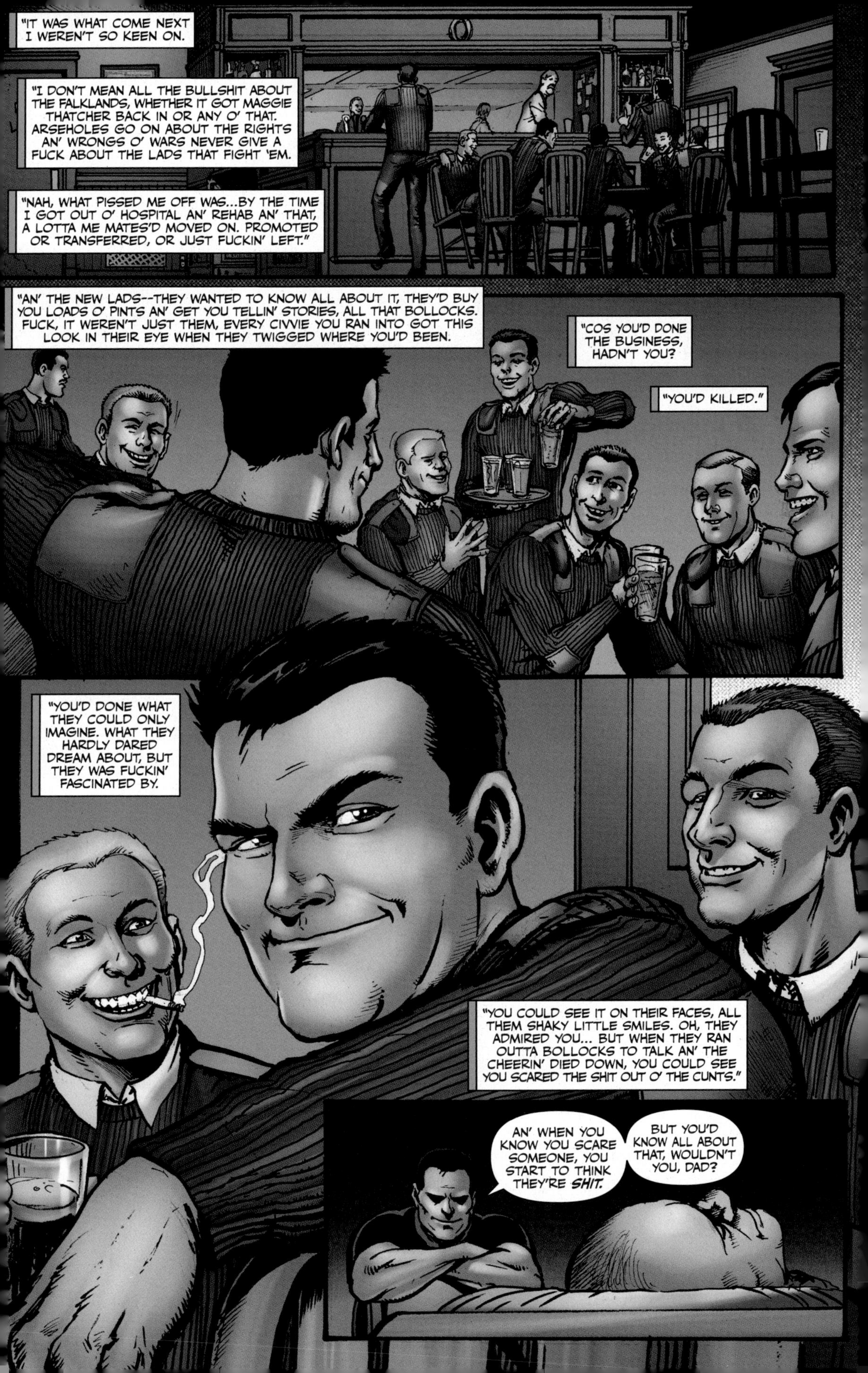
"IT WAS WHAT COME NEXT I WEREN'T SO KEEN ON.
"I DON'T MEAN ALL THE BULLSHIT ABOUT THE FALKLANDS, WHETHER IT GOT MAGGIE THATCHER BACK IN OR ANY O' THAT. ARSEHOLES GO ON ABOUT THE RIGHTS AN' WRONGS O' WARS NEVER GIVE A FUCK ABOUT THE LADS THAT FIGHT 'EM.
"NAH, WHAT PISSED ME OFF WAS...BY THE TIME I GOT OUT O' HOSPITAL AN' REHAB AN' THAT, A LOTTA ME MATES'D MOVED ON. PROMOTED OR TRANSFERRED, OR JUST FUCKIN' LEFT."
"AN' THE NEW LADS--THEY WANTED TO KNOW ALL ABOUT IT, THEY'D BUY YOU LOADS O' PINTS AN' GET YOU TELLIN' STORIES, ALL THAT BOLLOCKS. FUCK, IT WEREN'T JUST THEM, EVERY CIVVIE YOU RAN INTO GOT THIS LOOK IN THEIR EYE WHEN THEY TWIGGED WHERE YOU'D BEEN.
"COS YOU'D DONE THE BUSINESS, HADN'T YOU?
"YOU'D KILLED."
"YOU'D DONE WHAT THEY COULD ONLY IMAGINE. WHAT THEY HARDLY DARED DREAM ABOUT, BUT THEY WAS FUCKIN' FASCINATED BY.
"YOU COULD SEE IT ON THEIR FACES, ALL THEM SHAKY LITTLE SMILES. OH, THEY ADMIRED YOU... BUT WHEN THEY RAN OUTTA BOLLOCKS TO TALK AN' THE CHEERIN' DIED DOWN, YOU COULD SEE YOU SCARED THE SHIT OUT O' THE CUNTS."
AN' WHEN YOU KNOW YOU SCARE SOMEONE, YOU START TO THINK THEY'RE *SHIT.*
BUT YOU'D KNOW ALL ABOUT THAT, WOULDN'T YOU, DAD?

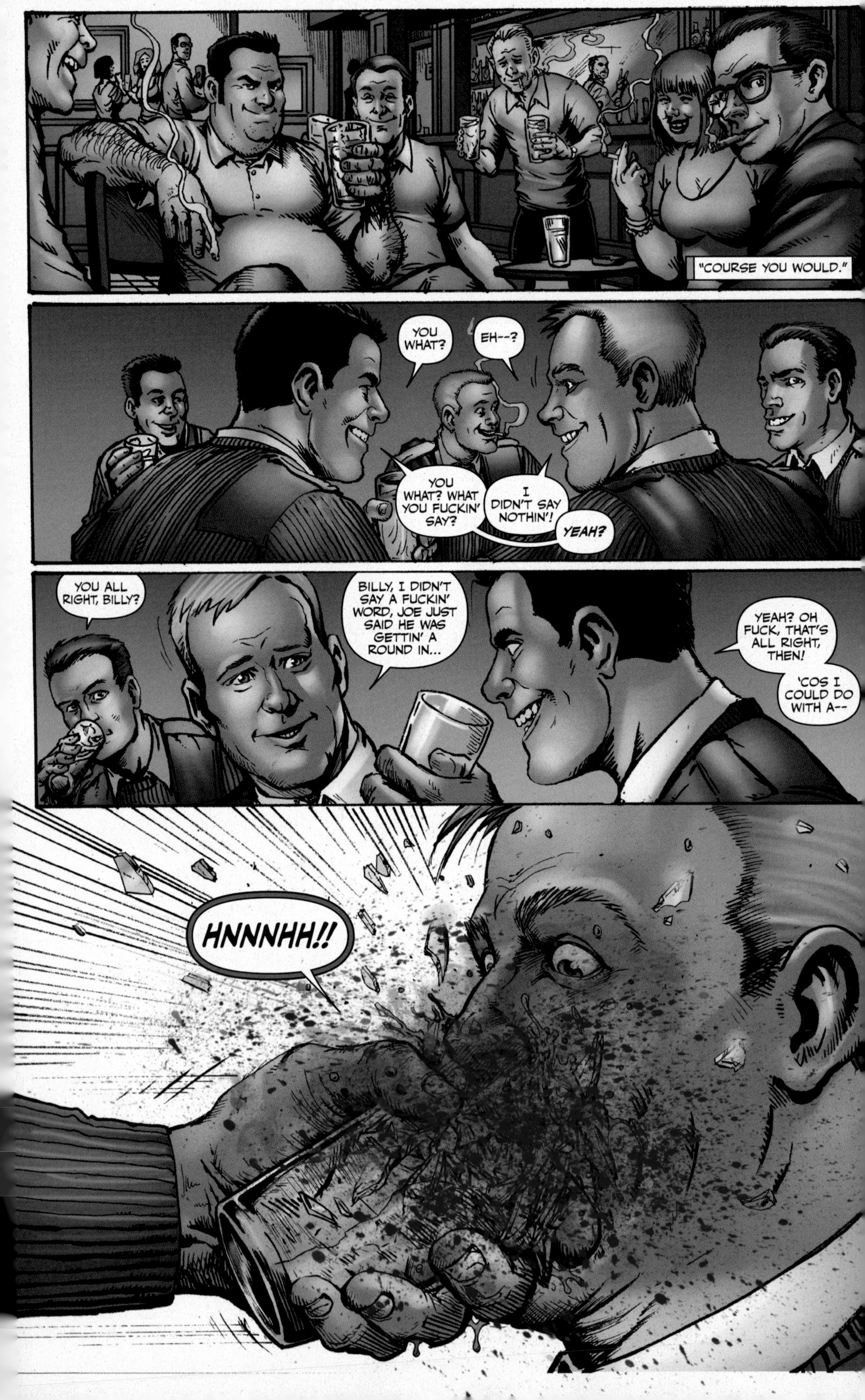
"COURSE YOU WOULD."
YOU WHAT?
EH--?
YOU WHAT? WHAT YOU FUCKIN' SAY?
I DIDN'T SAY NOTHIN'!
YEAH?
YOU ALL RIGHT, BILLY?
BILLY, I DIDN'T SAY A FUCKIN' WORD, JOE JUST SAID HE WAS GETTIN' A ROUND IN...
YEAH? OH FUCK, THAT'S ALL RIGHT, THEN!
'COS I COULD DO WITH A--
HNNNHH!!

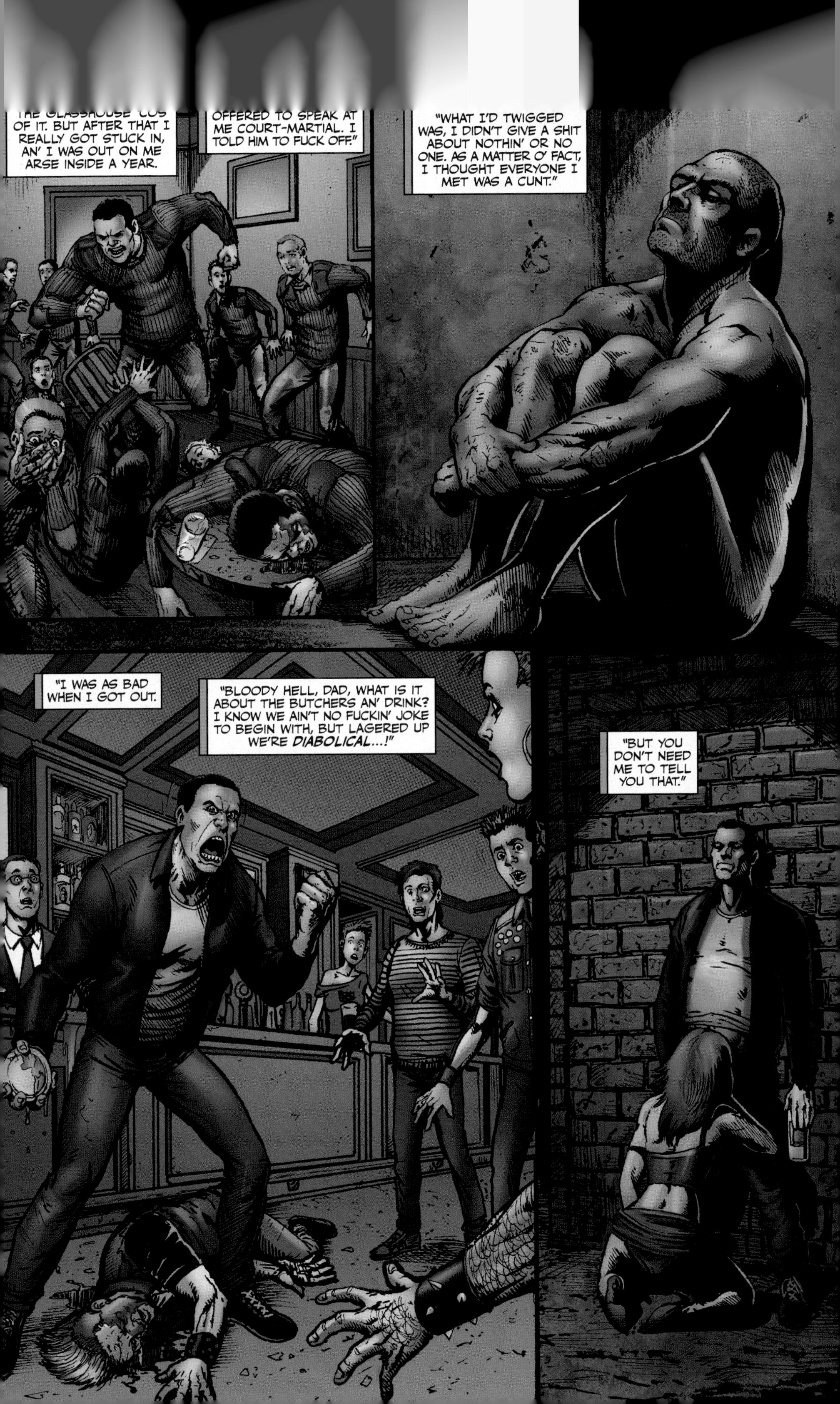
OF IT. BUT AFTER THAT I REALLY GOT STUCK IN, AN' I WAS OUT ON ME ARSE INSIDE A YEAR.
OFFERED TO SPEAK AT ME COURT-MARTIAL. I TOLD HIM TO FUCK OFF."
"WHAT I'D TWIGGED WAS, I DIDN'T GIVE A SHIT ABOUT NOTHIN' OR NO ONE. AS A MATTER O' FACT, I THOUGHT EVERYONE I MET WAS A CUNT."
"I WAS AS BAD WHEN I GOT OUT.
"BLOODY HELL, DAD, WHAT IS IT ABOUT THE BUTCHERS AN' DRINK? I KNOW WE AIN'T NO FUCKIN' JOKE TO BEGIN WITH, BUT LAGERED UP WE'RE *DIABOLICAL*...!"
"BUT YOU DON'T NEED ME TO TELL YOU THAT."

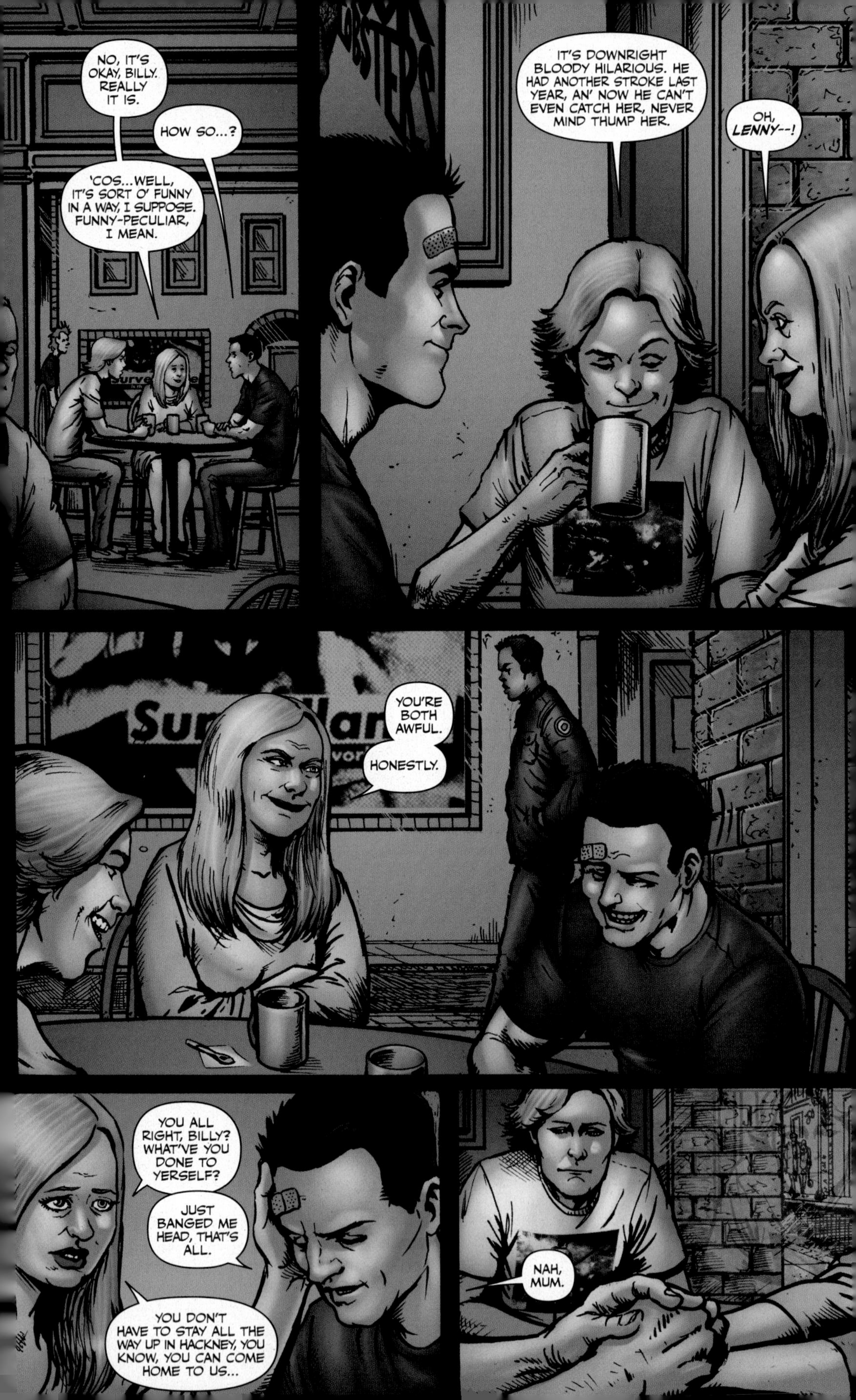
NO, IT'S OKAY, BILLY. REALLY IT IS.
HOW SO...?
'COS...WELL, IT'S SORT O' FUNNY IN A WAY, I SUPPOSE. FUNNY-PECULIAR, I MEAN.
IT'S DOWNRIGHT BLOODY HILARIOUS. HE HAD ANOTHER STROKE LAST YEAR, AN' NOW HE CAN'T EVEN CATCH HER, NEVER MIND THUMP HER.
OH, *LENNY*--!
YOU'RE BOTH AWFUL.
HONESTLY.
YOU ALL RIGHT, BILLY? WHAT'VE YOU DONE TO YERSELF?
JUST BANGED ME HEAD, THAT'S ALL.
YOU DON'T HAVE TO STAY ALL THE WAY UP IN HACKNEY, YOU KNOW, YOU CAN COME HOME TO US...
NAH, MUM.

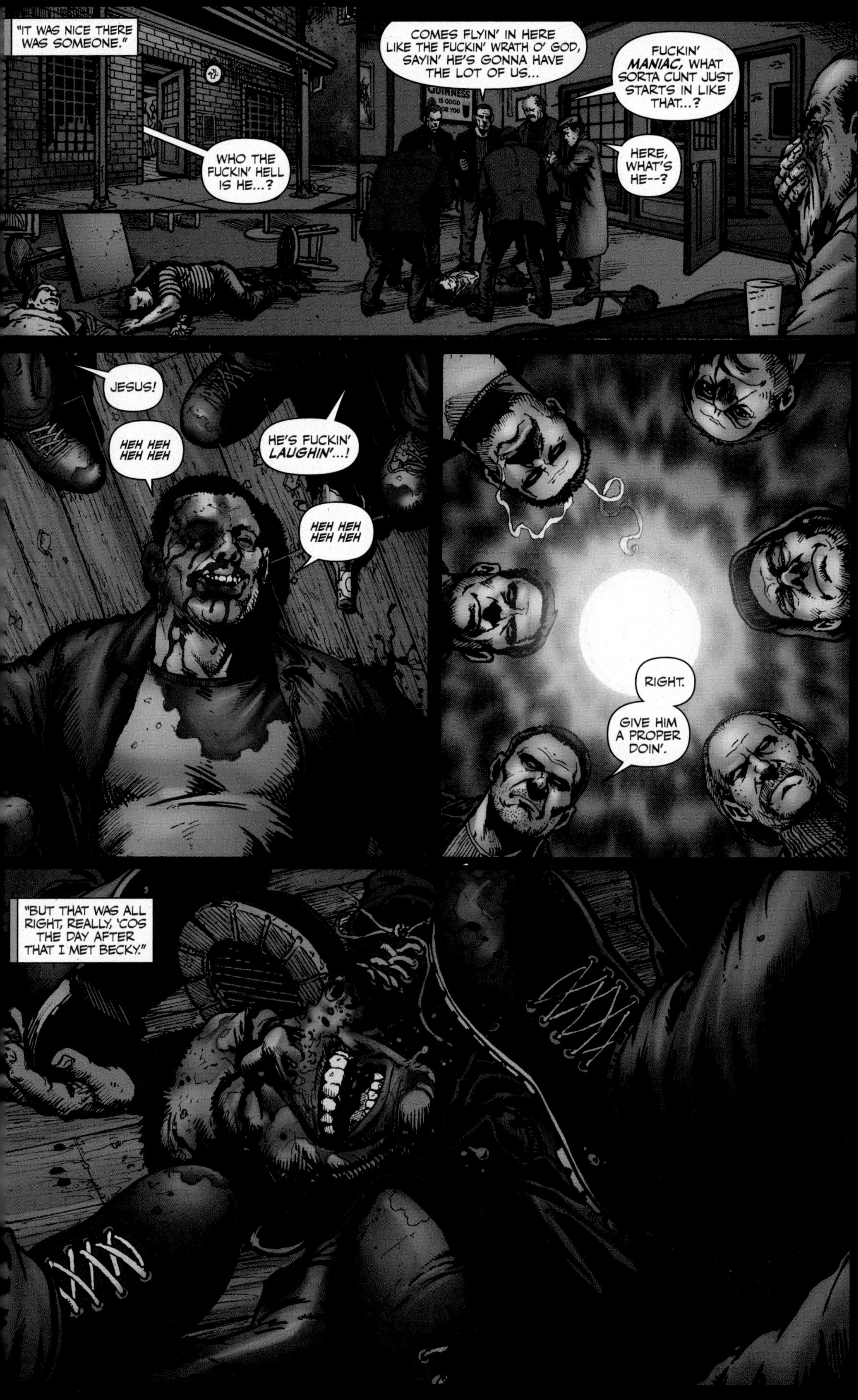

"IT WAS NICE THERE WAS SOMEONE."
WHO THE FUCKIN' HELL IS HE...?
COMES FLYIN' IN HERE LIKE THE FUCKIN' WRATH O' GOD, SAYIN' HE'S GONNA HAVE THE LOT OF US...
FUCKIN' MANIAC, WHAT SORTA CUNT JUST STARTS IN LIKE THAT...?
HERE, WHAT'S HE--?
JESUS!
HEH HEH HEH HEH
HE'S FUCKIN' LAUGHIN'...!
HEH HEH HEH HEH
RIGHT.
GIVE HIM A PROPER DOIN'.
"BUT THAT WAS ALL RIGHT, REALLY, 'COS THE DAY AFTER THAT I MET BECKY."

three

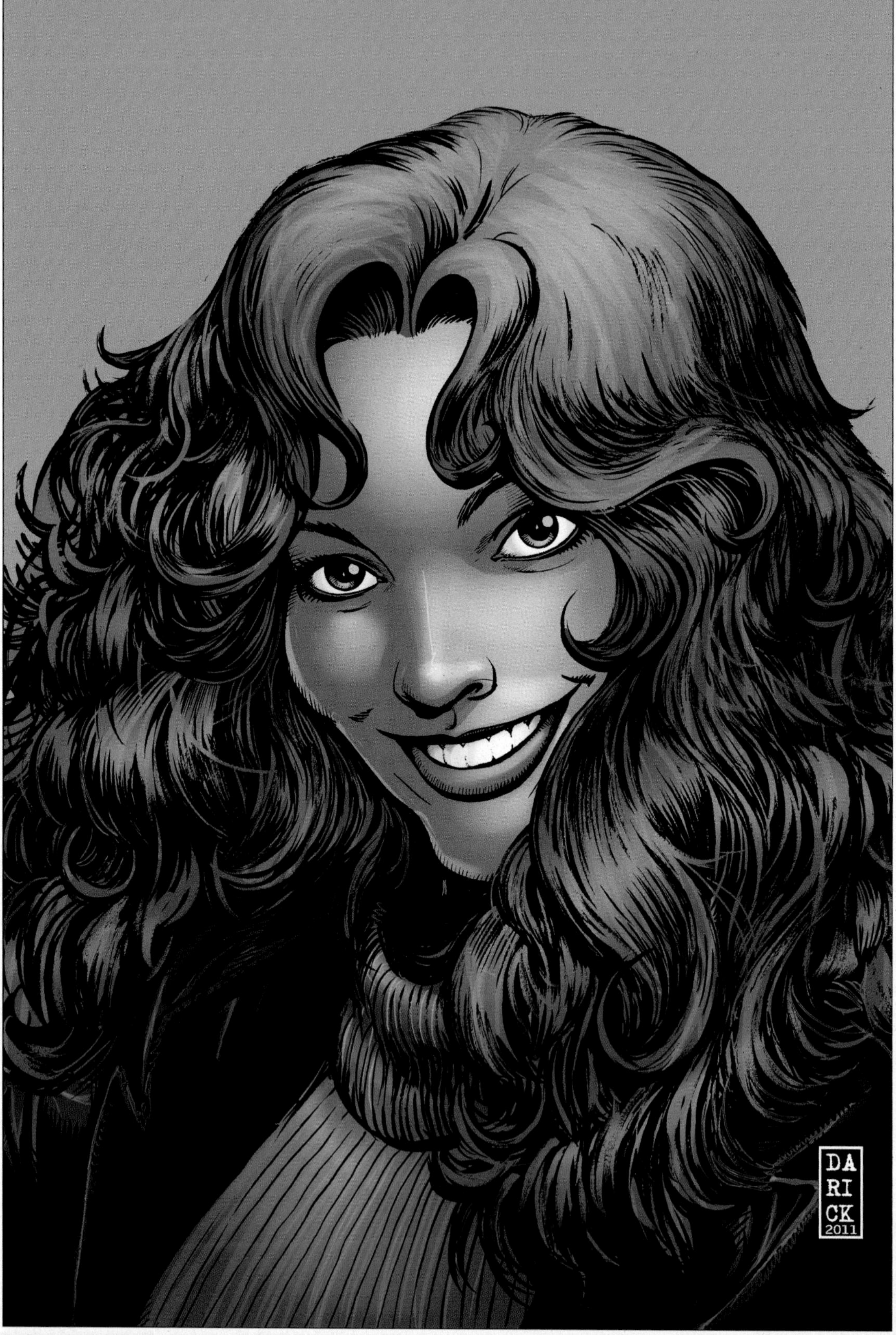
DA
RI
CK
2011

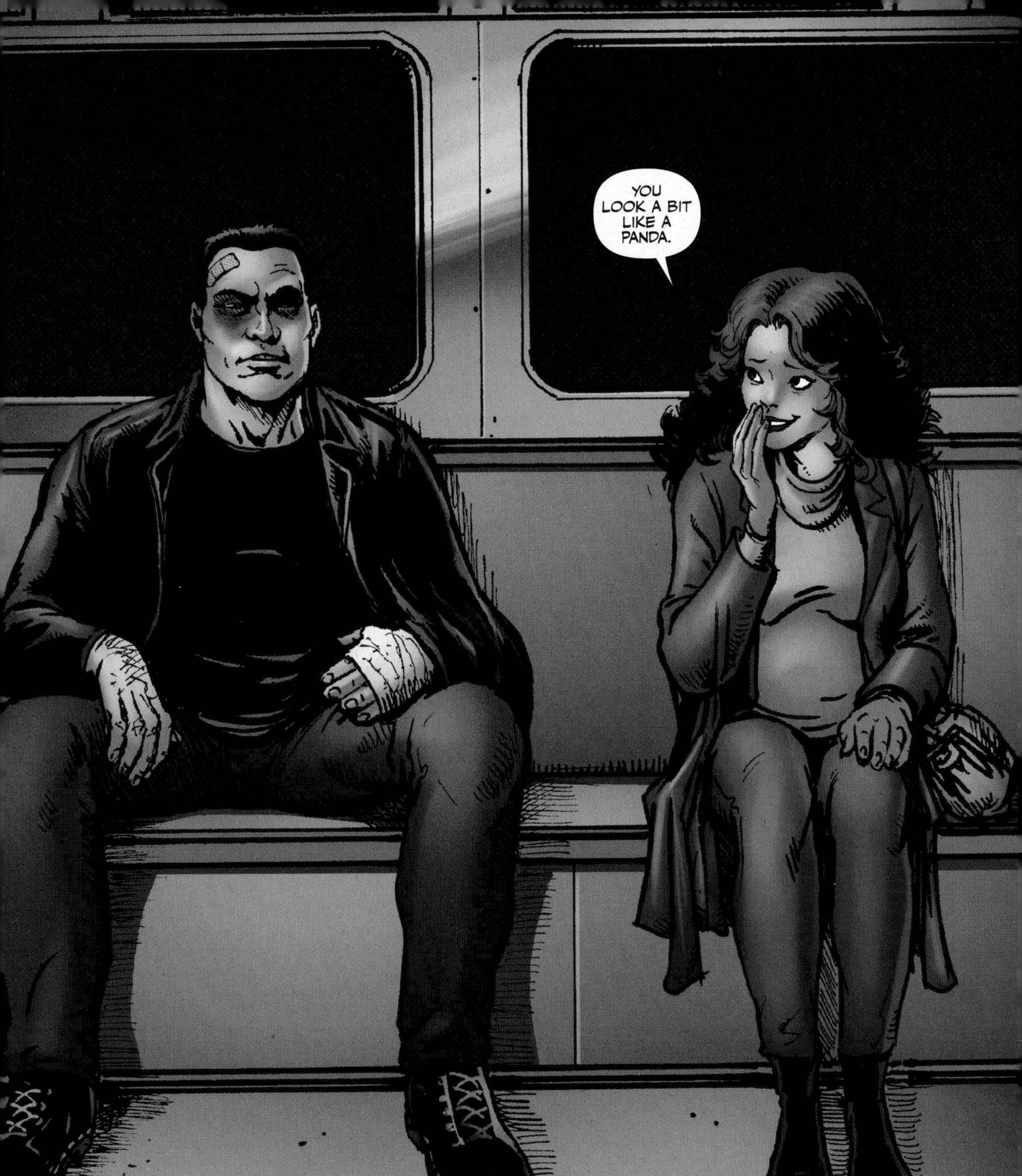
YOU LOOK A BIT LIKE A PANDA.

3: IT MUST BE LOVE. LOVE. LOVE

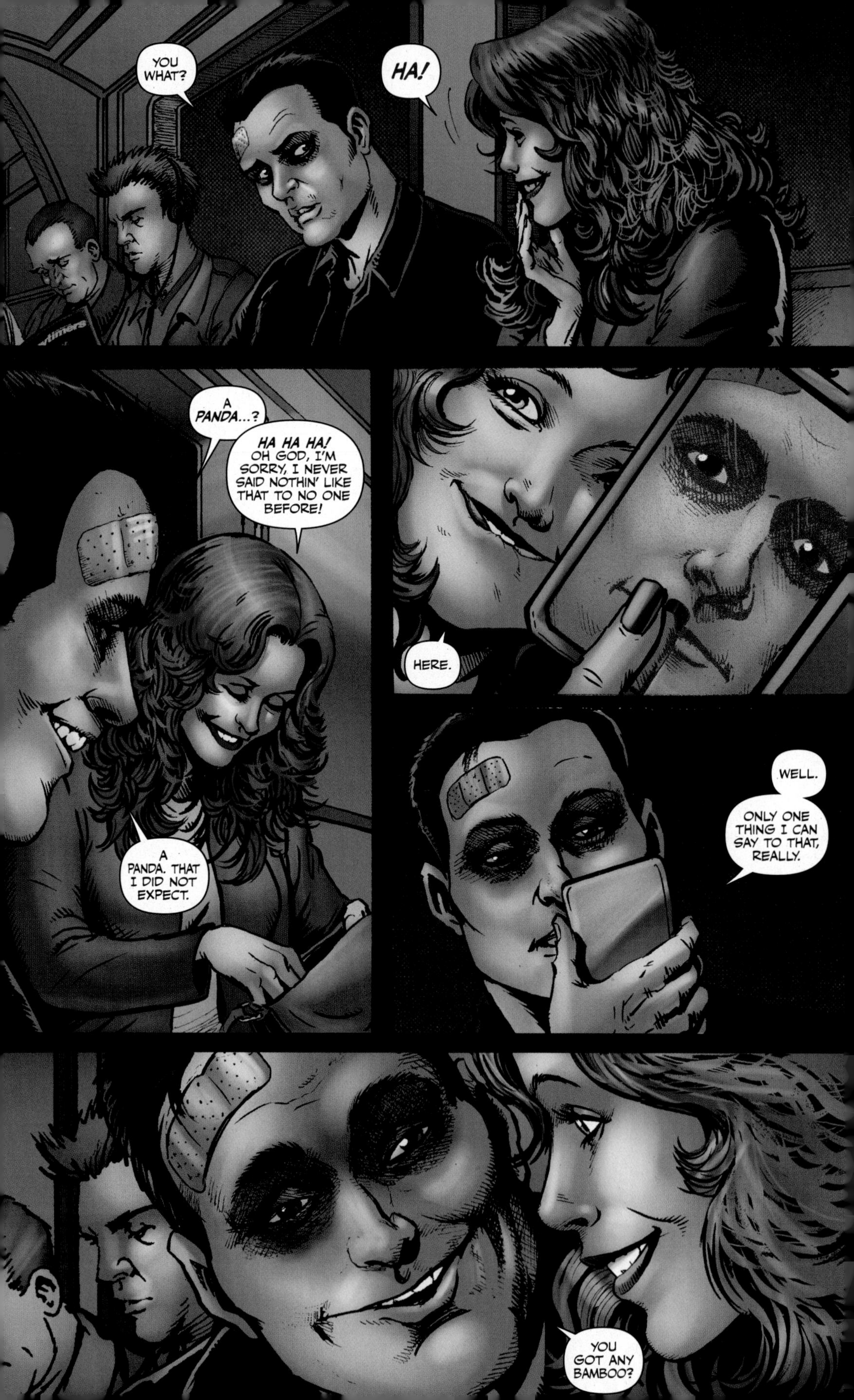
YOU WHAT?
HA!
A PANDA...?
HA HA HA! OH GOD, I'M SORRY, I NEVER SAID NOTHIN' LIKE THAT TO NO ONE BEFORE!
A PANDA. THAT I DID NOT EXPECT.
HERE.
WELL.
ONLY ONE THING I CAN SAY TO THAT, REALLY.
YOU GOT ANY BAMBOO?

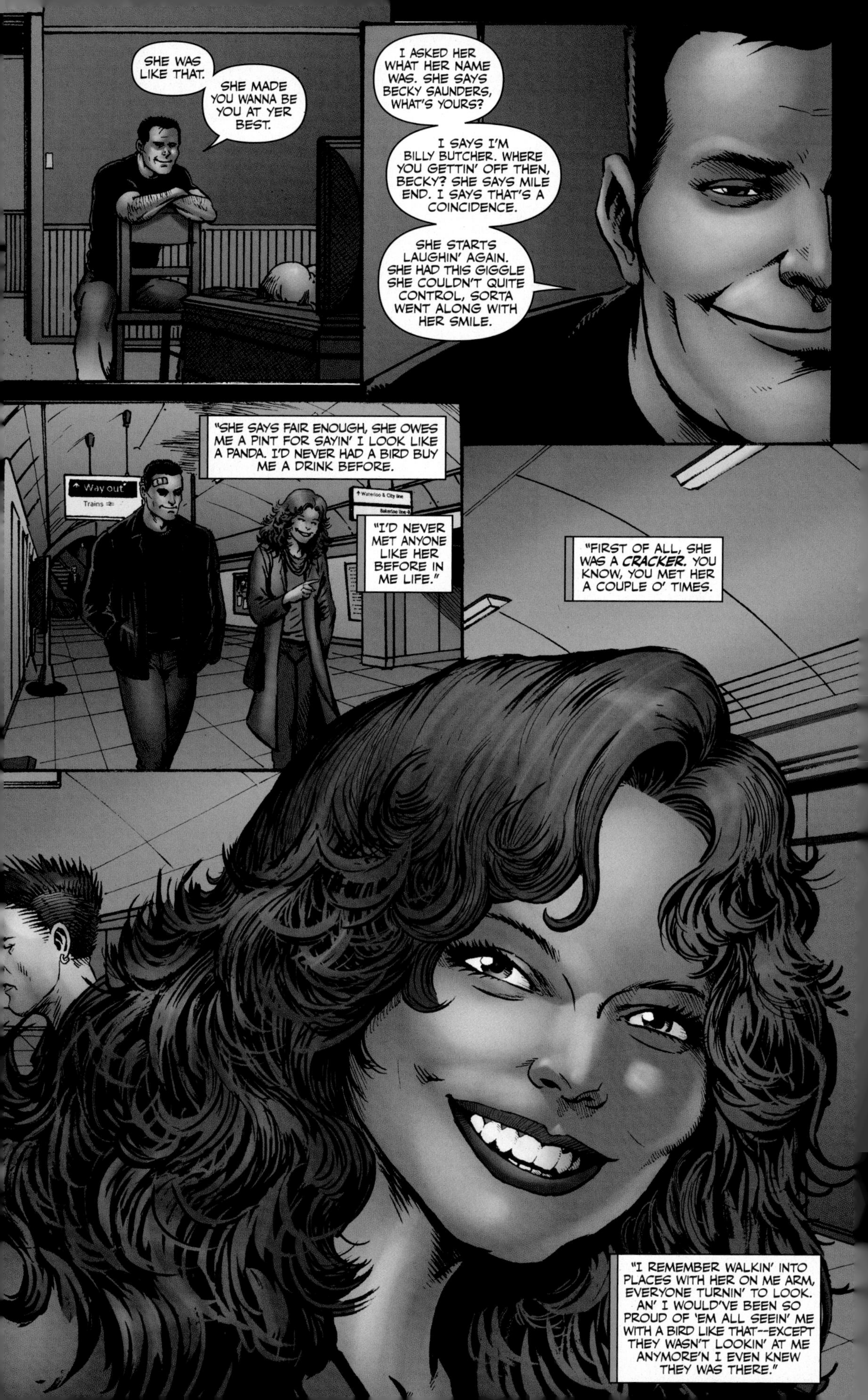
SHE WAS LIKE THAT.
SHE MADE YOU WANNA BE YOU AT YER BEST.
I ASKED HER WHAT HER NAME WAS. SHE SAYS BECKY SAUNDERS, WHAT'S YOURS?
I SAYS I'M BILLY BUTCHER. WHERE YOU GETTIN' OFF THEN, BECKY? SHE SAYS MILE END. I SAYS THAT'S A COINCIDENCE.
SHE STARTS LAUGHIN' AGAIN. SHE HAD THIS GIGGLE SHE COULDN'T QUITE CONTROL, SORTA WENT ALONG WITH HER SMILE.
"SHE SAYS FAIR ENOUGH, SHE OWES ME A PINT FOR SAYIN' I LOOK LIKE A PANDA. I'D NEVER HAD A BIRD BUY ME A DRINK BEFORE.
Way out
Trains
Waterloo & City line
Bakerloo line
"I'D NEVER MET ANYONE LIKE HER BEFORE IN ME LIFE."
"FIRST OF ALL, SHE WAS A CRACKER. YOU KNOW, YOU MET HER A COUPLE O' TIMES.
"I REMEMBER WALKIN' INTO PLACES WITH HER ON ME ARM, EVERYONE TURNIN' TO LOOK. AN' I WOULD'VE BEEN SO PROUD OF 'EM ALL SEEIN' ME WITH A BIRD LIKE THAT--EXCEPT THEY WASN'T LOOKIN' AT ME ANYMORE'N I EVEN KNEW THEY WAS THERE."

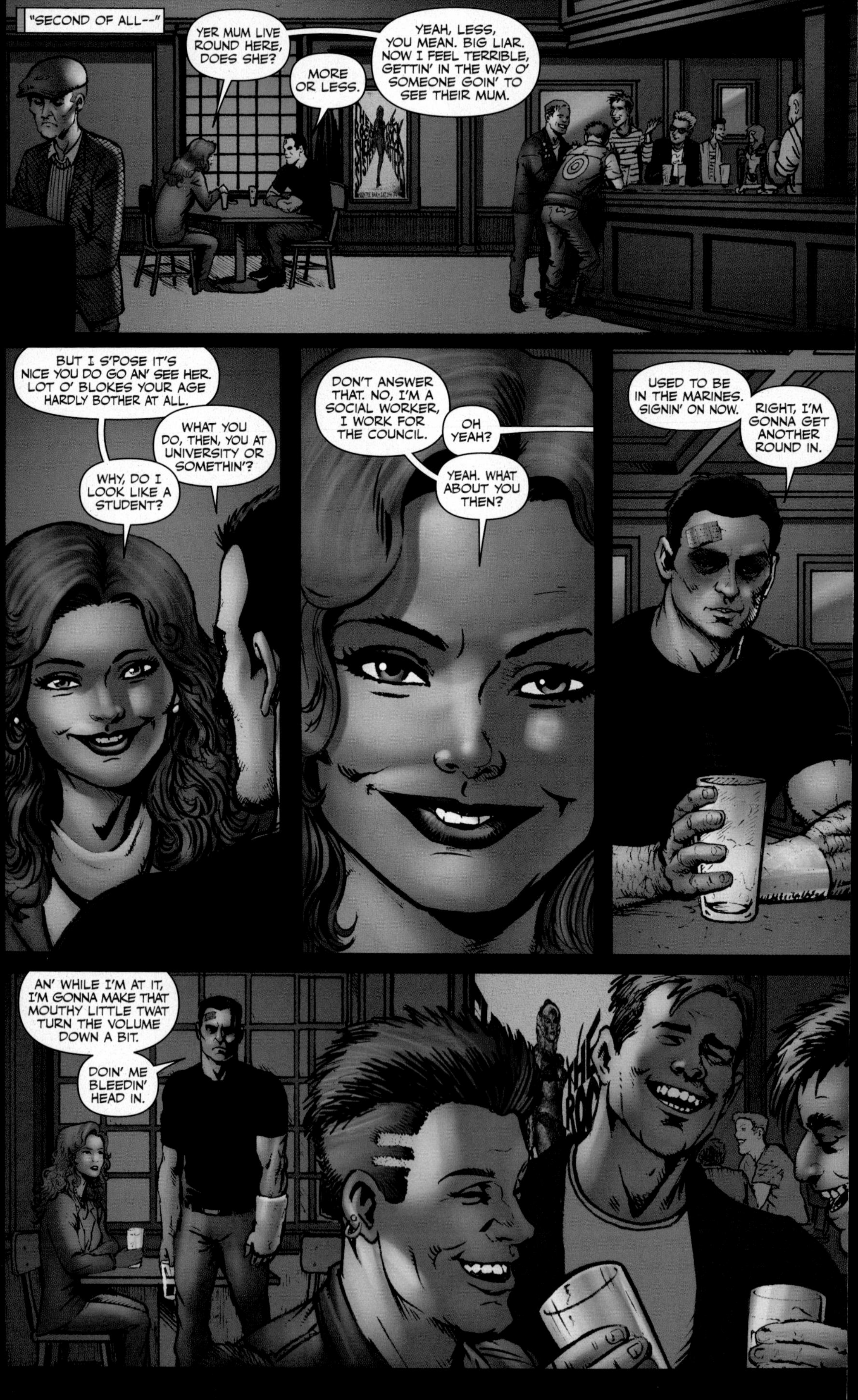
"SECOND OF ALL--"
YER MUM LIVE ROUND HERE, DOES SHE?
MORE OR LESS.
YEAH, LESS, YOU MEAN. BIG LIAR. NOW I FEEL TERRIBLE, GETTIN' IN THE WAY O' SOMEONE GOIN' TO SEE THEIR MUM.
BUT I S'POSE IT'S NICE YOU DO GO AN' SEE HER. LOT O' BLOKES YOUR AGE HARDLY BOTHER AT ALL.
WHAT YOU DO, THEN, YOU AT UNIVERSITY OR SOMETHIN'?
WHY, DO I LOOK LIKE A STUDENT?
DON'T ANSWER THAT. NO, I'M A SOCIAL WORKER, I WORK FOR THE COUNCIL.
OH YEAH?
YEAH. WHAT ABOUT YOU THEN?
USED TO BE IN THE MARINES. SIGNIN' ON NOW.
RIGHT, I'M GONNA GET ANOTHER ROUND IN.
AN' WHILE I'M AT IT, I'M GONNA MAKE THAT MOUTHY LITTLE TWAT TURN THE VOLUME DOWN A BIT.
DOIN' ME BLEEDIN' HEAD IN.

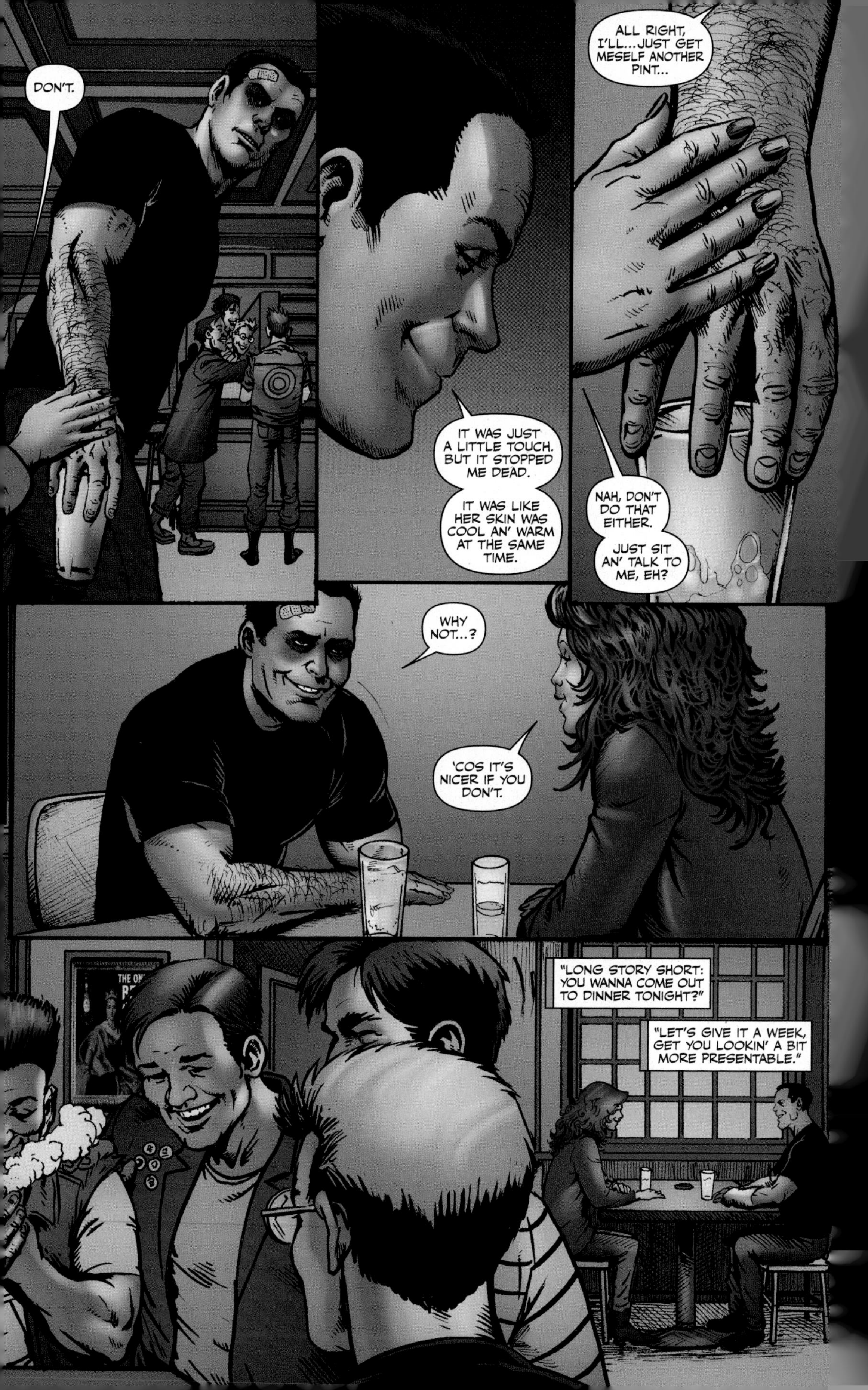
DON'T.
IT WAS JUST A LITTLE TOUCH. BUT IT STOPPED ME DEAD.
IT WAS LIKE HER SKIN WAS COOL AN' WARM AT THE SAME TIME.
ALL RIGHT, I'LL...JUST GET MESELF ANOTHER PINT...
NAH, DON'T DO THAT EITHER.
JUST SIT AN' TALK TO ME, EH?
WHY NOT...?
'COS IT'S NICER IF YOU DON'T.
"LONG STORY SHORT: YOU WANNA COME OUT TO DINNER TONIGHT?"
"LET'S GIVE IT A WEEK, GET YOU LOOKIN' A BIT MORE PRESENTABLE."

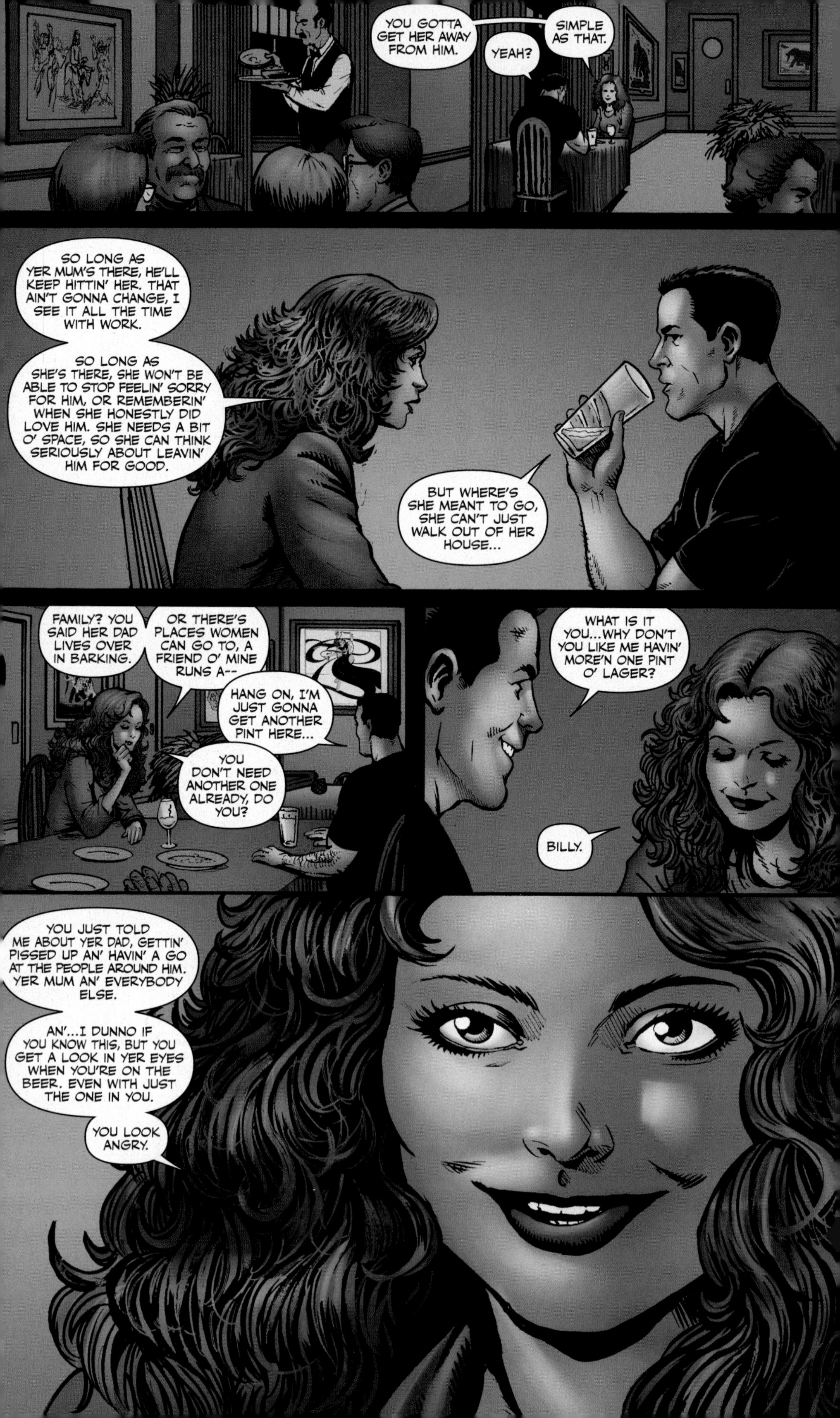

YOU GOTTA GET HER AWAY FROM HIM.
SIMPLE AS THAT.
YEAH?
SO LONG AS YER MUM'S THERE, HE'LL KEEP HITTIN' HER. THAT AIN'T GONNA CHANGE, I SEE IT ALL THE TIME WITH WORK.
SO LONG AS SHE'S THERE, SHE WON'T BE ABLE TO STOP FEELIN' SORRY FOR HIM, OR REMEMBERIN' WHEN SHE HONESTLY DID LOVE HIM. SHE NEEDS A BIT O' SPACE, SO SHE CAN THINK SERIOUSLY ABOUT LEAVIN' HIM FOR GOOD.
BUT WHERE'S SHE MEANT TO GO, SHE CAN'T JUST WALK OUT OF HER HOUSE...
FAMILY? YOU SAID HER DAD LIVES OVER IN BARKING.
OR THERE'S PLACES WOMEN CAN GO TO, A FRIEND O' MINE RUNS A--
HANG ON, I'M JUST GONNA GET ANOTHER PINT HERE...
YOU DON'T NEED ANOTHER ONE ALREADY, DO YOU?
WHAT IS IT YOU...WHY DON'T YOU LIKE ME HAVIN' MORE'N ONE PINT O' LAGER?
BILLY.
YOU JUST TOLD ME ABOUT YER DAD, GETTIN' PISSED UP AN' HAVIN' A GO AT THE PEOPLE AROUND HIM. YER MUM AN' EVERYBODY ELSE.
AN'...I DUNNO IF YOU KNOW THIS, BUT YOU GET A LOOK IN YER EYES WHEN YOU'RE ON THE BEER. EVEN WITH JUST THE ONE IN YOU.
YOU LOOK ANGRY.

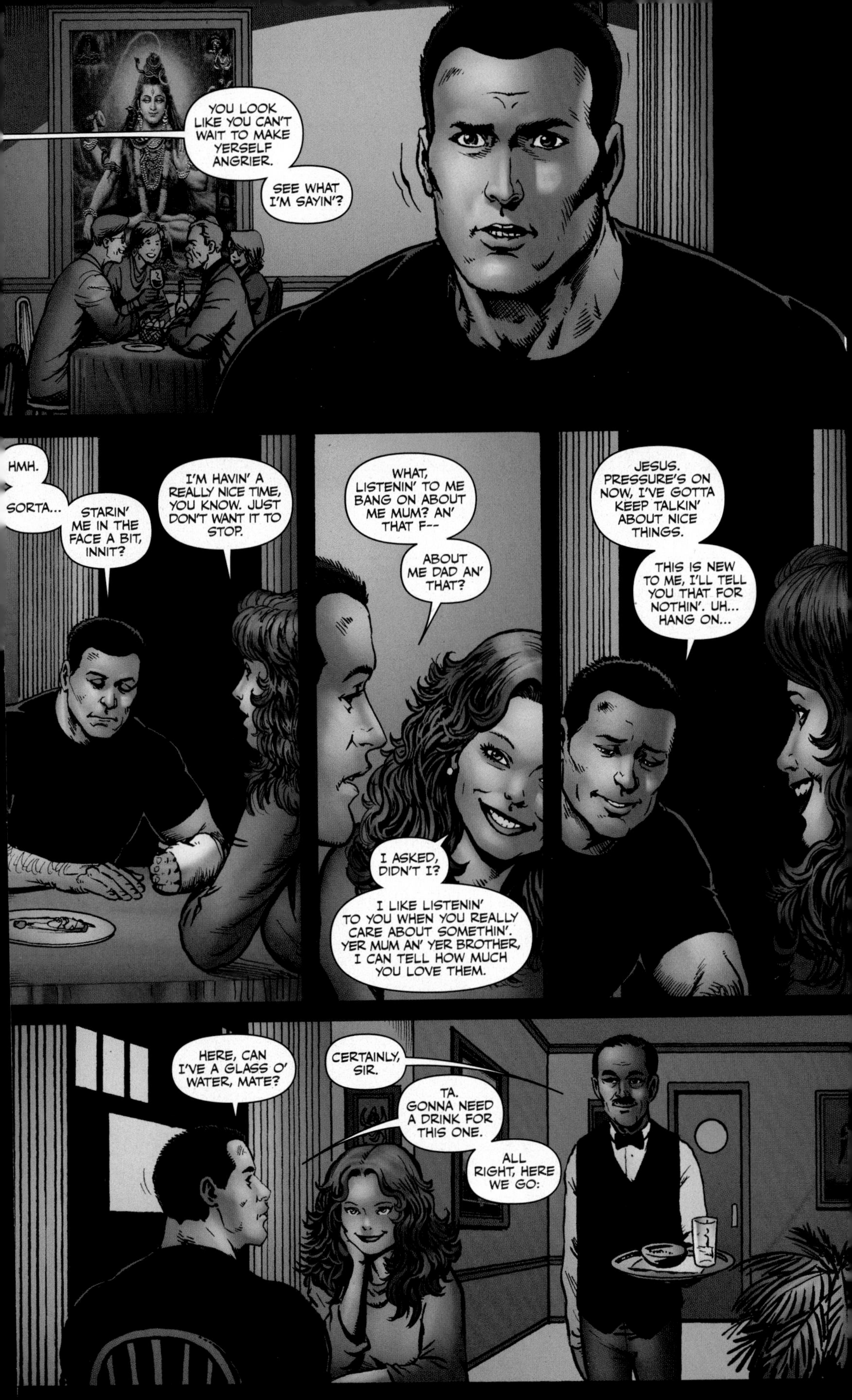

YOU LOOK LIKE YOU CAN'T WAIT TO MAKE YERSELF ANGRIER.
SEE WHAT I'M SAYIN'?
HMH.
SORTA...
STARIN' ME IN THE FACE A BIT, INNIT?
I'M HAVIN' A REALLY NICE TIME, YOU KNOW. JUST DON'T WANT IT TO STOP.
WHAT, LISTENIN' TO ME BANG ON ABOUT ME MUM? AN' THAT F--
ABOUT ME DAD AN' THAT?
I ASKED, DIDN'T I?
I LIKE LISTENIN' TO YOU WHEN YOU REALLY CARE ABOUT SOMETHIN'. YER MUM AN' YER BROTHER, I CAN TELL HOW MUCH YOU LOVE THEM.
JESUS. PRESSURE'S ON NOW, I'VE GOTTA KEEP TALKIN' ABOUT NICE THINGS.
THIS IS NEW TO ME, I'LL TELL YOU THAT FOR NOTHIN'. UH... HANG ON...
HERE, CAN I'VE A GLASS O' WATER, MATE?
CERTAINLY, SIR.
TA. GONNA NEED A DRINK FOR THIS ONE.
ALL RIGHT, HERE WE GO:

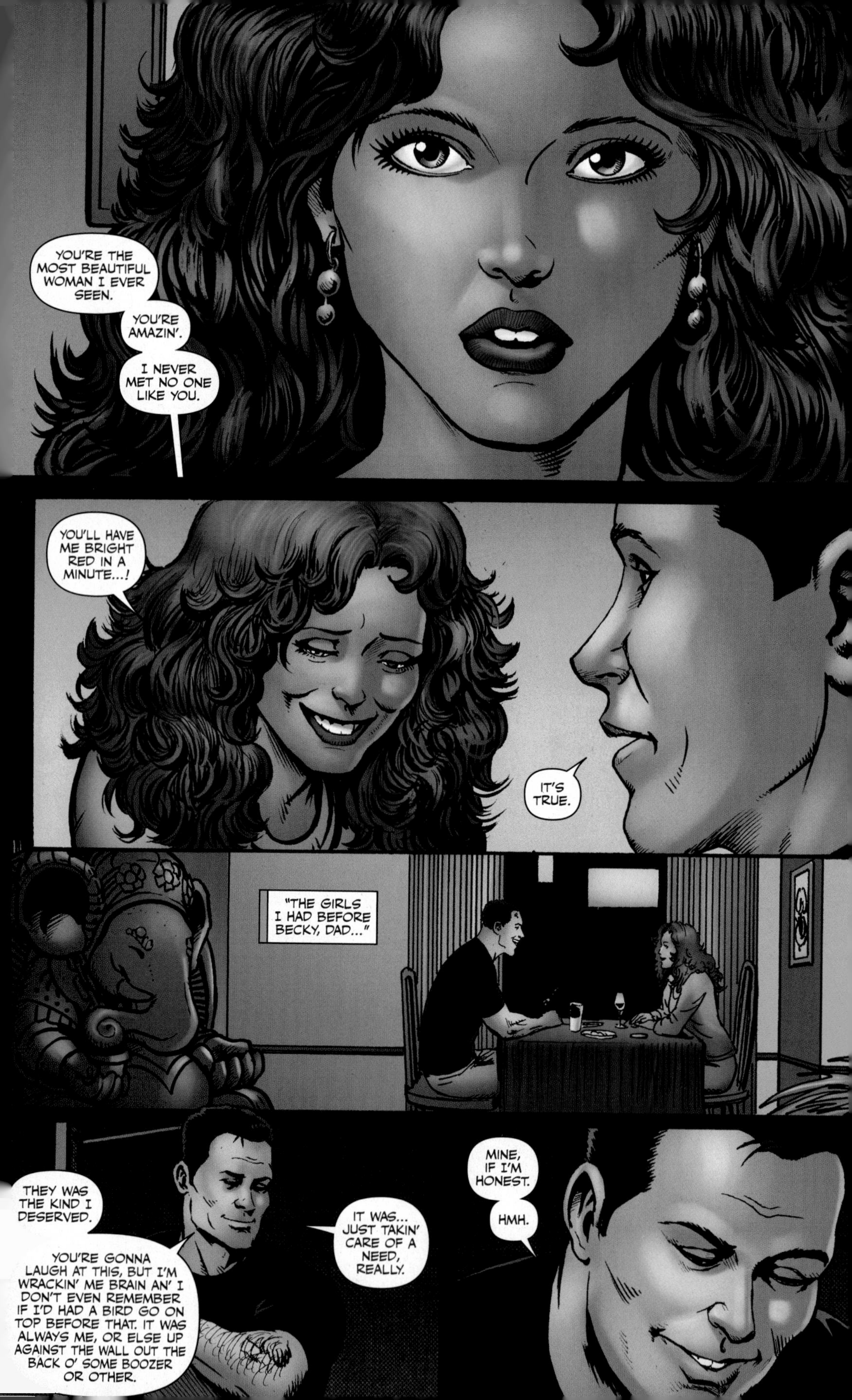
YOU'RE THE MOST BEAUTIFUL WOMAN I EVER SEEN.
YOU'RE AMAZIN'.
I NEVER MET NO ONE LIKE YOU.
YOU'LL HAVE ME BRIGHT RED IN A MINUTE...!
IT'S TRUE.
"THE GIRLS I HAD BEFORE BECKY, DAD..."
THEY WAS THE KIND I DESERVED.
YOU'RE GONNA LAUGH AT THIS, BUT I'M WRACKIN' ME BRAIN AN' I DON'T EVEN REMEMBER IF I'D HAD A BIRD GO ON TOP BEFORE THAT. IT WAS ALWAYS ME, OR ELSE UP AGAINST THE WALL OUT THE BACK O' SOME BOOZER OR OTHER.
IT WAS... JUST TAKIN' CARE OF A NEED, REALLY.
MINE, IF I'M HONEST.
HMH.

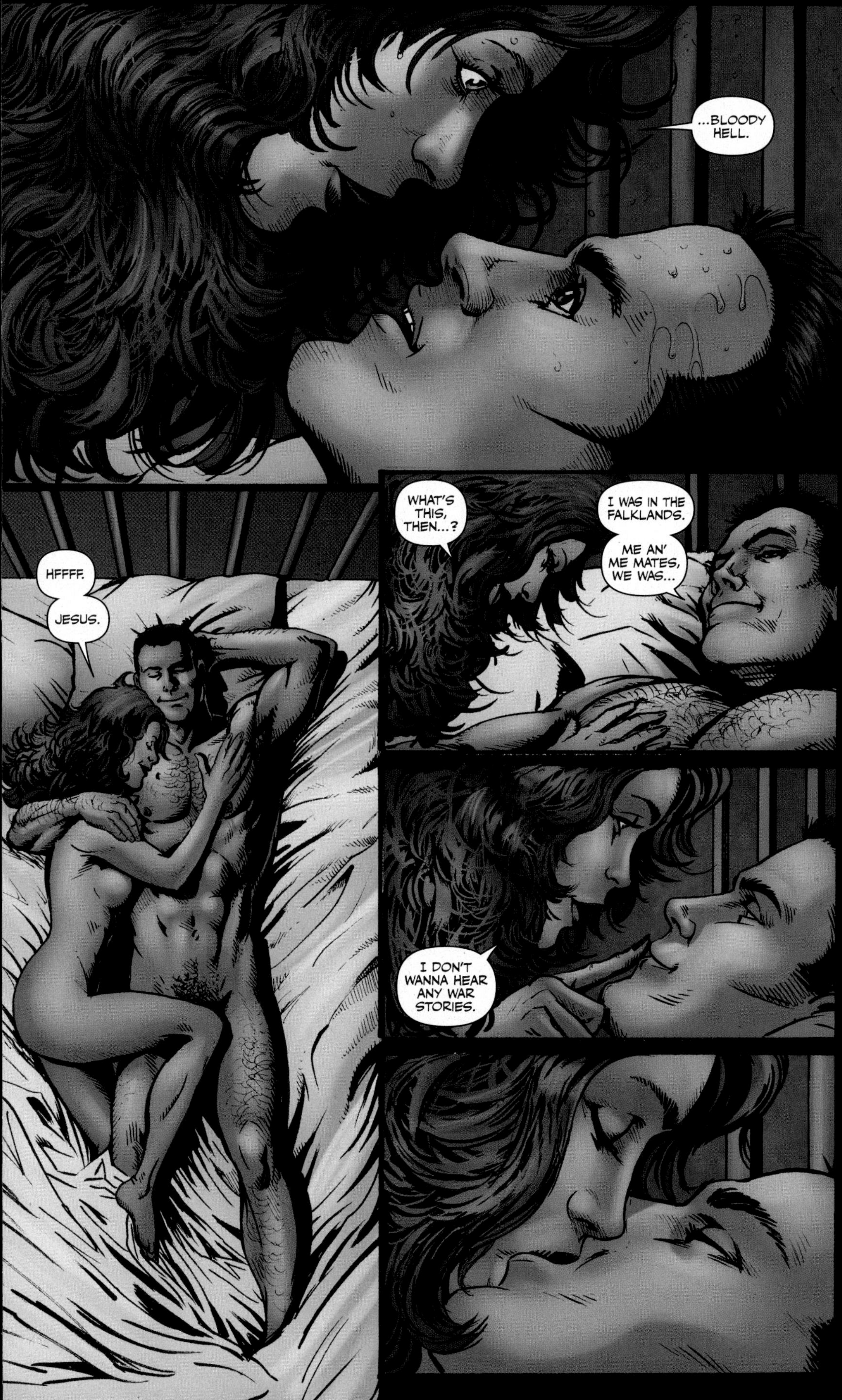
...BLOODY HELL.
HFFFF.
JESUS.
WHAT'S THIS, THEN...?
I WAS IN THE FALKLANDS.
ME AN' ME MATES, WE WAS...
I DON'T WANNA HEAR ANY WAR STORIES.

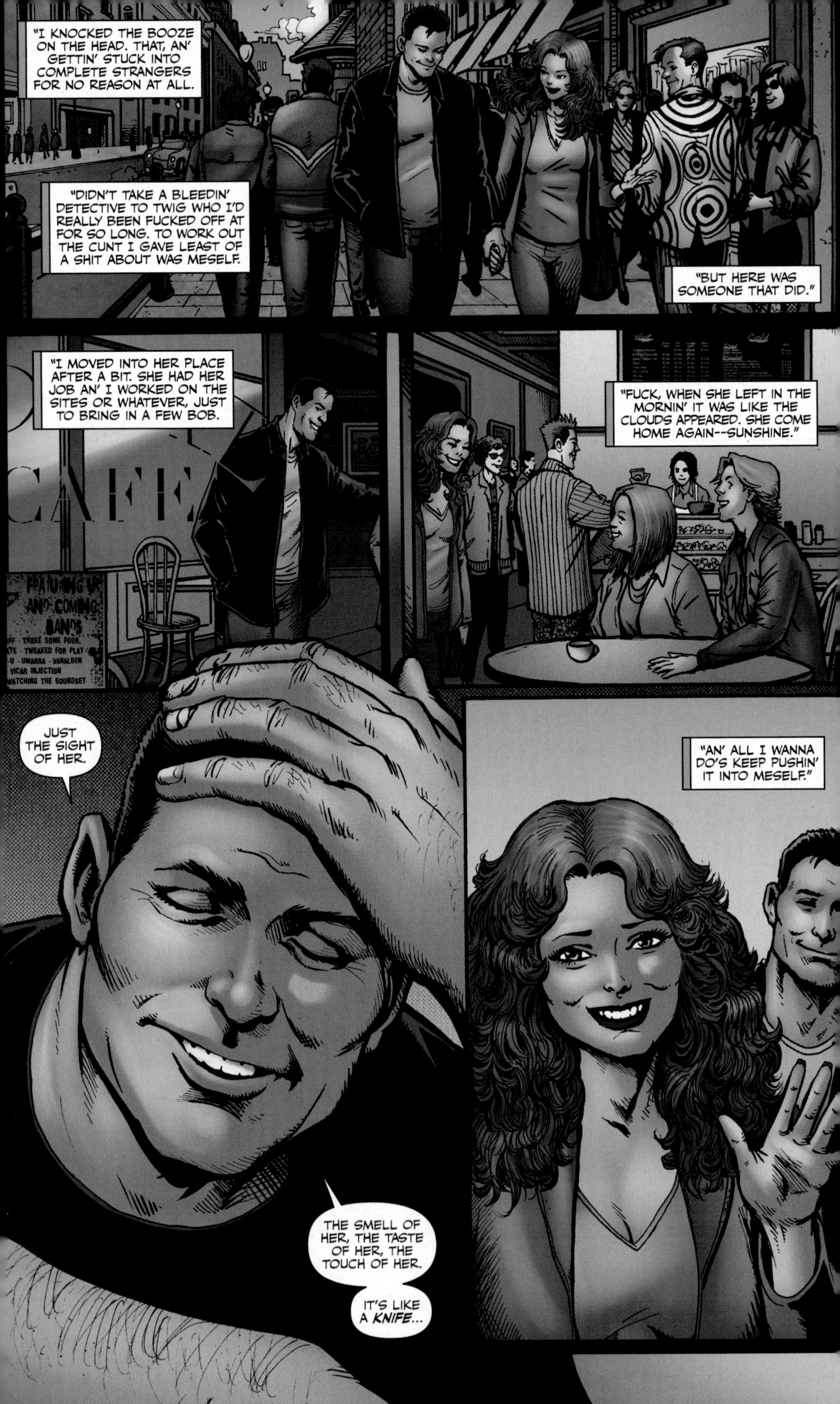
"I KNOCKED THE BOOZE ON THE HEAD. THAT, AN' GETTIN' STUCK INTO COMPLETE STRANGERS FOR NO REASON AT ALL.
"DIDN'T TAKE A BLEEDIN' DETECTIVE TO TWIG WHO I'D REALLY BEEN FUCKED OFF AT FOR SO LONG. TO WORK OUT THE CUNT I GAVE LEAST OF A SHIT ABOUT WAS MESELF.
"BUT HERE WAS SOMEONE THAT DID."
"I MOVED INTO HER PLACE AFTER A BIT. SHE HAD HER JOB AN' I WORKED ON THE SITES OR WHATEVER, JUST TO BRING IN A FEW BOB.
CAFE
"FUCK, WHEN SHE LEFT IN THE MORNIN' IT WAS LIKE THE CLOUDS APPEARED. SHE COME HOME AGAIN--SUNSHINE."
JUST THE SIGHT OF HER.
"AN' ALL I WANNA DO'S KEEP PUSHIN' IT INTO MESELF."
THE SMELL OF HER, THE TASTE OF HER, THE TOUCH OF HER.
IT'S LIKE A KNIFE...

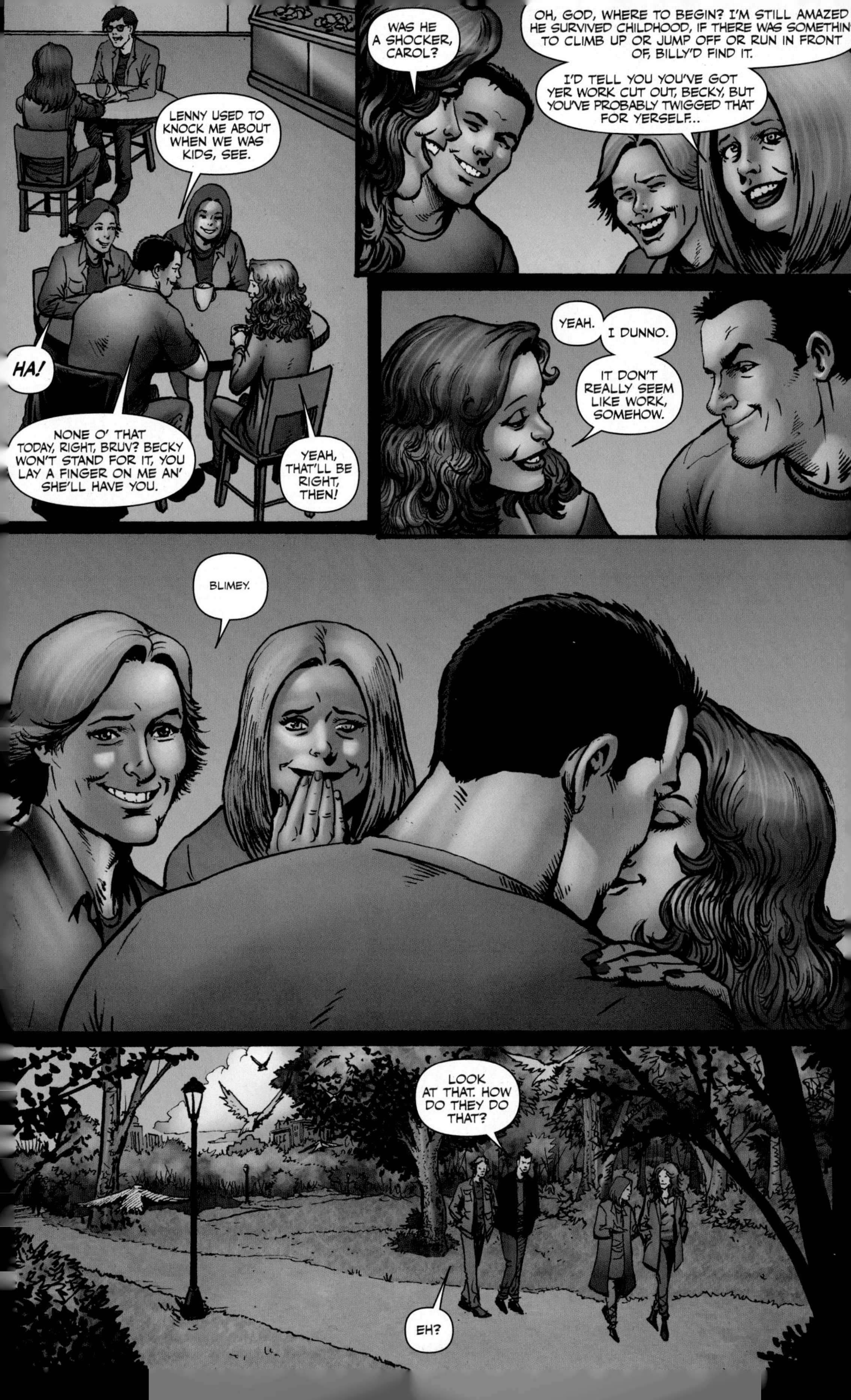
LENNY USED TO KNOCK ME ABOUT WHEN WE WAS KIDS, SEE.
HA!
NONE O' THAT TODAY, RIGHT, BRUV? BECKY WON'T STAND FOR IT, YOU LAY A FINGER ON ME AN' SHE'LL HAVE YOU.
YEAH, THAT'LL BE RIGHT, THEN!
WAS HE A SHOCKER, CAROL?
OH, GOD, WHERE TO BEGIN? I'M STILL AMAZED HE SURVIVED CHILDHOOD, IF THERE WAS SOMETHIN' TO CLIMB UP OR JUMP OFF OR RUN IN FRONT OF, BILLY'D FIND IT.
I'D TELL YOU YOU'VE GOT YER WORK CUT OUT, BECKY, BUT YOU'VE PROBABLY TWIGGED THAT FOR YERSELF...
YEAH.
I DUNNO.
IT DON'T REALLY SEEM LIKE WORK, SOMEHOW.
BLIMEY.
LOOK AT THAT. HOW DO THEY DO THAT?
EH?

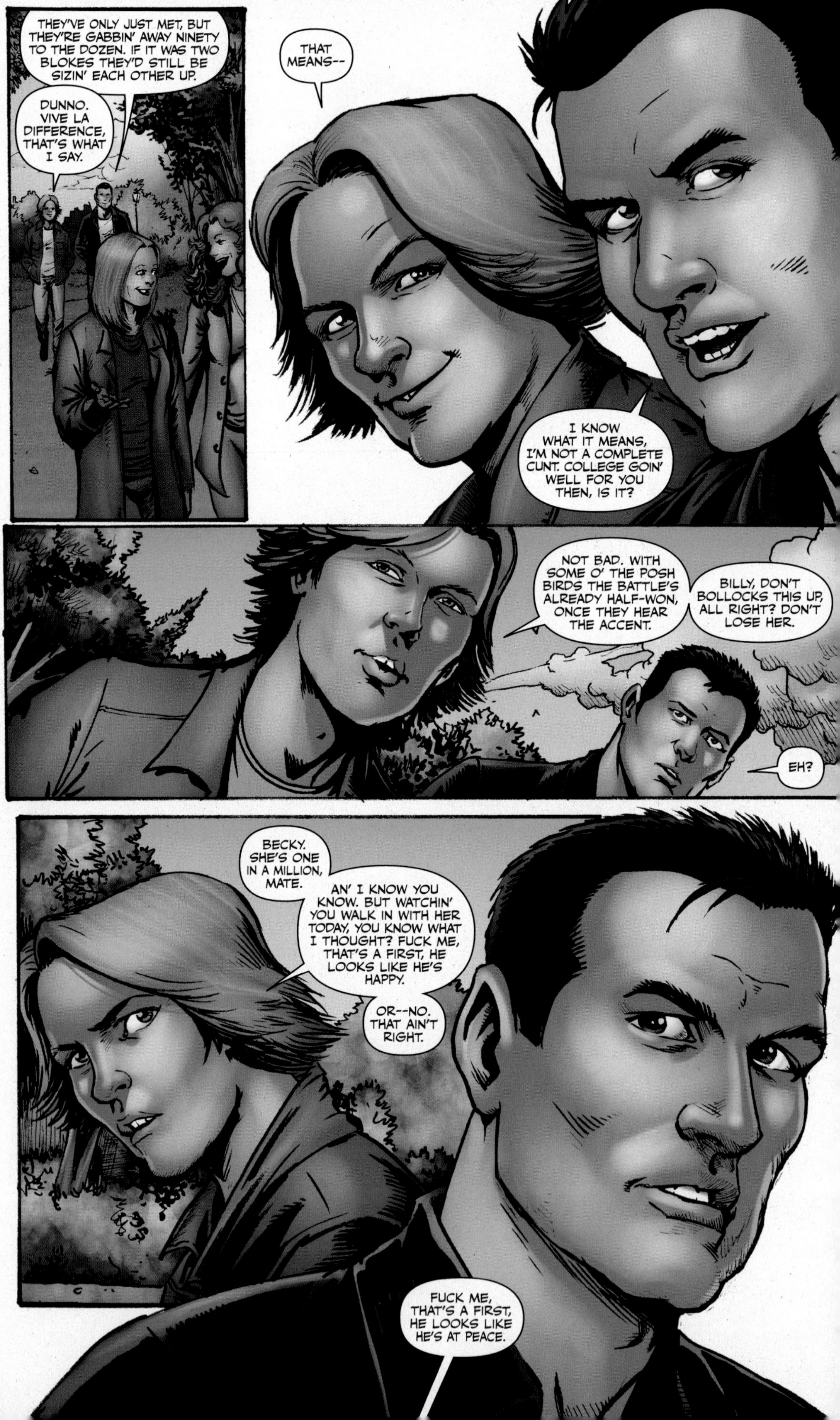
THEY'VE ONLY JUST MET, BUT THEY'RE GABBIN' AWAY NINETY TO THE DOZEN. IF IT WAS TWO BLOKES THEY'D STILL BE SIZIN' EACH OTHER UP.
DUNNO. VIVE LA DIFFERENCE, THAT'S WHAT I SAY.
THAT MEANS--
I KNOW WHAT IT MEANS, I'M NOT A COMPLETE CUNT. COLLEGE GOIN' WELL FOR YOU THEN, IS IT?
NOT BAD. WITH SOME O' THE POSH BIRDS THE BATTLE'S ALREADY HALF-WON, ONCE THEY HEAR THE ACCENT.
BILLY, DON'T BOLLOCKS THIS UP, ALL RIGHT? DON'T LOSE HER.
EH?
BECKY. SHE'S ONE IN A MILLION, MATE.
AN' I KNOW YOU KNOW. BUT WATCHIN' YOU WALK IN WITH HER TODAY, YOU KNOW WHAT I THOUGHT? FUCK ME, THAT'S A FIRST, HE LOOKS LIKE HE'S HAPPY.
OR--NO. THAT AIN'T RIGHT.
FUCK ME, THAT'S A FIRST, HE LOOKS LIKE HE'S AT PEACE.

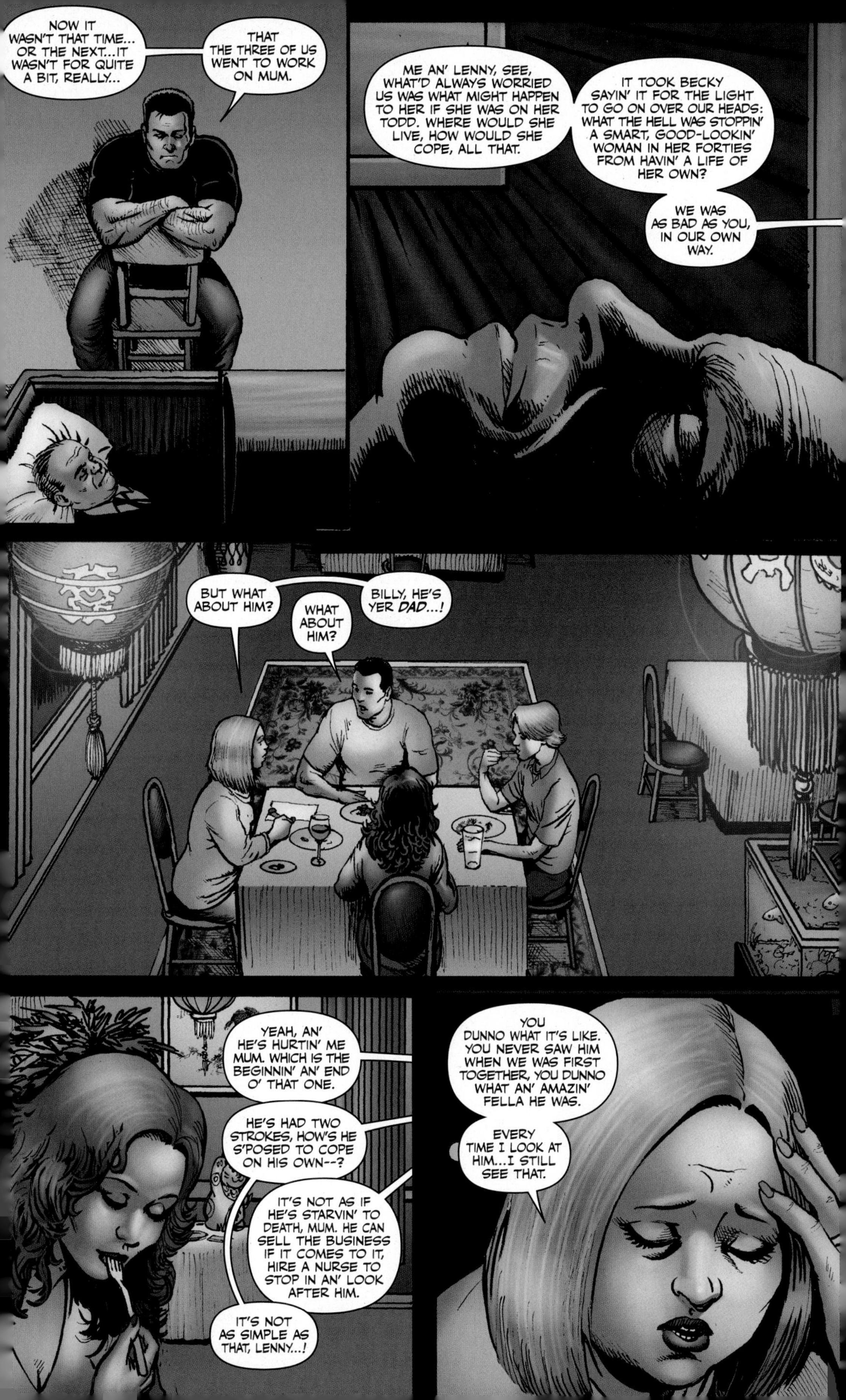
NOW IT WASN'T THAT TIME... OR THE NEXT...IT WASN'T FOR QUITE A BIT, REALLY...
THAT THE THREE OF US WENT TO WORK ON MUM.
ME AN' LENNY, SEE, WHAT'D ALWAYS WORRIED US WAS WHAT MIGHT HAPPEN TO HER IF SHE WAS ON HER TODD. WHERE WOULD SHE LIVE, HOW WOULD SHE COPE, ALL THAT.
IT TOOK BECKY SAYIN' IT FOR THE LIGHT TO GO ON OVER OUR HEADS: WHAT THE HELL WAS STOPPIN' A SMART, GOOD-LOOKIN' WOMAN IN HER FORTIES FROM HAVIN' A LIFE OF HER OWN?
WE WAS AS BAD AS YOU, IN OUR OWN WAY.
BUT WHAT ABOUT HIM?
WHAT ABOUT HIM?
BILLY, HE'S YER *DAD*...!
YEAH, AN' HE'S HURTIN' ME MUM. WHICH IS THE BEGINNIN' AN' END O' THAT ONE.
HE'S HAD TWO STROKES, HOW'S HE S'POSED TO COPE ON HIS OWN--?
IT'S NOT AS IF HE'S STARVIN' TO DEATH, MUM. HE CAN SELL THE BUSINESS IF IT COMES TO IT, HIRE A NURSE TO STOP IN AN' LOOK AFTER HIM.
IT'S NOT AS SIMPLE AS THAT, LENNY...!
YOU DUNNO WHAT IT'S LIKE. YOU NEVER SAW HIM WHEN WE WAS FIRST TOGETHER, YOU DUNNO WHAT AN' AMAZIN' FELLA HE WAS.
EVERY TIME I LOOK AT HIM...I STILL SEE THAT.

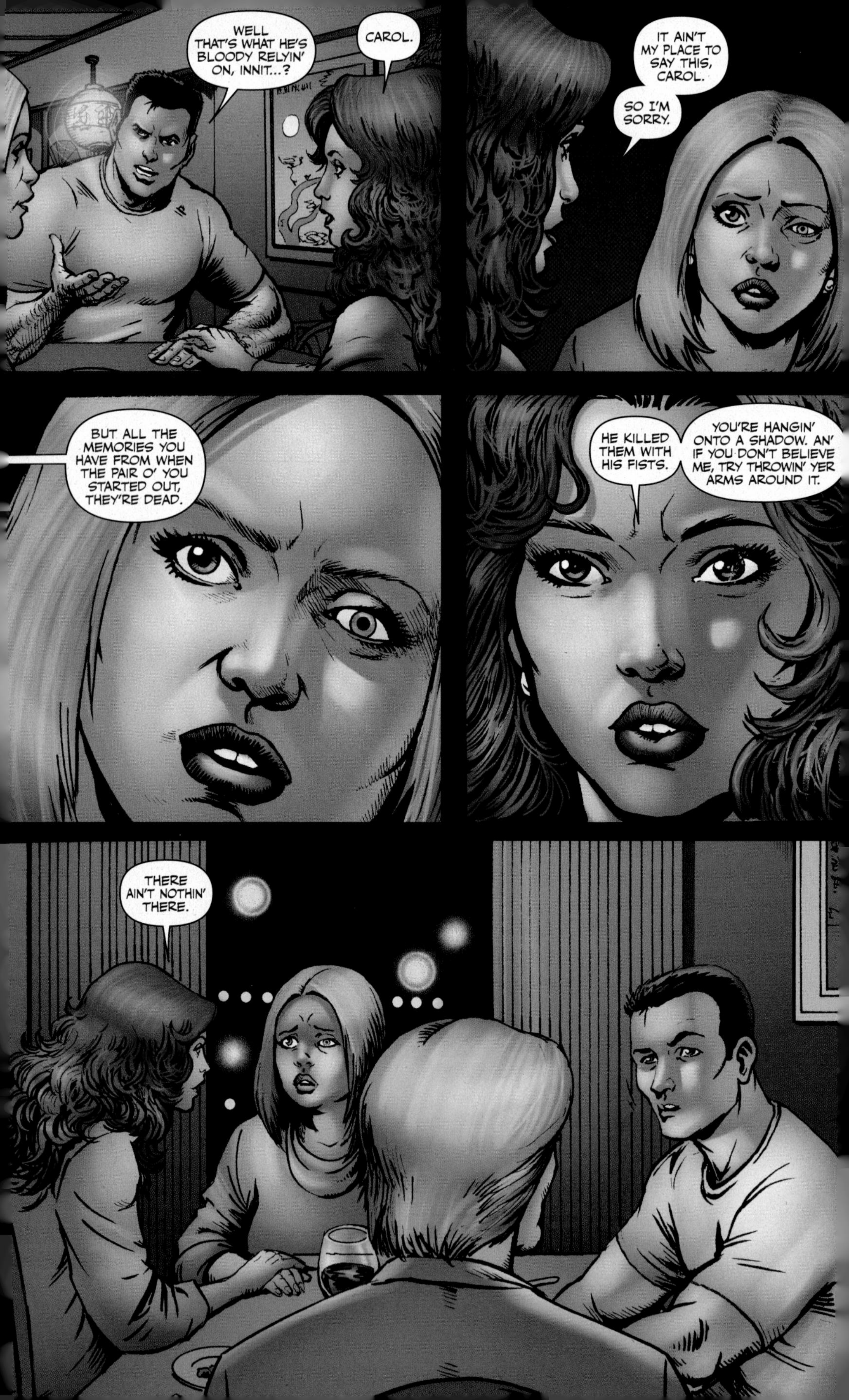

WELL THAT'S WHAT HE'S BLOODY RELYIN' ON, INNIT...?
CAROL.
IT AIN'T MY PLACE TO SAY THIS, CAROL.
SO I'M SORRY.
BUT ALL THE MEMORIES YOU HAVE FROM WHEN THE PAIR O' YOU STARTED OUT, THEY'RE DEAD.
HE KILLED THEM WITH HIS FISTS.
YOU'RE HANGIN' ONTO A SHADOW. AN' IF YOU DON'T BELIEVE ME, TRY THROWIN' YER ARMS AROUND IT.
THERE AIN'T NOTHIN' THERE.

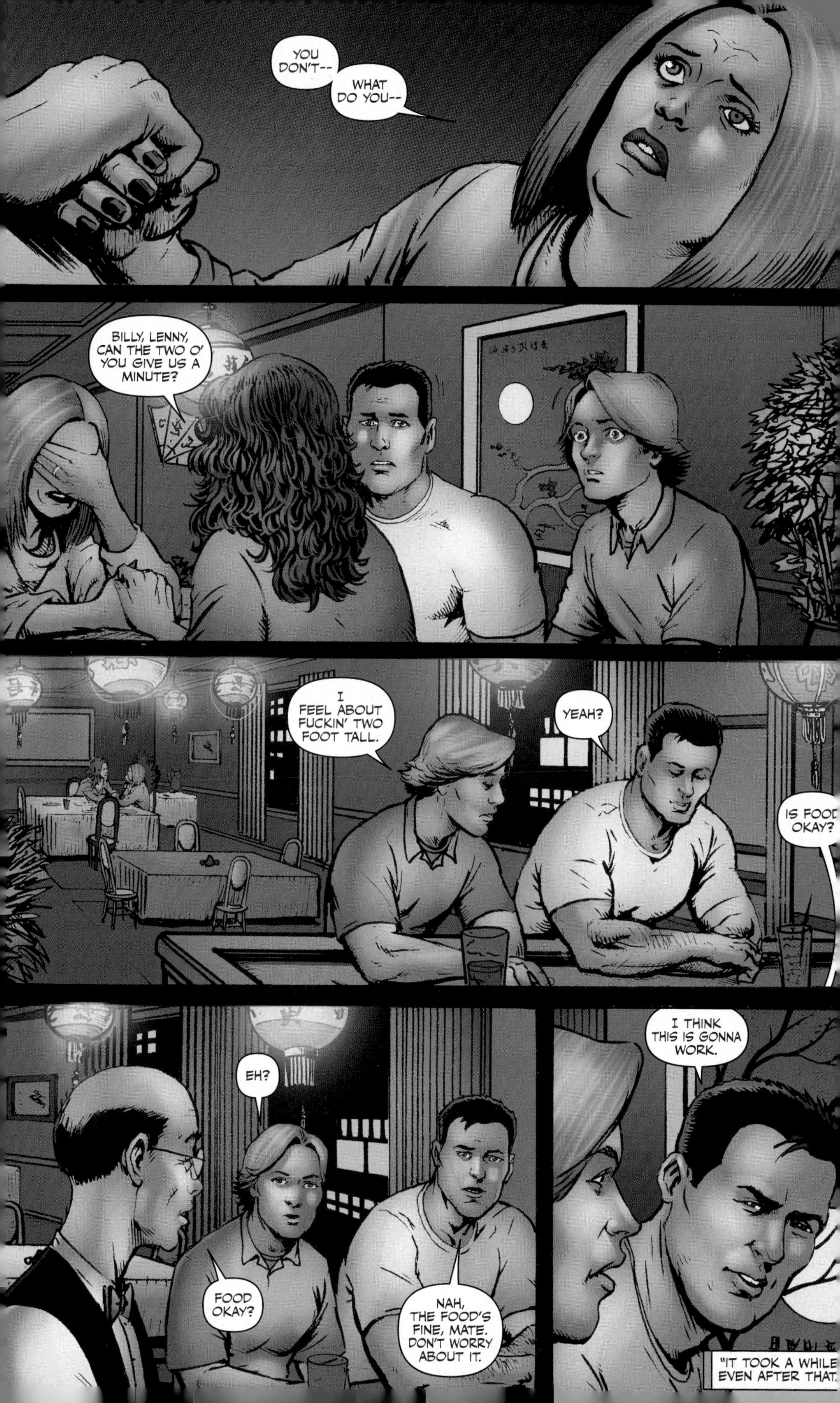
YOU DON'T--
WHAT DO YOU--
BILLY, LENNY, CAN THE TWO O' YOU GIVE US A MINUTE?
I FEEL ABOUT FUCKIN' TWO FOOT TALL.
YEAH?
IS FOOD OKAY?
EH?
FOOD OKAY?
NAH, THE FOOD'S FINE, MATE. DON'T WORRY ABOUT IT.
I THINK THIS IS GONNA WORK.
"IT TOOK A WHILE EVEN AFTER THAT.

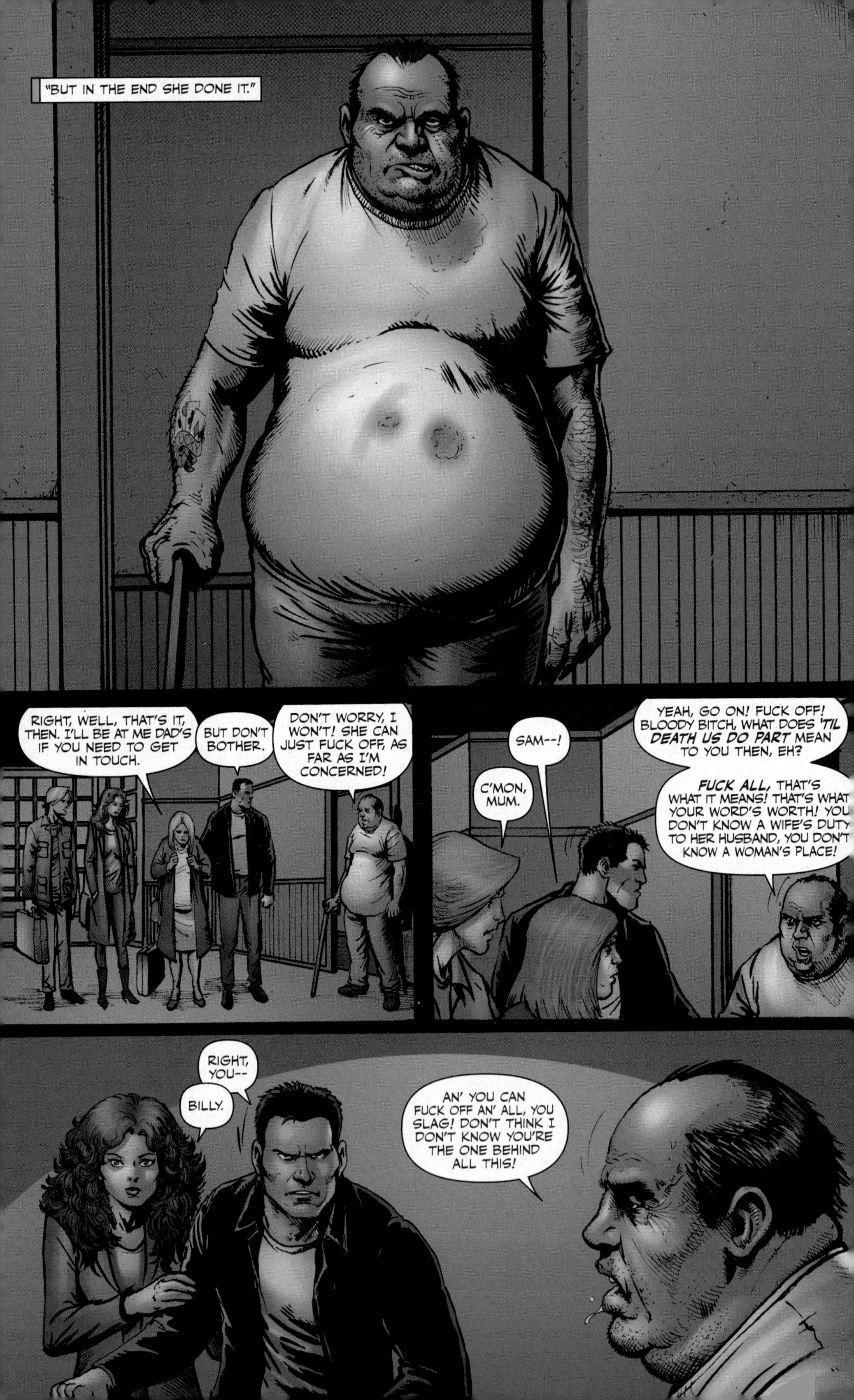
"BUT IN THE END SHE DONE IT."
RIGHT, WELL, THAT'S IT, THEN. I'LL BE AT ME DAD'S IF YOU NEED TO GET IN TOUCH.
BUT DON'T BOTHER.
DON'T WORRY, I WON'T! SHE CAN JUST FUCK OFF, AS FAR AS I'M CONCERNED!
SAM--!
C'MON, MUM.
YEAH, GO ON! FUCK OFF! BLOODY BITCH, WHAT DOES 'TIL DEATH US DO PART MEAN TO YOU THEN, EH?
FUCK ALL, THAT'S WHAT IT MEANS! THAT'S WHAT YOUR WORD'S WORTH! YOU DON'T KNOW A WIFE'S DUTY TO HER HUSBAND, YOU DON'T KNOW A WOMAN'S PLACE!
RIGHT, YOU--
BILLY.
AN' YOU CAN FUCK OFF AN' ALL, YOU SLAG! DON'T THINK I DON'T KNOW YOU'RE THE ONE BEHIND ALL THIS!

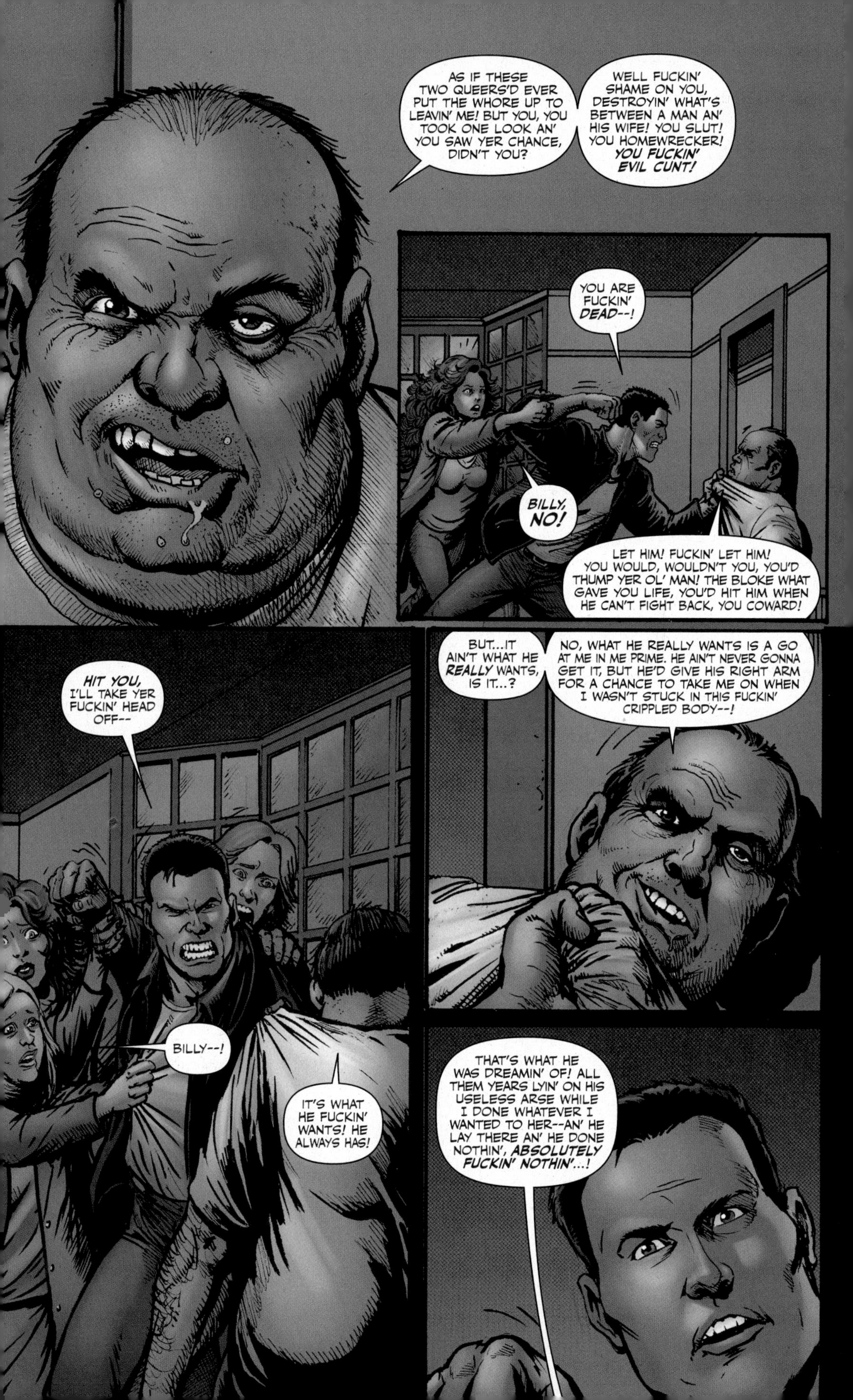
AS IF THESE TWO QUEERS'D EVER PUT THE WHORE UP TO LEAVIN' ME! BUT YOU, YOU TOOK ONE LOOK AN' YOU SAW YER CHANCE, DIDN'T YOU?
WELL FUCKIN' SHAME ON YOU, DESTROYIN' WHAT'S BETWEEN A MAN AN' HIS WIFE! YOU SLUT! YOU HOMEWRECKER! YOU FUCKIN' EVIL CUNT!
YOU ARE FUCKIN' DEAD--!
BILLY, NO!
LET HIM! FUCKIN' LET HIM! YOU WOULD, WOULDN'T YOU, YOU'D THUMP YER OL' MAN! THE BLOKE WHAT GAVE YOU LIFE, YOU'D HIT HIM WHEN HE CAN'T FIGHT BACK, YOU COWARD!
HIT YOU, I'LL TAKE YER FUCKIN' HEAD OFF--
BILLY--!
IT'S WHAT HE FUCKIN' WANTS! HE ALWAYS HAS!
BUT...IT AIN'T WHAT HE REALLY WANTS, IS IT...?
NO, WHAT HE REALLY WANTS IS A GO AT ME IN ME PRIME. HE AIN'T NEVER GONNA GET IT, BUT HE'D GIVE HIS RIGHT ARM FOR A CHANCE TO TAKE ME ON WHEN I WASN'T STUCK IN THIS FUCKIN' CRIPPLED BODY--!
THAT'S WHAT HE WAS DREAMIN' OF! ALL THEM YEARS LYIN' ON HIS USELESS ARSE WHILE I DONE WHATEVER I WANTED TO HER--AN' HE LAY THERE AN' HE DONE NOTHIN', ABSOLUTELY FUCKIN' NOTHIN'...!

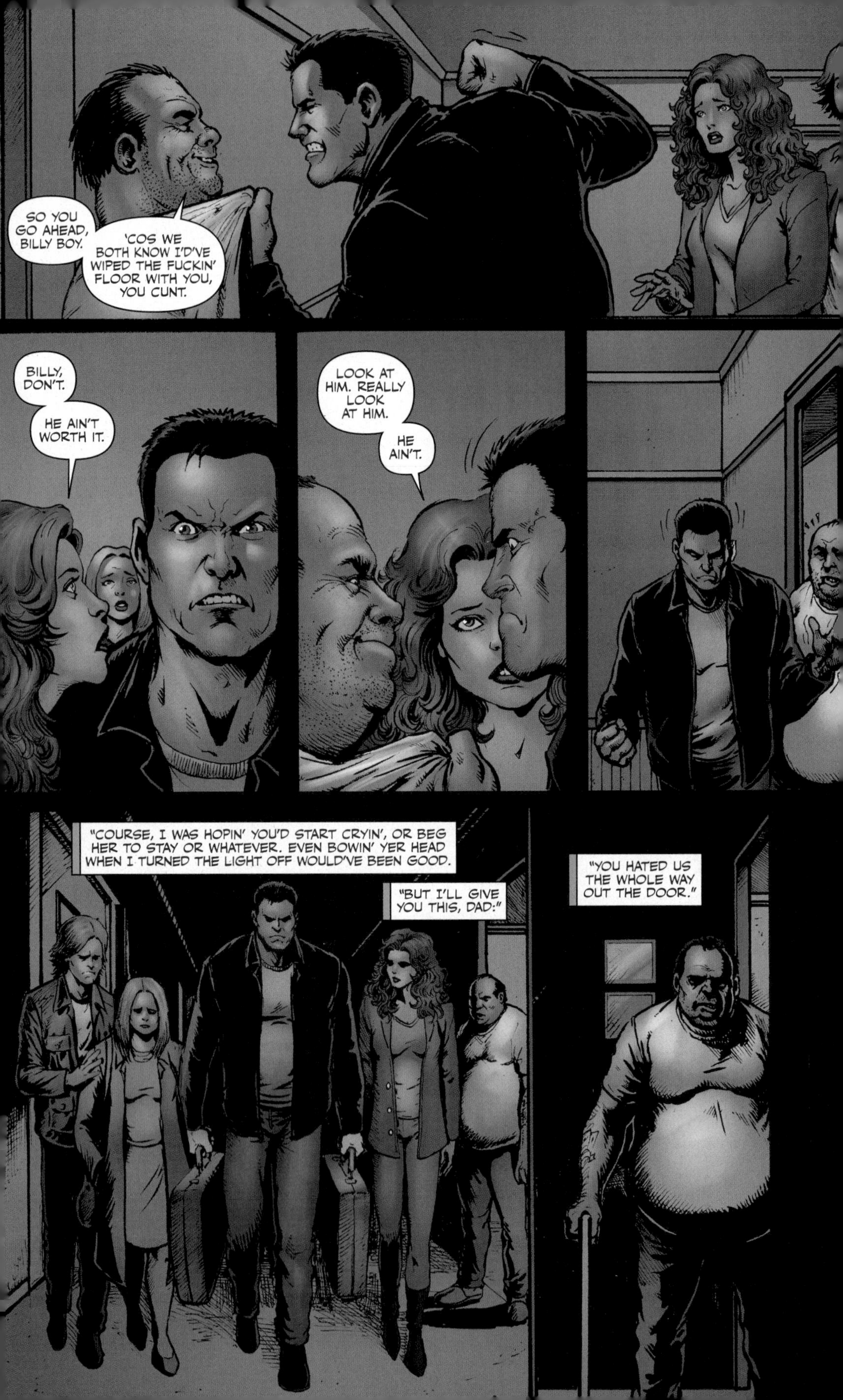
SO YOU GO AHEAD, BILLY BOY.
'COS WE BOTH KNOW I'D'VE WIPED THE FUCKIN' FLOOR WITH YOU, YOU CUNT.
BILLY, DON'T.
HE AIN'T WORTH IT.
LOOK AT HIM. REALLY LOOK AT HIM.
HE AIN'T.
"COURSE, I WAS HOPIN' YOU'D START CRYIN', OR BEG HER TO STAY OR WHATEVER. EVEN BOWIN' YER HEAD WHEN I TURNED THE LIGHT OFF WOULD'VE BEEN GOOD.
"BUT I'LL GIVE YOU THIS, DAD:"
"YOU HATED US THE WHOLE WAY OUT THE DOOR."

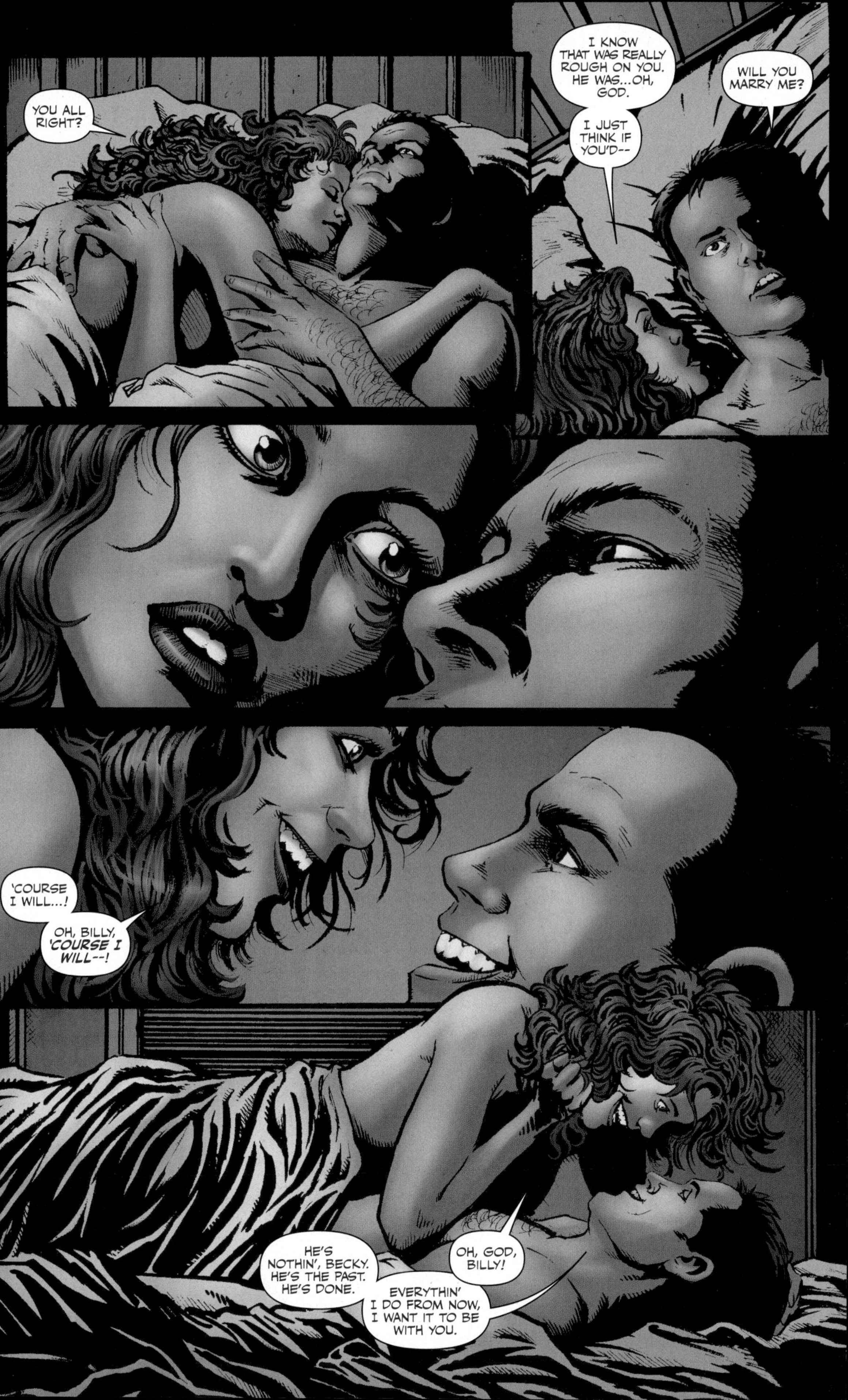
YOU ALL RIGHT?
I KNOW THAT WAS REALLY ROUGH ON YOU. HE WAS...OH, GOD.
I JUST THINK IF YOU'D--
WILL YOU MARRY ME?
'COURSE I WILL...!
OH, BILLY, 'COURSE I WILL--!
HE'S NOTHIN', BECKY. HE'S THE PAST. HE'S DONE.
OH, GOD, BILLY!
EVERYTHIN' I DO FROM NOW, I WANT IT TO BE WITH YOU.

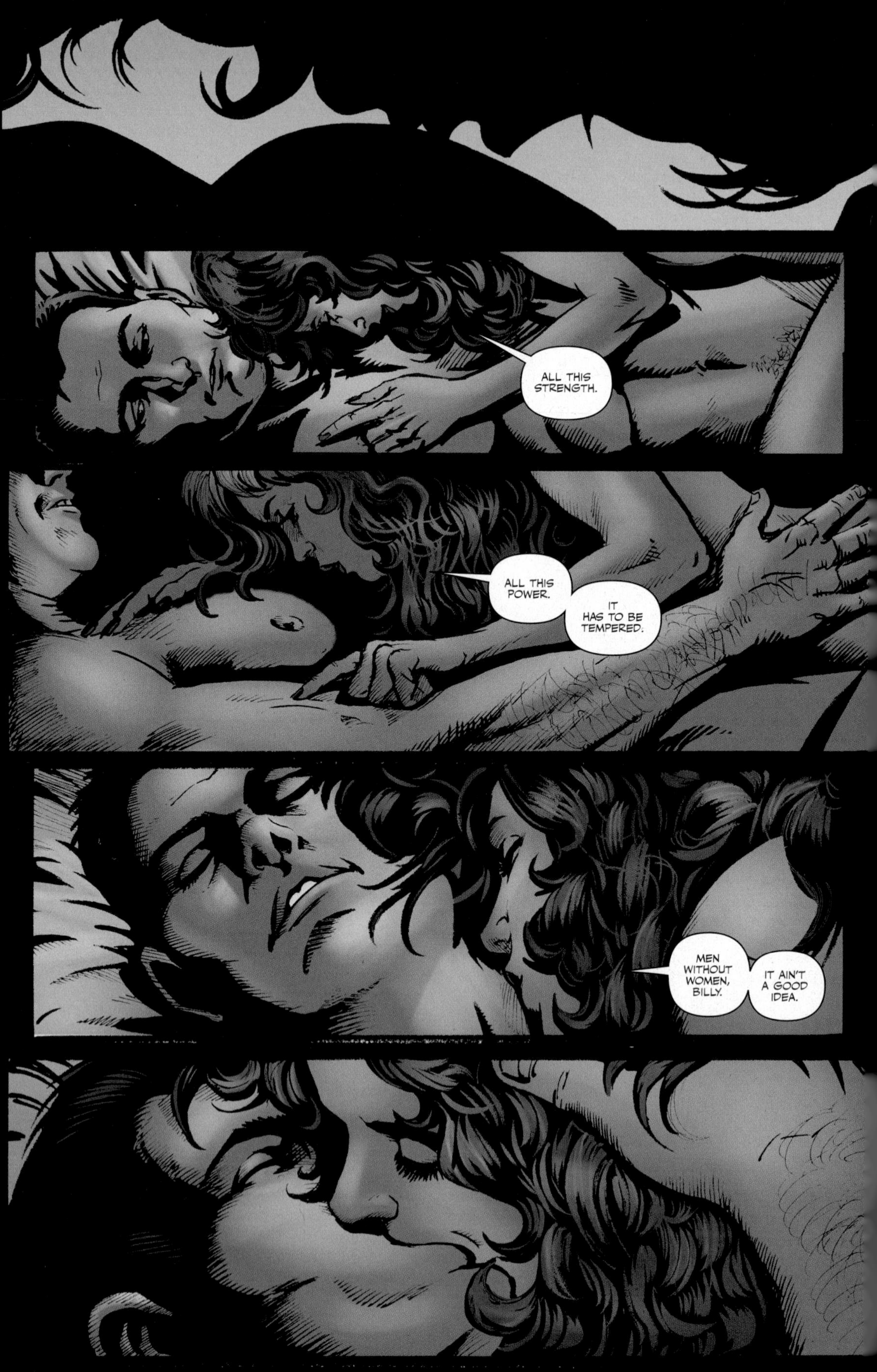
ALL THIS STRENGTH.
ALL THIS POWER.
IT HAS TO BE TEMPERED.
MEN WITHOUT WOMEN, BILLY.
IT AIN'T A GOOD IDEA.

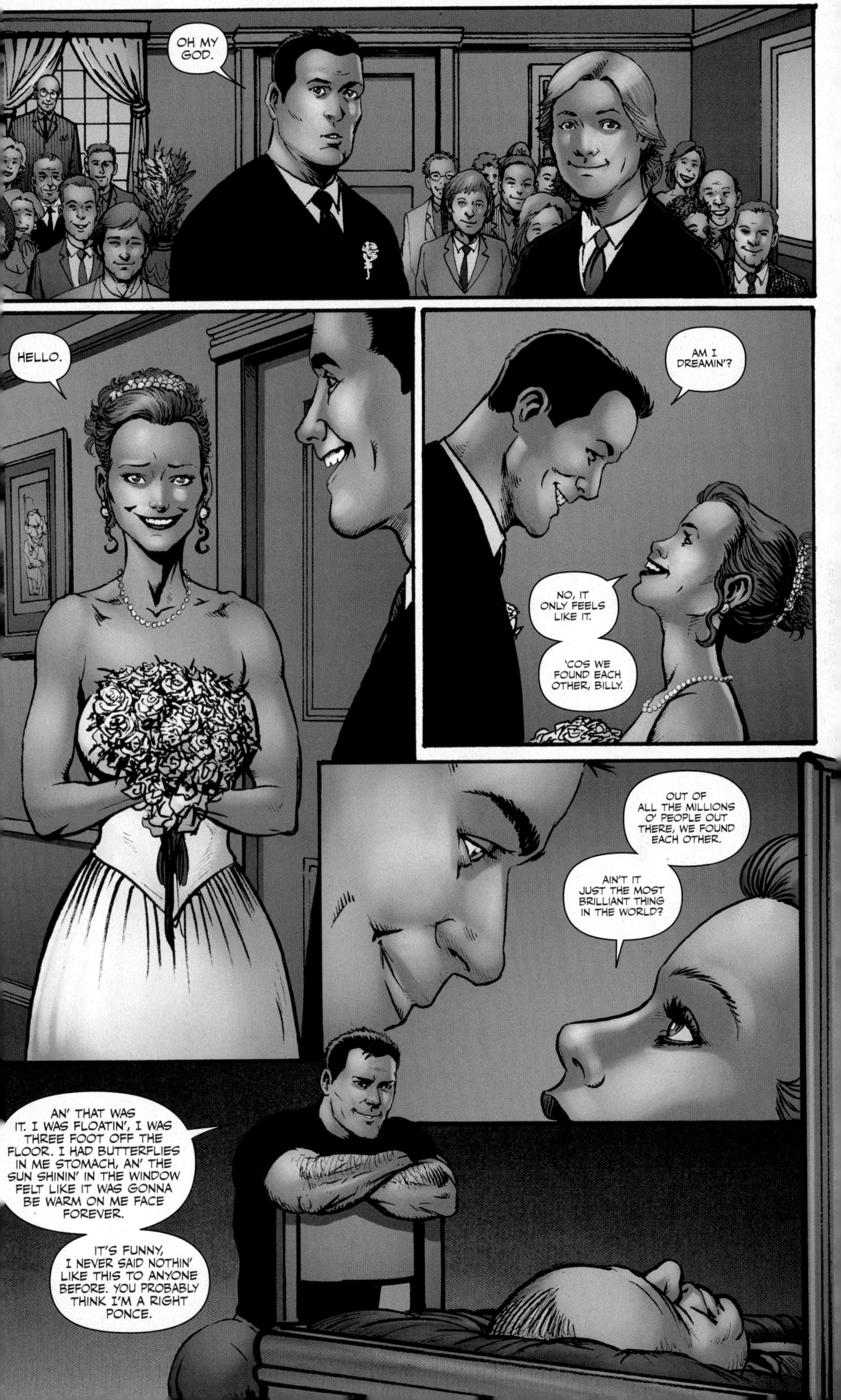
OH MY GOD.
HELLO.
AM I DREAMIN'?
NO, IT ONLY FEELS LIKE IT.
'COS WE FOUND EACH OTHER, BILLY.
OUT OF ALL THE MILLIONS O' PEOPLE OUT THERE, WE FOUND EACH OTHER.
AIN'T IT JUST THE MOST BRILLIANT THING IN THE WORLD?
AN' THAT WAS IT. I WAS FLOATIN', I WAS THREE FOOT OFF THE FLOOR. I HAD BUTTERFLIES IN ME STOMACH, AN' THE SUN SHININ' IN THE WINDOW FELT LIKE IT WAS GONNA BE WARM ON ME FACE FOREVER.
IT'S FUNNY, I NEVER SAID NOTHIN' LIKE THIS TO ANYONE BEFORE. YOU PROBABLY THINK I'M A RIGHT PONCE.

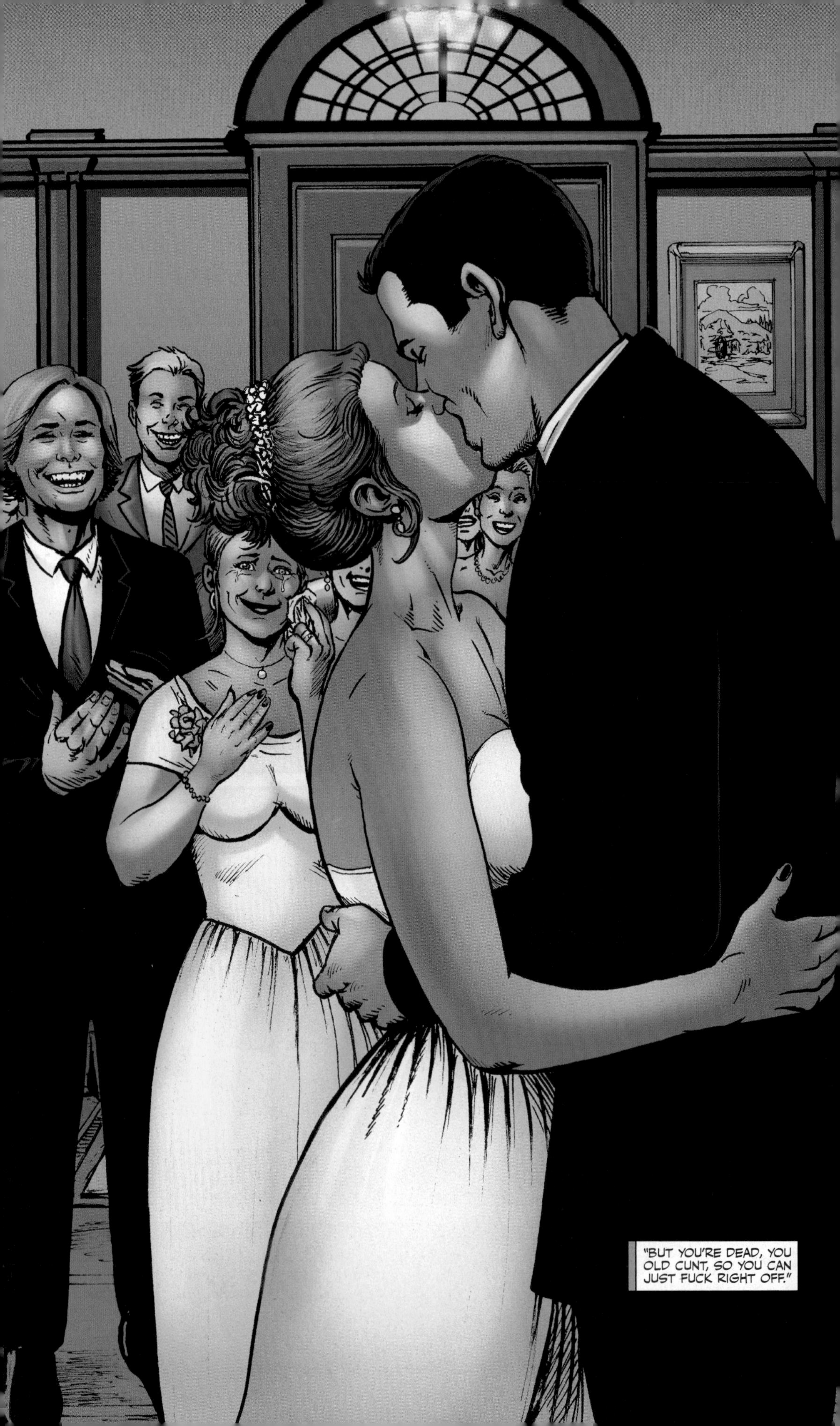
"BUT YOU'RE DEAD, YOU OLD CUNT, SO YOU CAN JUST FUCK RIGHT OFF."

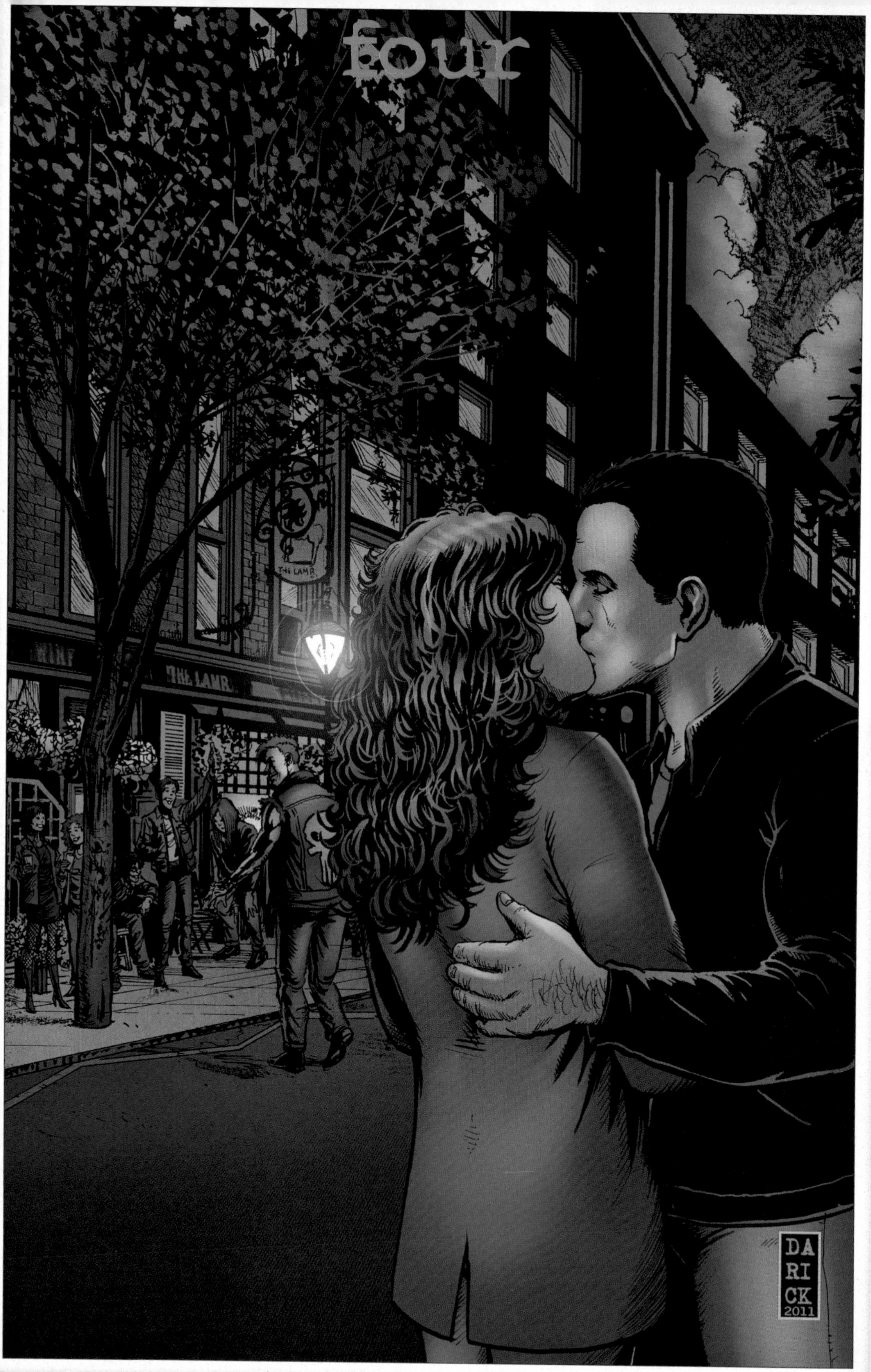
four
THE LAMB
DA
RI
CK
2011

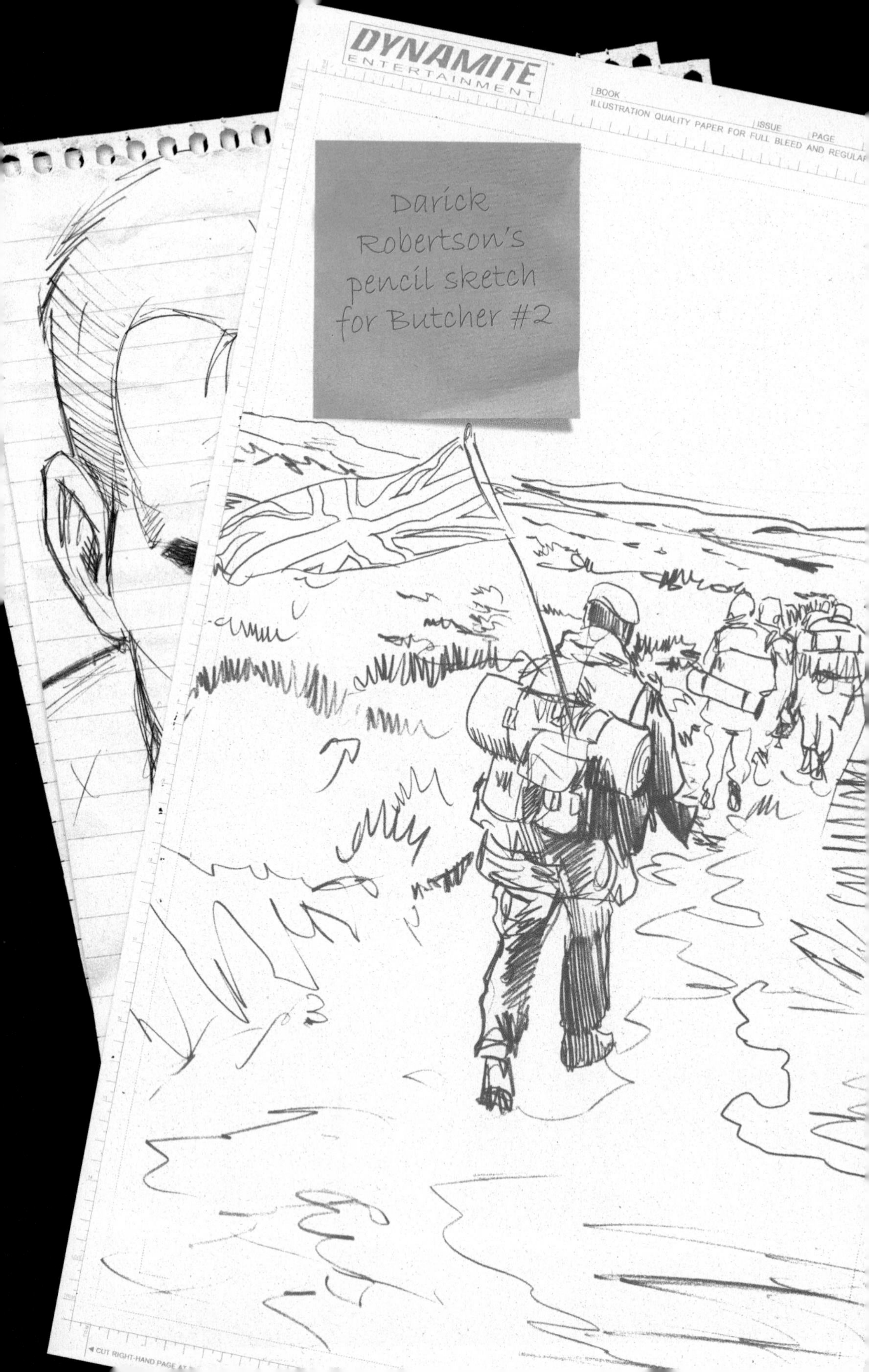
DYNAMITE
ENTERTAINMENT
BOOK
ILLUSTRATION QUALITY PAPER FOR FULL BLEED AND REGULAR
ISSUE
PAGE
Darick Robertson's pencil sketch for Butcher #2
CUT RIGHT-HAND PAGE AT

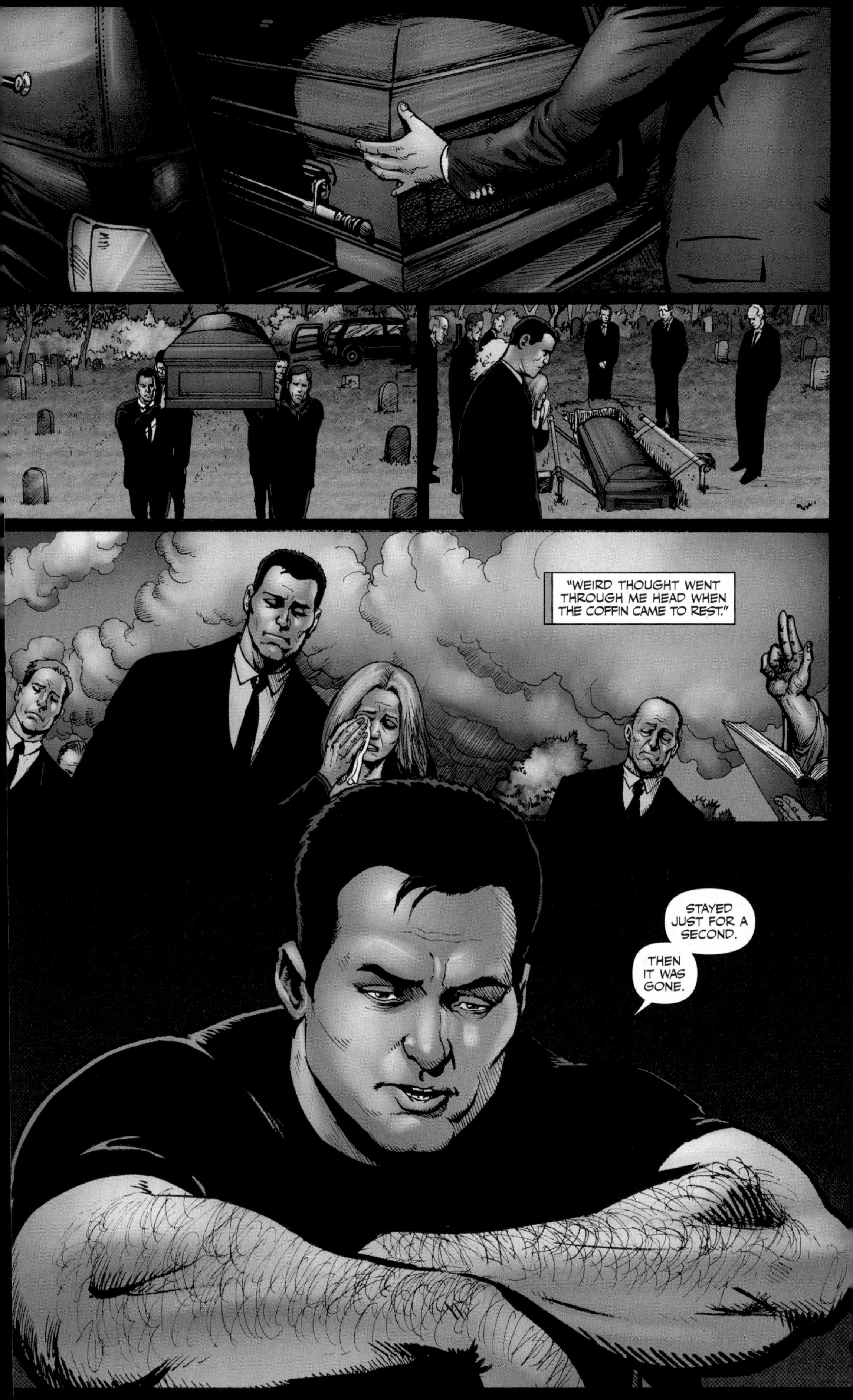
"WEIRD THOUGHT WENT THROUGH ME HEAD WHEN THE COFFIN CAME TO REST."
STAYED JUST FOR A SECOND.
THEN IT WAS GONE.

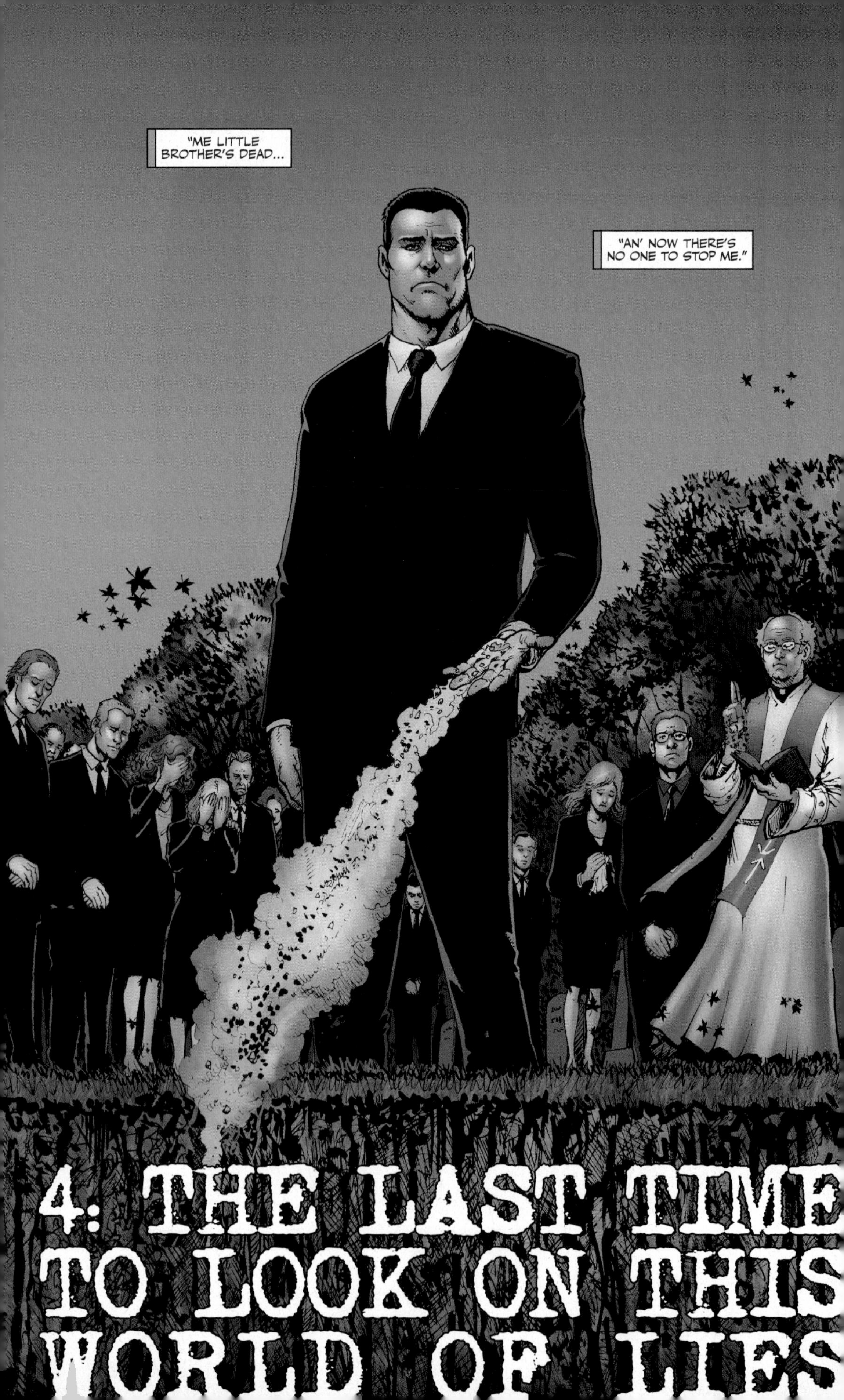
"ME LITTLE BROTHER'S DEAD...
"AN' NOW THERE'S NO ONE TO STOP ME."
4: THE LAST TIME TO LOOK ON THIS WORLD OF LIES

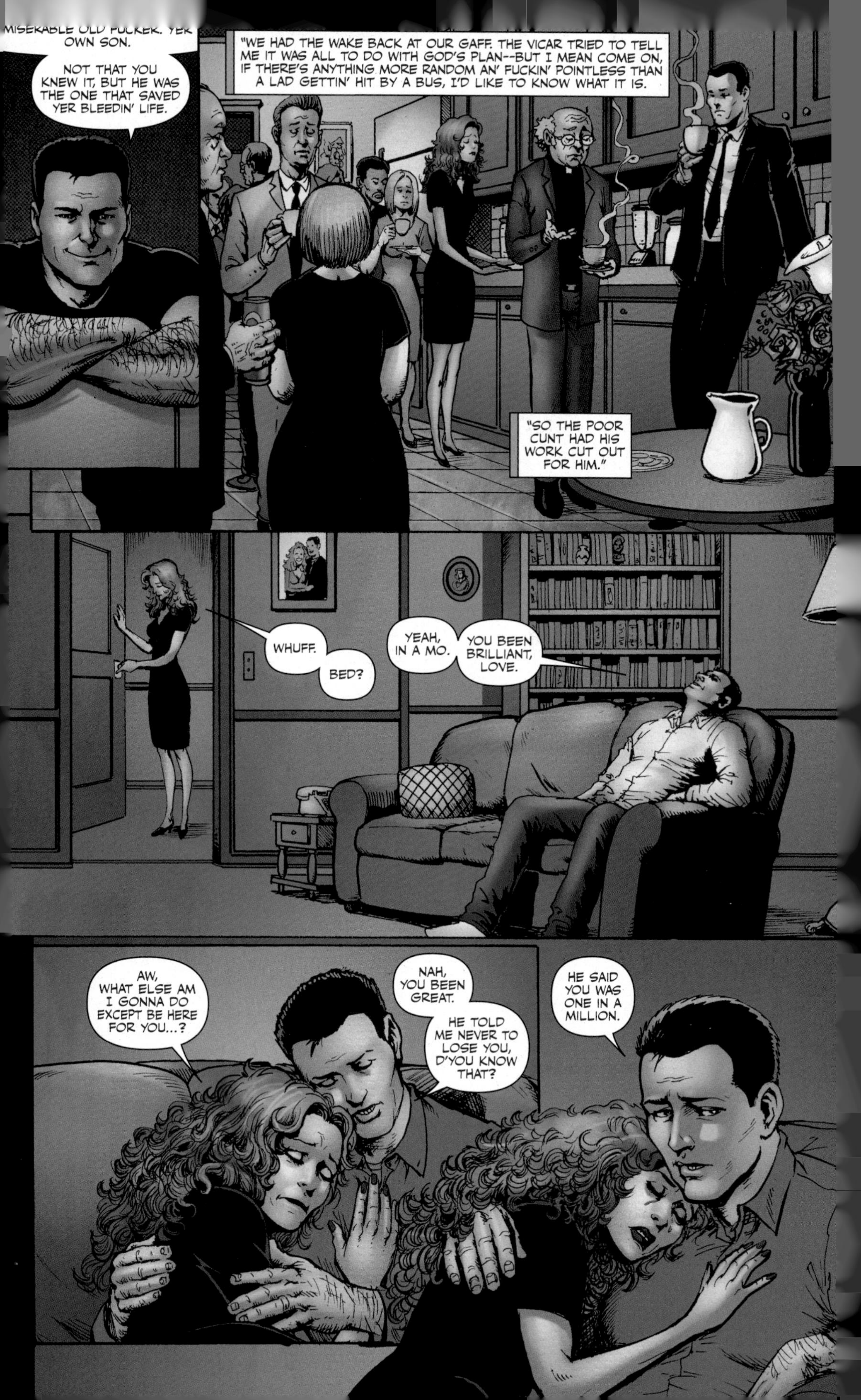
MISERABLE OLD FUCKER. YER OWN SON.
NOT THAT YOU KNEW IT, BUT HE WAS THE ONE THAT SAVED YER BLEEDIN' LIFE.
"WE HAD THE WAKE BACK AT OUR GAFF. THE VICAR TRIED TO TELL ME IT WAS ALL TO DO WITH GOD'S PLAN--BUT I MEAN COME ON, IF THERE'S ANYTHING MORE RANDOM AN' FUCKIN' POINTLESS THAN A LAD GETTIN' HIT BY A BUS, I'D LIKE TO KNOW WHAT IT IS.
"SO THE POOR CUNT HAD HIS WORK CUT OUT FOR HIM."
WHUFF.
BED?
YEAH, IN A MO.
YOU BEEN BRILLIANT, LOVE.
AW, WHAT ELSE AM I GONNA DO EXCEPT BE HERE FOR YOU...?
NAH, YOU BEEN GREAT.
HE TOLD ME NEVER TO LOSE YOU, D'YOU KNOW THAT?
HE SAID YOU WAS ONE IN A MILLION.

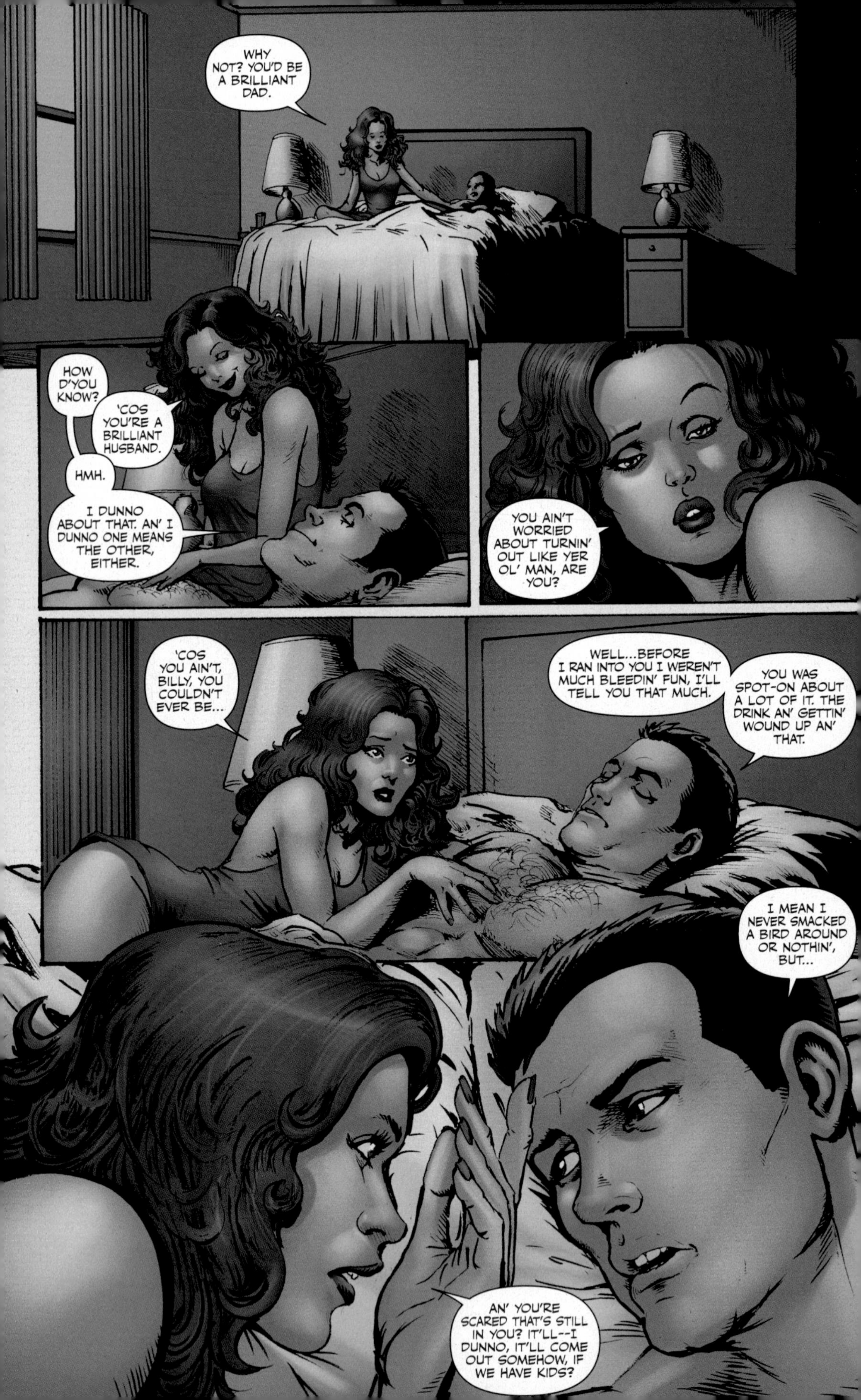
WHY NOT? YOU'D BE A BRILLIANT DAD.
HOW D'YOU KNOW?
'COS YOU'RE A BRILLIANT HUSBAND.
HMH.
I DUNNO ABOUT THAT. AN' I DUNNO ONE MEANS THE OTHER, EITHER.
YOU AIN'T WORRIED ABOUT TURNIN' OUT LIKE YER OL' MAN, ARE YOU?
'COS YOU AIN'T, BILLY, YOU COULDN'T EVER BE...
WELL...BEFORE I RAN INTO YOU I WEREN'T MUCH BLEEDIN' FUN, I'LL TELL YOU THAT MUCH.
YOU WAS SPOT-ON ABOUT A LOT OF IT. THE DRINK AN' GETTIN' WOUND UP AN' THAT.
I MEAN I NEVER SMACKED A BIRD AROUND OR NOTHIN', BUT...
AN' YOU'RE SCARED THAT'S STILL IN YOU? IT'LL--I DUNNO, IT'LL COME OUT SOMEHOW, IF WE HAVE KIDS?

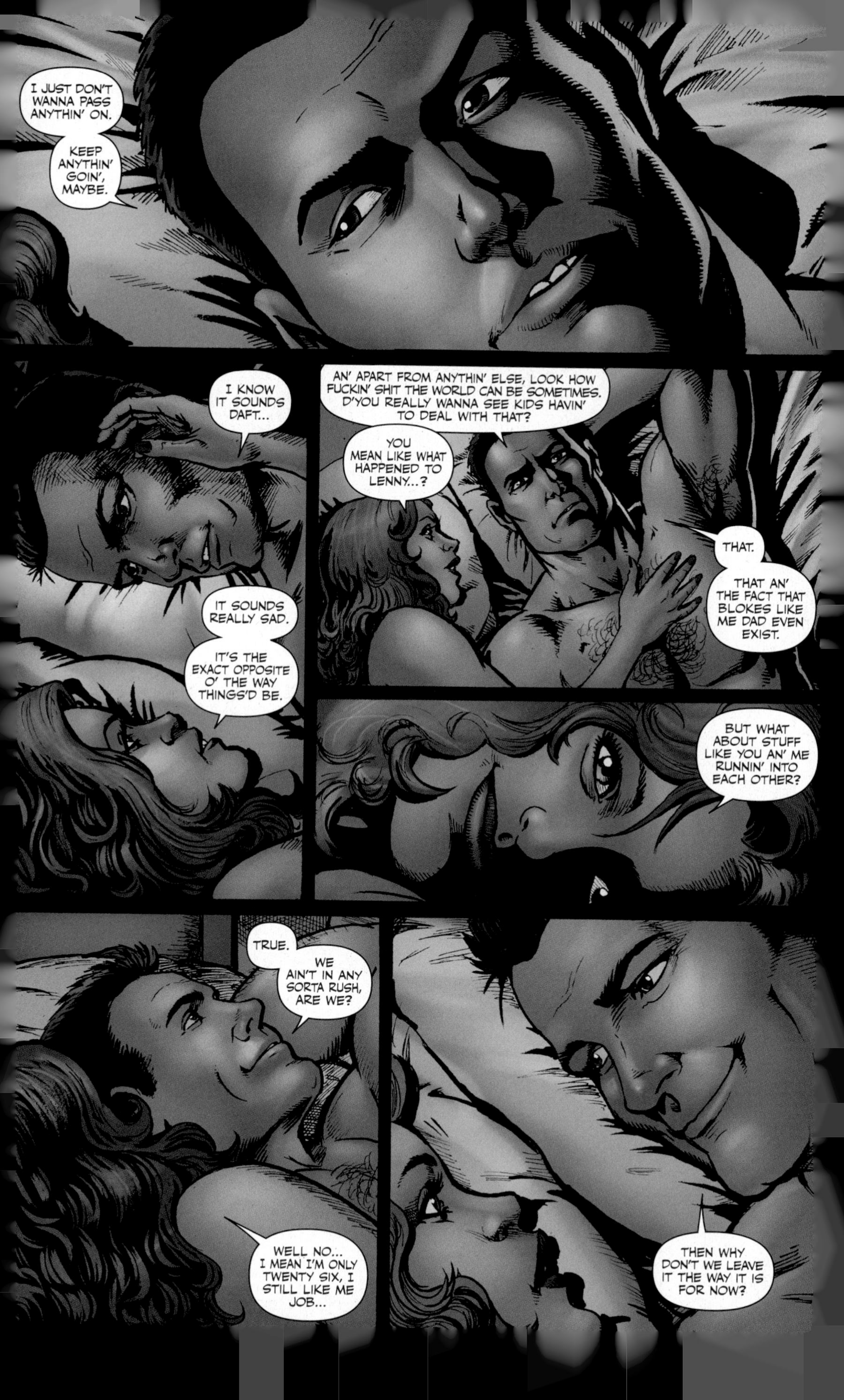
I JUST DON'T WANNA PASS ANYTHIN' ON.
KEEP ANYTHIN' GOIN', MAYBE.
I KNOW IT SOUNDS DAFT...
IT SOUNDS REALLY SAD.
IT'S THE EXACT OPPOSITE O' THE WAY THINGS'D BE.
AN' APART FROM ANYTHIN' ELSE, LOOK HOW FUCKIN' SHIT THE WORLD CAN BE SOMETIMES. D'YOU REALLY WANNA SEE KIDS HAVIN' TO DEAL WITH THAT?
YOU MEAN LIKE WHAT HAPPENED TO LENNY...?
THAT.
THAT AN' THE FACT THAT BLOKES LIKE ME DAD EVEN EXIST.
BUT WHAT ABOUT STUFF LIKE YOU AN' ME RUNNIN' INTO EACH OTHER?
TRUE.
WE AIN'T IN ANY SORTA RUSH, ARE WE?
WELL NO... I MEAN I'M ONLY TWENTY SIX, I STILL LIKE ME JOB...
THEN WHY DON'T WE LEAVE IT THE WAY IT IS FOR NOW?

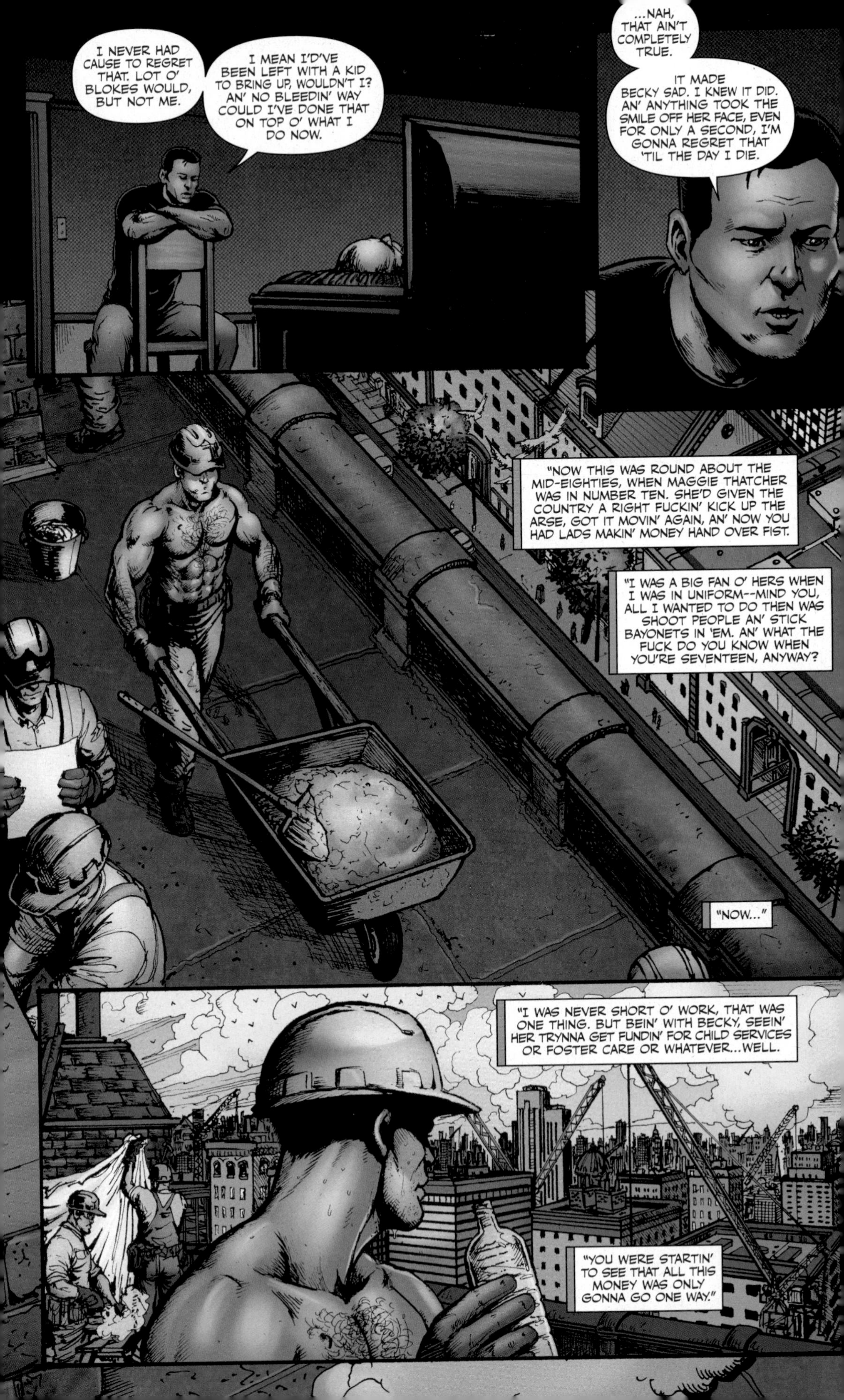

I NEVER HAD CAUSE TO REGRET THAT. LOT O' BLOKES WOULD, BUT NOT ME.
I MEAN I'D'VE BEEN LEFT WITH A KID TO BRING UP, WOULDN'T I? AN' NO BLEEDIN' WAY COULD I'VE DONE THAT ON TOP O' WHAT I DO NOW.
...NAH, THAT AIN'T COMPLETELY TRUE.
IT MADE BECKY SAD. I KNEW IT DID. AN' ANYTHING TOOK THE SMILE OFF HER FACE, EVEN FOR ONLY A SECOND, I'M GONNA REGRET THAT 'TIL THE DAY I DIE.
"NOW THIS WAS ROUND ABOUT THE MID-EIGHTIES, WHEN MAGGIE THATCHER WAS IN NUMBER TEN. SHE'D GIVEN THE COUNTRY A RIGHT FUCKIN' KICK UP THE ARSE, GOT IT MOVIN' AGAIN, AN' NOW YOU HAD LADS MAKIN' MONEY HAND OVER FIST.
"I WAS A BIG FAN O' HERS WHEN I WAS IN UNIFORM--MIND YOU, ALL I WANTED TO DO THEN WAS SHOOT PEOPLE AN' STICK BAYONETS IN 'EM. AN' WHAT THE FUCK DO YOU KNOW WHEN YOU'RE SEVENTEEN, ANYWAY?
"NOW..."
"I WAS NEVER SHORT O' WORK, THAT WAS ONE THING. BUT BEIN' WITH BECKY, SEEIN' HER TRYNNA GET FUNDIN' FOR CHILD SERVICES OR FOSTER CARE OR WHATEVER...WELL.
"YOU WERE STARTIN' TO SEE THAT ALL THIS MONEY WAS ONLY GONNA GO ONE WAY."

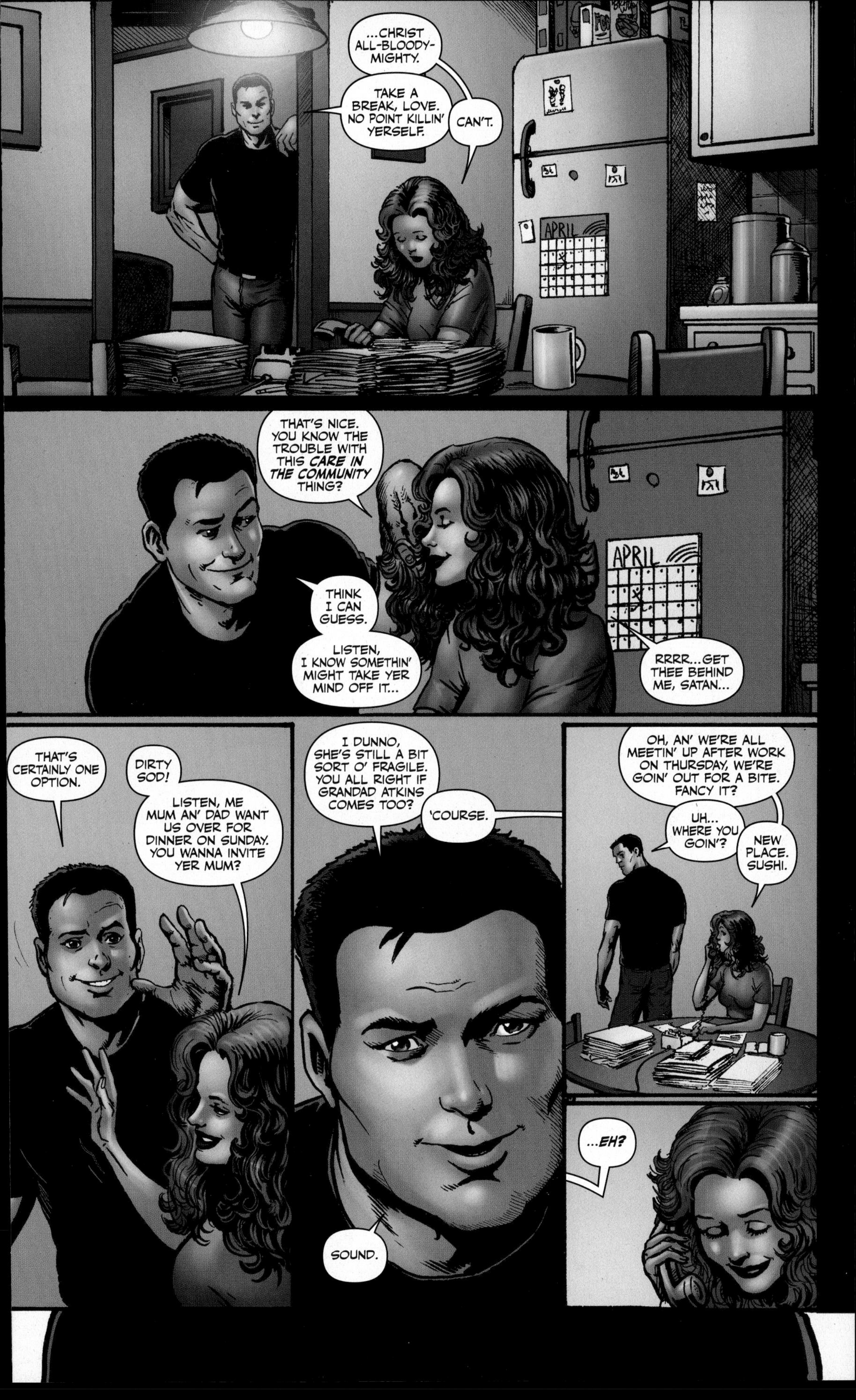
...CHRIST ALL-BLOODY-MIGHTY.
TAKE A BREAK, LOVE. NO POINT KILLIN' YERSELF.
CAN'T.
THAT'S NICE. YOU KNOW THE TROUBLE WITH THIS CARE IN THE COMMUNITY THING?
THINK I CAN GUESS.
LISTEN, I KNOW SOMETHIN' MIGHT TAKE YER MIND OFF IT...
RRRR...GET THEE BEHIND ME, SATAN...
THAT'S CERTAINLY ONE OPTION.
DIRTY SOD!
LISTEN, ME MUM AN' DAD WANT US OVER FOR DINNER ON SUNDAY. YOU WANNA INVITE YER MUM?
I DUNNO, SHE'S STILL A BIT SORT O' FRAGILE. YOU ALL RIGHT IF GRANDAD ATKINS COMES TOO?
'COURSE.
SOUND.
OH, AN' WE'RE ALL MEETIN' UP AFTER WORK ON THURSDAY, WE'RE GOIN' OUT FOR A BITE. FANCY IT?
UH... WHERE YOU GOIN'?
NEW PLACE. SUSHI.
...EH?

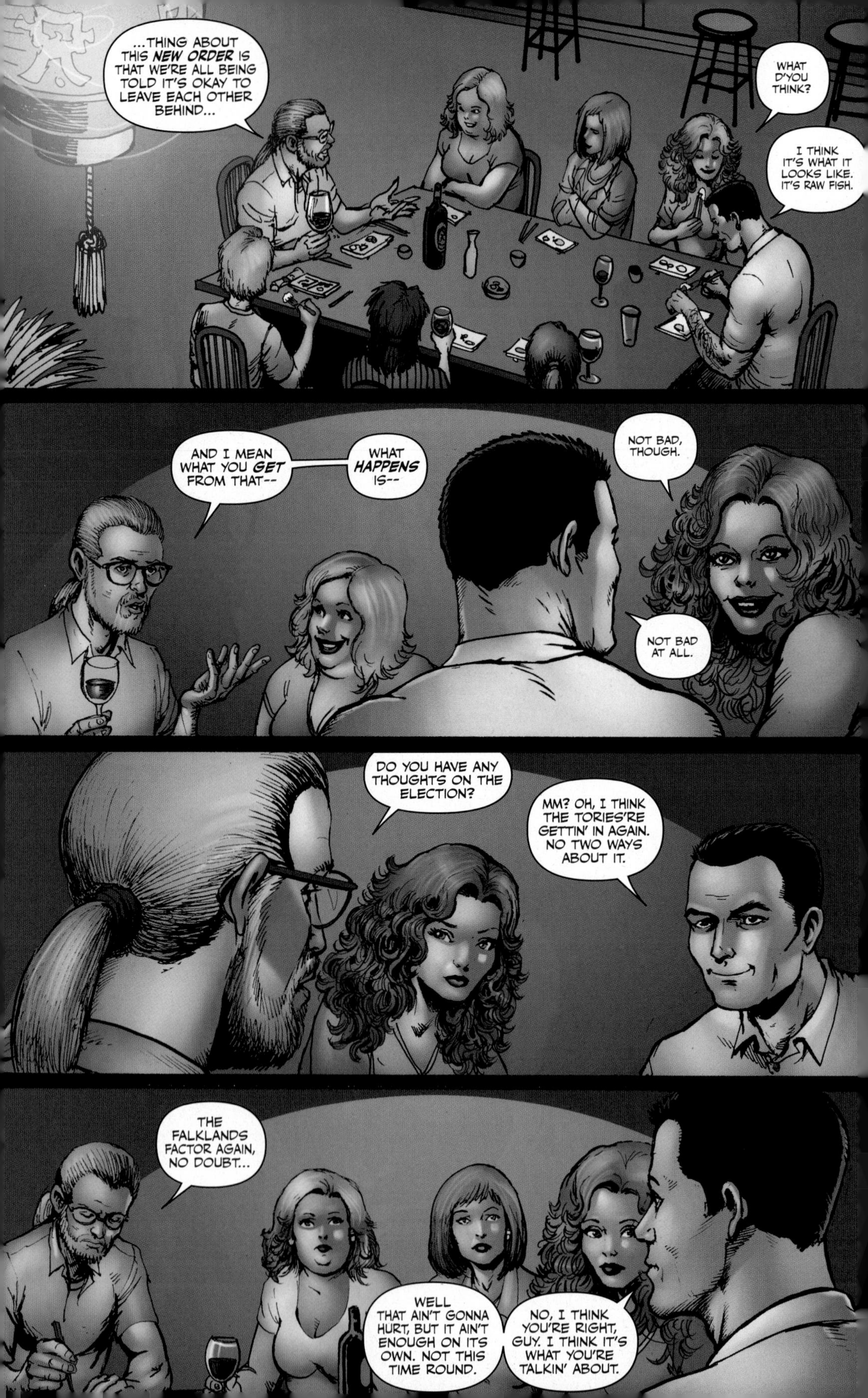
...THING ABOUT THIS NEW ORDER IS THAT WE'RE ALL BEING TOLD IT'S OKAY TO LEAVE EACH OTHER BEHIND...
WHAT D'YOU THINK?
I THINK IT'S WHAT IT LOOKS LIKE. IT'S RAW FISH.
AND I MEAN WHAT YOU GET FROM THAT--
WHAT HAPPENS IS--
NOT BAD, THOUGH.
NOT BAD AT ALL.
DO YOU HAVE ANY THOUGHTS ON THE ELECTION?
MM? OH, I THINK THE TORIES'RE GETTIN' IN AGAIN. NO TWO WAYS ABOUT IT.
THE FALKLANDS FACTOR AGAIN, NO DOUBT...
WELL THAT AIN'T GONNA HURT, BUT IT AIN'T ENOUGH ON ITS OWN. NOT THIS TIME ROUND.
NO, I THINK YOU'RE RIGHT, GUY. I THINK IT'S WHAT YOU'RE TALKIN' ABOUT.

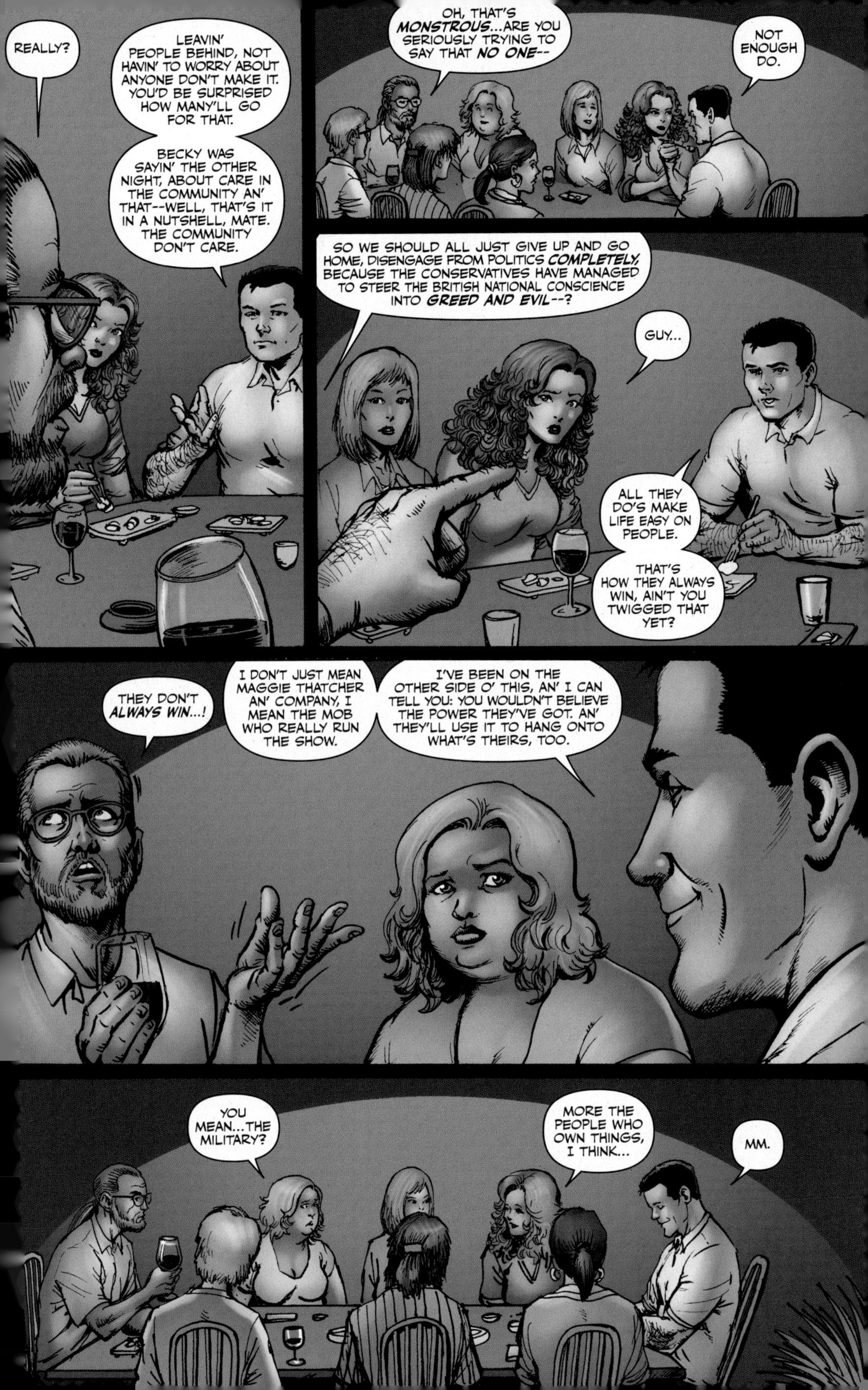
REALLY?
LEAVIN' PEOPLE BEHIND, NOT HAVIN' TO WORRY ABOUT ANYONE DON'T MAKE IT. YOU'D BE SURPRISED HOW MANY'LL GO FOR THAT.
BECKY WAS SAYIN' THE OTHER NIGHT, ABOUT CARE IN THE COMMUNITY AN' THAT--WELL, THAT'S IT IN A NUTSHELL, MATE. THE COMMUNITY DON'T CARE.
OH, THAT'S MONSTROUS...ARE YOU SERIOUSLY TRYING TO SAY THAT NO ONE--
NOT ENOUGH DO.
SO WE SHOULD ALL JUST GIVE UP AND GO HOME, DISENGAGE FROM POLITICS COMPLETELY, BECAUSE THE CONSERVATIVES HAVE MANAGED TO STEER THE BRITISH NATIONAL CONSCIENCE INTO GREED AND EVIL--?
GUY...
ALL THEY DO'S MAKE LIFE EASY ON PEOPLE.
THAT'S HOW THEY ALWAYS WIN, AIN'T YOU TWIGGED THAT YET?
THEY DON'T ALWAYS WIN...!
I DON'T JUST MEAN MAGGIE THATCHER AN' COMPANY, I MEAN THE MOB WHO REALLY RUN THE SHOW.
I'VE BEEN ON THE OTHER SIDE O' THIS, AN' I CAN TELL YOU: YOU WOULDN'T BELIEVE THE POWER THEY'VE GOT. AN' THEY'LL USE IT TO HANG ONTO WHAT'S THEIRS, TOO.
YOU MEAN...THE MILITARY?
MORE THE PEOPLE WHO OWN THINGS, I THINK...
MM.

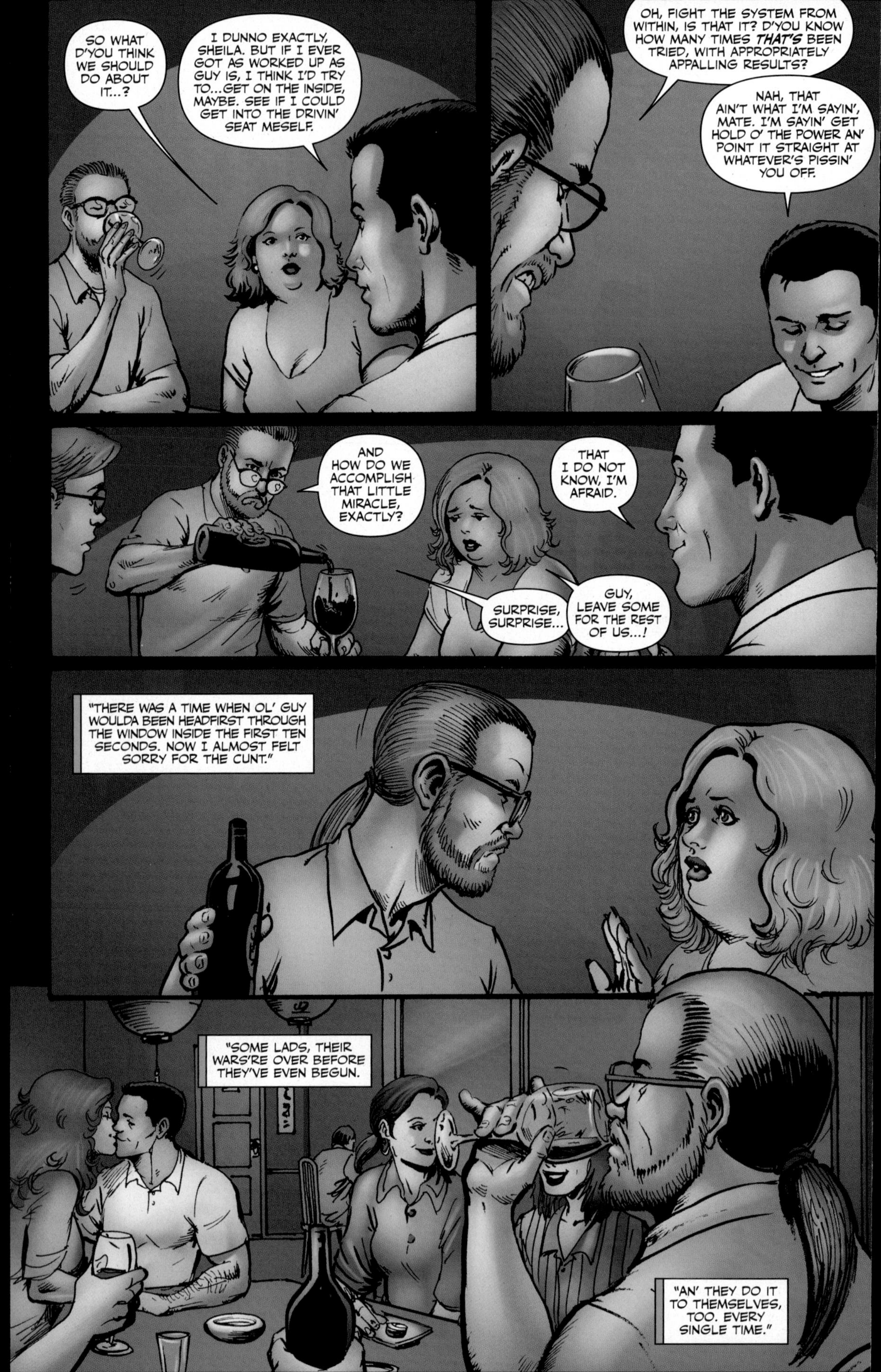

SO WHAT D'YOU THINK WE SHOULD DO ABOUT IT...?
I DUNNO EXACTLY, SHEILA. BUT IF I EVER GOT AS WORKED UP AS GUY IS, I THINK I'D TRY TO...GET ON THE INSIDE, MAYBE. SEE IF I COULD GET INTO THE DRIVIN' SEAT MESELF.
OH, FIGHT THE SYSTEM FROM WITHIN, IS THAT IT? D'YOU KNOW HOW MANY TIMES *THAT'S* BEEN TRIED, WITH APPROPRIATELY APPALLING RESULTS?
NAH, THAT AIN'T WHAT I'M SAYIN', MATE. I'M SAYIN' GET HOLD O' THE POWER AN' POINT IT STRAIGHT AT WHATEVER'S PISSIN' YOU OFF.
AND HOW DO WE ACCOMPLISH THAT LITTLE MIRACLE, EXACTLY?
THAT I DO NOT KNOW, I'M AFRAID.
SURPRISE, SURPRISE...
GUY, LEAVE SOME FOR THE REST OF US...!
"THERE WAS A TIME WHEN OL' GUY WOULDA BEEN HEADFIRST THROUGH THE WINDOW INSIDE THE FIRST TEN SECONDS. NOW I ALMOST FELT SORRY FOR THE CUNT."
"SOME LADS, THEIR WARS'RE OVER BEFORE THEY'VE EVEN BEGUN.
"AN' THEY DO IT TO THEMSELVES, TOO. EVERY SINGLE TIME."

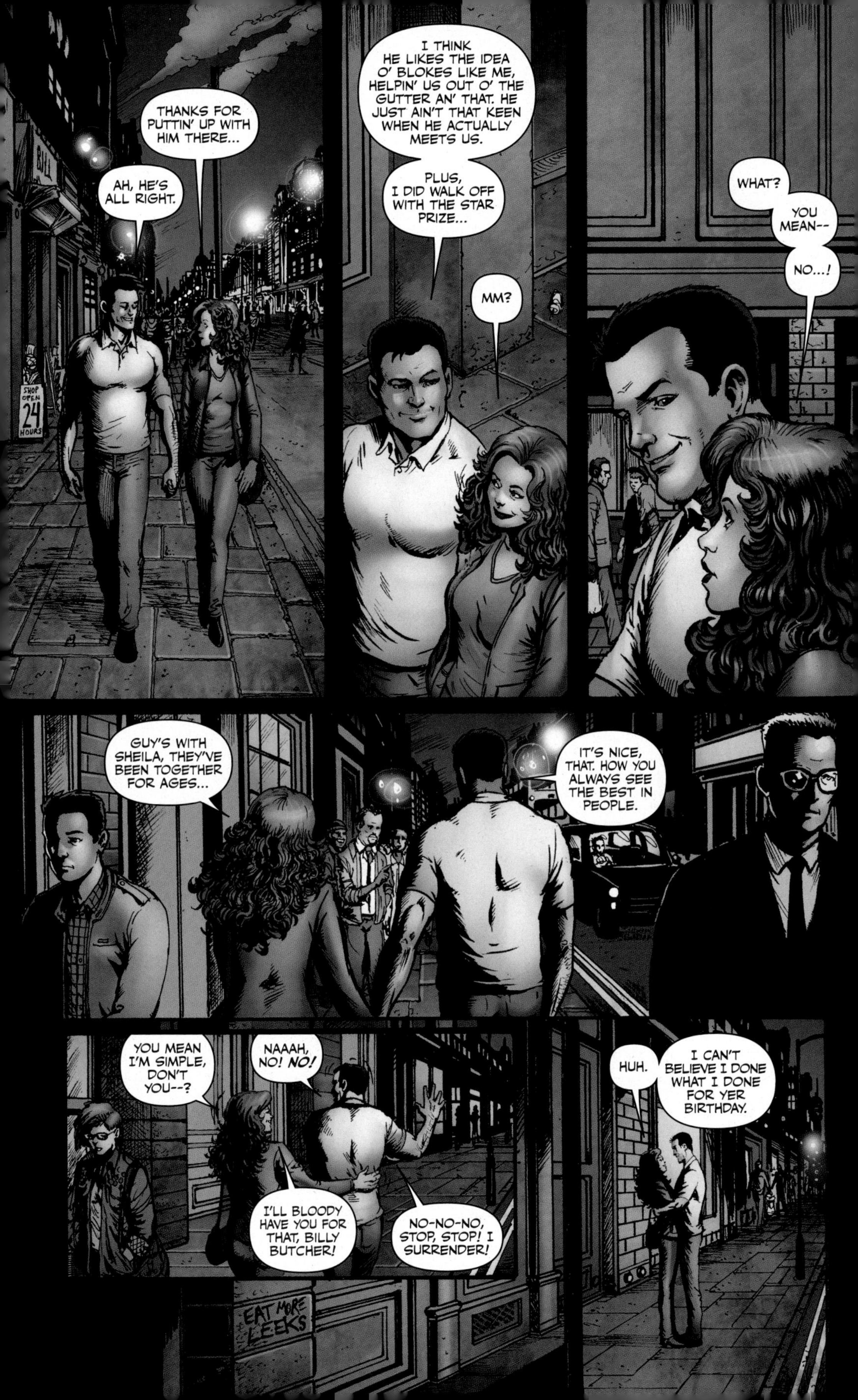
THANKS FOR PUTTIN' UP WITH HIM THERE...
AH, HE'S ALL RIGHT.
SHOP OPEN 24 HOURS
I THINK HE LIKES THE IDEA O' BLOKES LIKE ME, HELPIN' US OUT O' THE GUTTER AN' THAT. HE JUST AIN'T THAT KEEN WHEN HE ACTUALLY MEETS US.
PLUS, I DID WALK OFF WITH THE STAR PRIZE...
MM?
WHAT?
YOU MEAN--
NO...!
GUY'S WITH SHEILA, THEY'VE BEEN TOGETHER FOR AGES...
IT'S NICE, THAT. HOW YOU ALWAYS SEE THE BEST IN PEOPLE.
YOU MEAN I'M SIMPLE, DON'T YOU--?
NAAAH, NO! *NO!*
I'LL BLOODY HAVE YOU FOR THAT, BILLY BUTCHER!
NO-NO-NO, STOP, STOP! I SURRENDER!
EAT MORE LEEKS
HUH.
I CAN'T BELIEVE I DONE WHAT I DONE FOR YER BIRTHDAY.

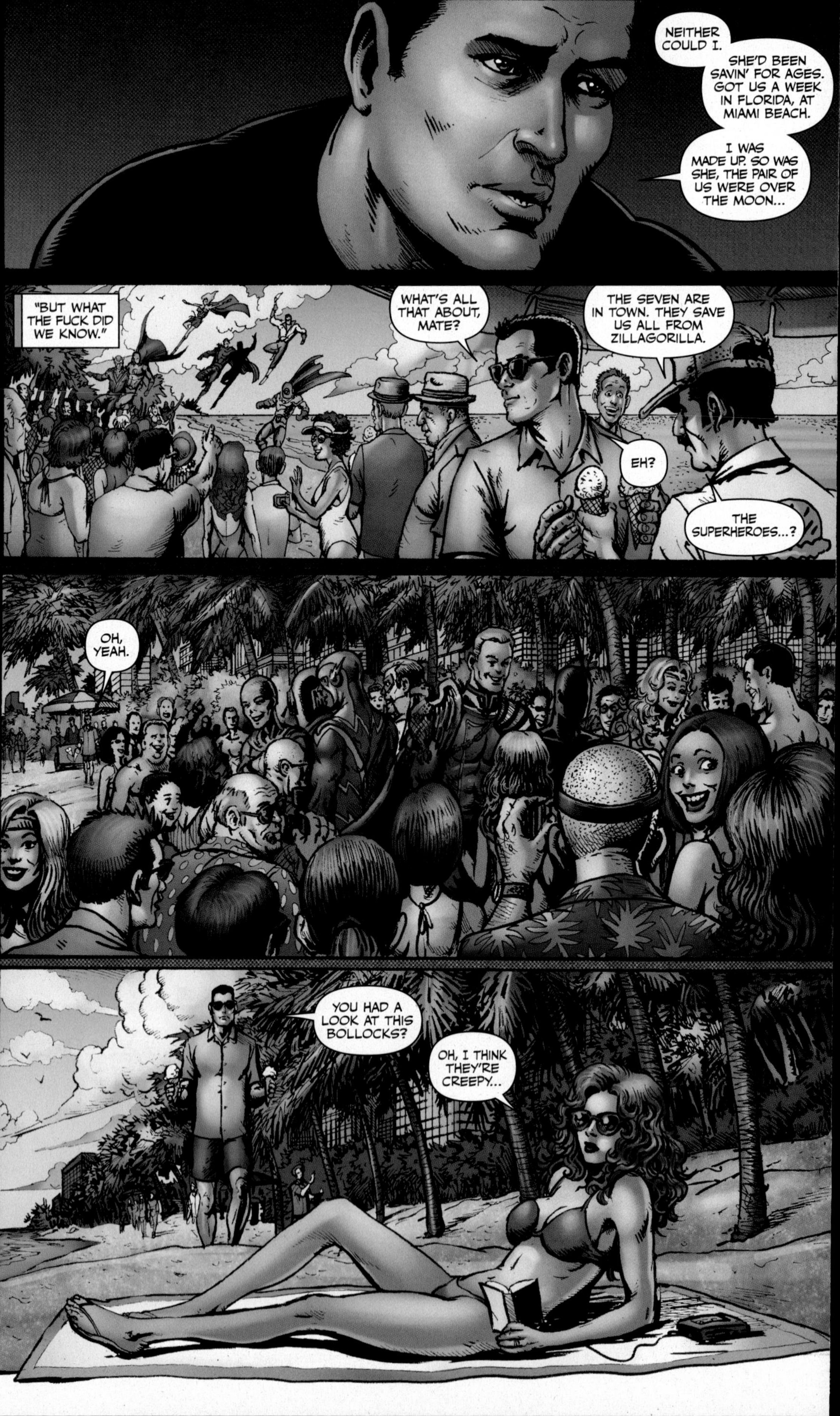
NEITHER COULD I.
SHE'D BEEN SAVIN' FOR AGES. GOT US A WEEK IN FLORIDA, AT MIAMI BEACH.
I WAS MADE UP. SO WAS SHE, THE PAIR OF US WERE OVER THE MOON...
"BUT WHAT THE FUCK DID WE KNOW."
WHAT'S ALL THAT ABOUT, MATE?
THE SEVEN ARE IN TOWN. THEY SAVE US ALL FROM ZILLAGORILLA.
EH?
THE SUPERHEROES...?
OH, YEAH.
YOU HAD A LOOK AT THIS BOLLOCKS?
OH, I THINK THEY'RE CREEPY...

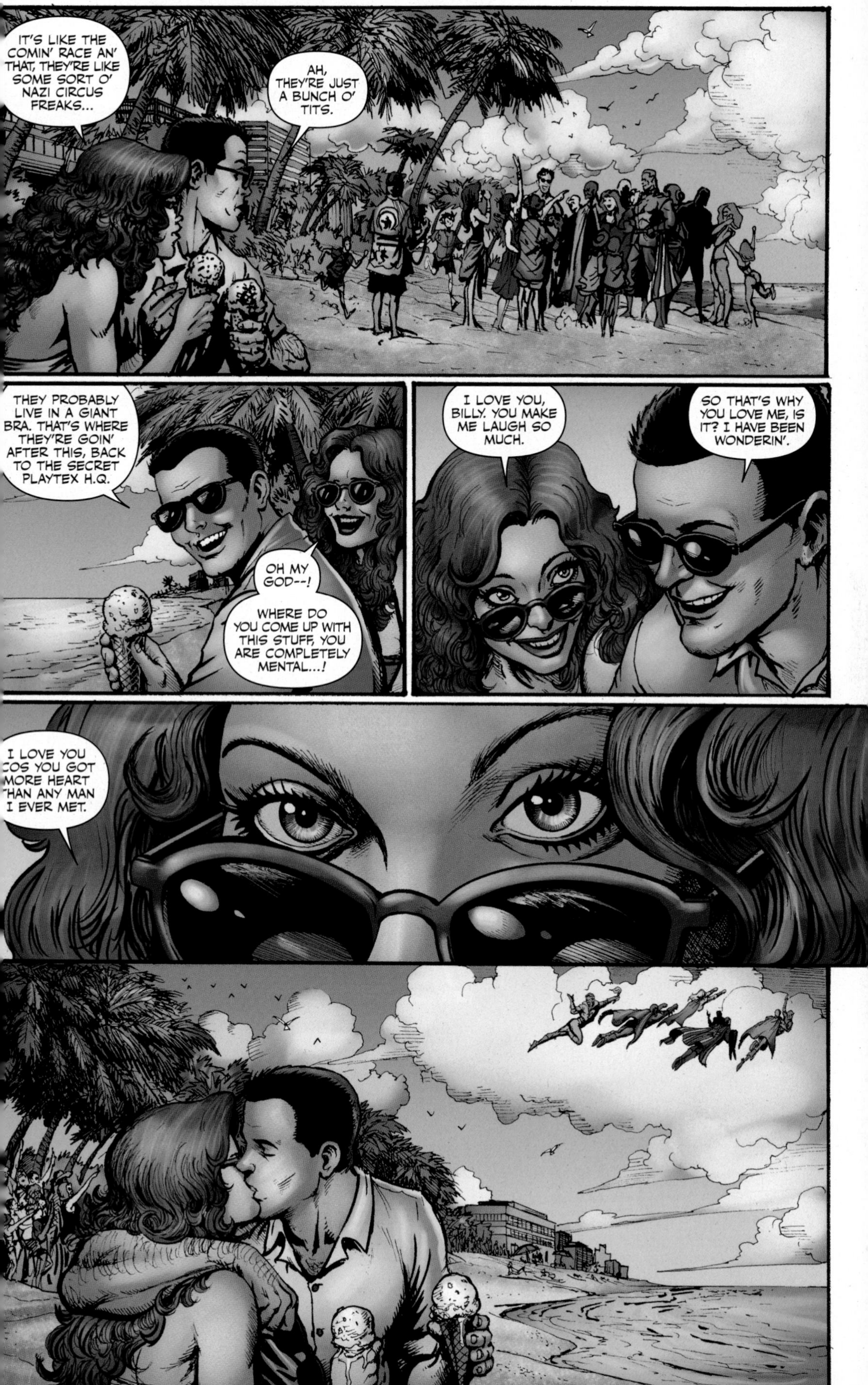
IT'S LIKE THE COMIN' RACE AN' THAT, THEY'RE LIKE SOME SORT O' NAZI CIRCUS FREAKS...
AH, THEY'RE JUST A BUNCH O' TITS.
THEY PROBABLY LIVE IN A GIANT BRA. THAT'S WHERE THEY'RE GOIN' AFTER THIS, BACK TO THE SECRET PLAYTEX H.Q.
OH MY GOD--!
WHERE DO YOU COME UP WITH THIS STUFF, YOU ARE COMPLETELY MENTAL...!
I LOVE YOU, BILLY. YOU MAKE ME LAUGH SO MUCH.
SO THAT'S WHY YOU LOVE ME, IS IT? I HAVE BEEN WONDERIN'.
I LOVE YOU COS YOU GOT MORE HEART THAN ANY MAN I EVER MET.

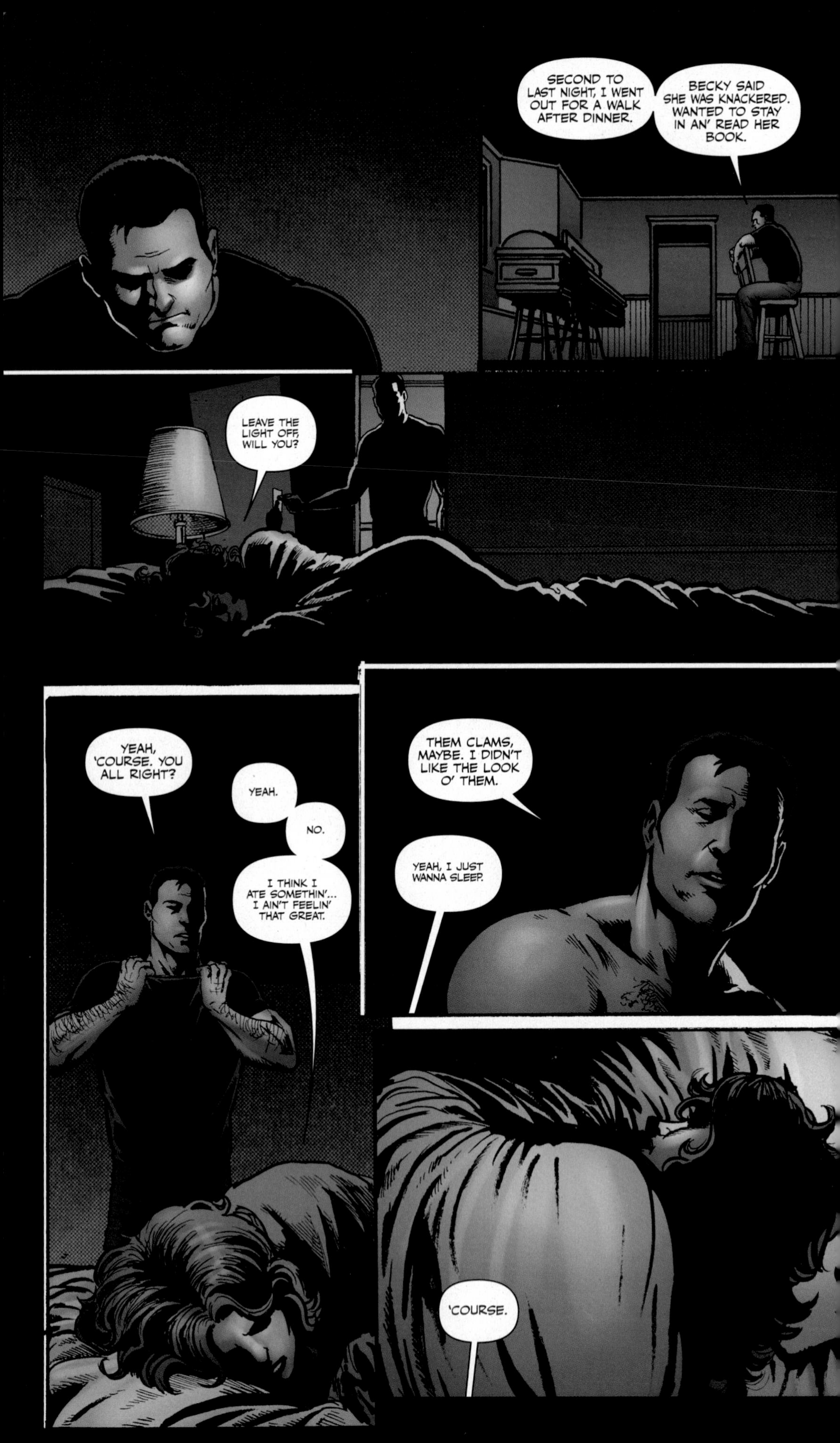
SECOND TO LAST NIGHT, I WENT OUT FOR A WALK AFTER DINNER.
BECKY SAID SHE WAS KNACKERED. WANTED TO STAY IN AN' READ HER BOOK.
LEAVE THE LIGHT OFF, WILL YOU?
YEAH, 'COURSE. YOU ALL RIGHT?
YEAH.
NO.
I THINK I ATE SOMETHIN'... I AIN'T FEELIN' THAT GREAT.
THEM CLAMS, MAYBE. I DIDN'T LIKE THE LOOK O' THEM.
YEAH, I JUST WANNA SLEEP.
'COURSE.

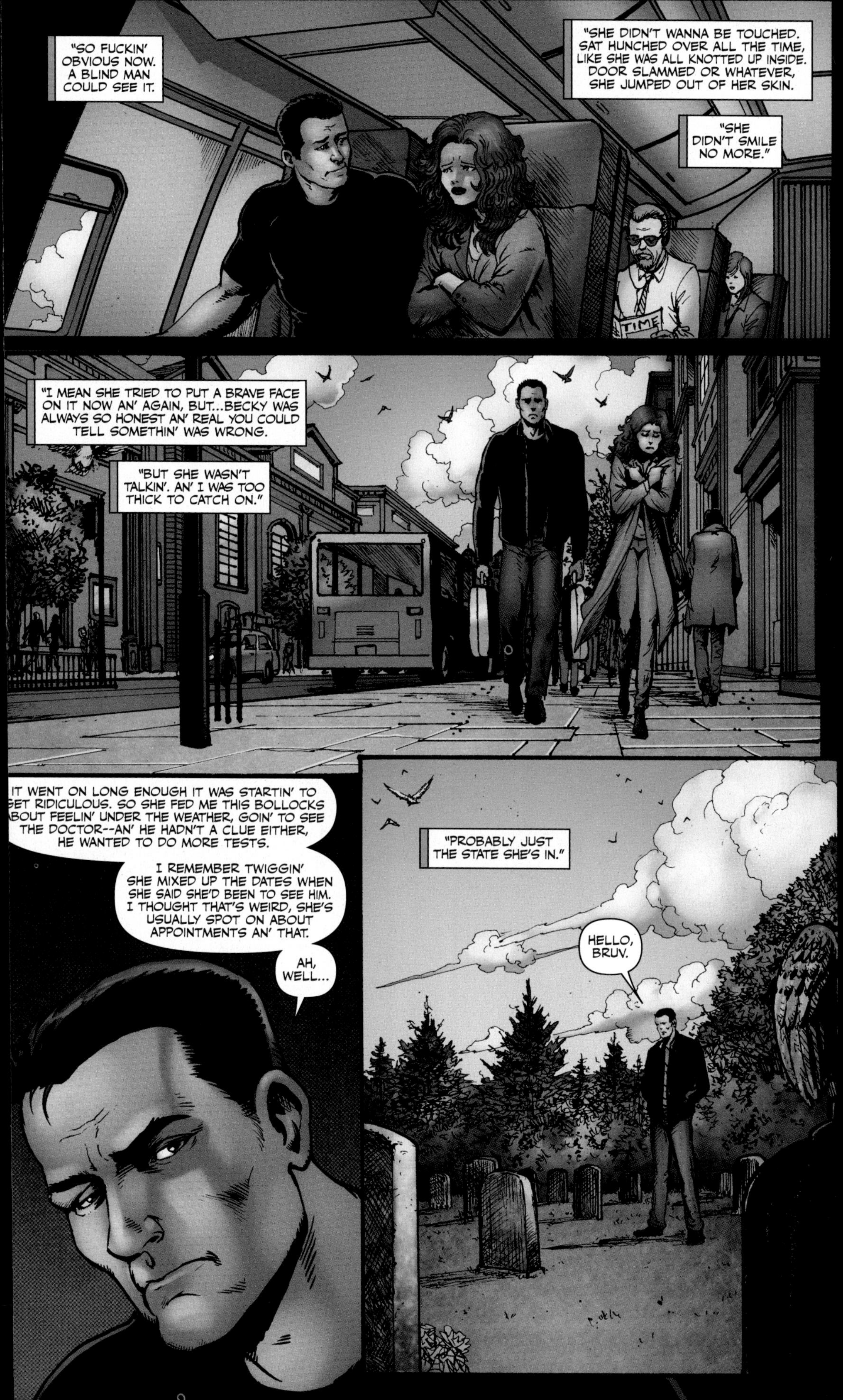
"SO FUCKIN' OBVIOUS NOW. A BLIND MAN COULD SEE IT.
"SHE DIDN'T WANNA BE TOUCHED. SAT HUNCHED OVER ALL THE TIME, LIKE SHE WAS ALL KNOTTED UP INSIDE. DOOR SLAMMED OR WHATEVER, SHE JUMPED OUT OF HER SKIN.
"SHE DIDN'T SMILE NO MORE."
TIME
"I MEAN SHE TRIED TO PUT A BRAVE FACE ON IT NOW AN' AGAIN, BUT...BECKY WAS ALWAYS SO HONEST AN' REAL YOU COULD TELL SOMETHIN' WAS WRONG.
"BUT SHE WASN'T TALKIN'. AN' I WAS TOO THICK TO CATCH ON."
IT WENT ON LONG ENOUGH IT WAS STARTIN' TO GET RIDICULOUS. SO SHE FED ME THIS BOLLOCKS ABOUT FEELIN' UNDER THE WEATHER, GOIN' TO SEE THE DOCTOR--AN' HE HADN'T A CLUE EITHER, HE WANTED TO DO MORE TESTS.
I REMEMBER TWIGGIN' SHE MIXED UP THE DATES WHEN SHE SAID SHE'D BEEN TO SEE HIM. I THOUGHT THAT'S WEIRD, SHE'S USUALLY SPOT ON ABOUT APPOINTMENTS AN' THAT.
AH, WELL...
"PROBABLY JUST THE STATE SHE'S IN."
HELLO, BRUV.

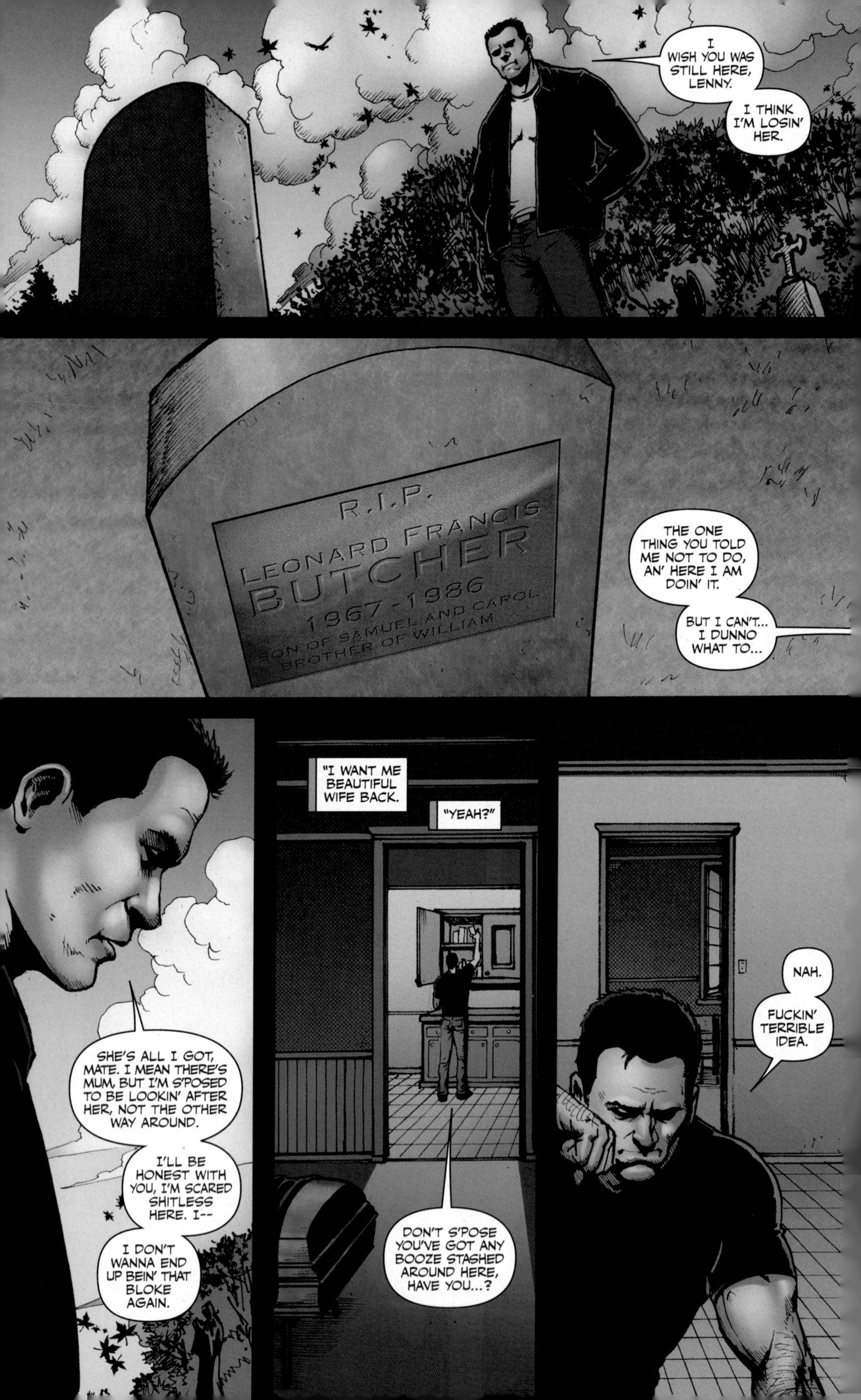
I WISH YOU WAS STILL HERE, LENNY.
I THINK I'M LOSIN' HER.
R.I.P.
LEONARD FRANCIS BUTCHER
1967-1986
SON OF SAMUEL AND CAROL
BROTHER OF WILLIAM
THE ONE THING YOU TOLD ME NOT TO DO, AN' HERE I AM DOIN' IT.
BUT I CAN'T... I DUNNO WHAT TO...
SHE'S ALL I GOT, MATE. I MEAN THERE'S MUM, BUT I'M S'POSED TO BE LOOKIN' AFTER HER, NOT THE OTHER WAY AROUND.
I'LL BE HONEST WITH YOU, I'M SCARED SHITLESS HERE. I--
I DON'T WANNA END UP BEIN' THAT BLOKE AGAIN.
"I WANT ME BEAUTIFUL WIFE BACK.
"YEAH?"
DON'T S'POSE YOU'VE GOT ANY BOOZE STASHED AROUND HERE, HAVE YOU...?
NAH.
FUCKIN' TERRIBLE IDEA.

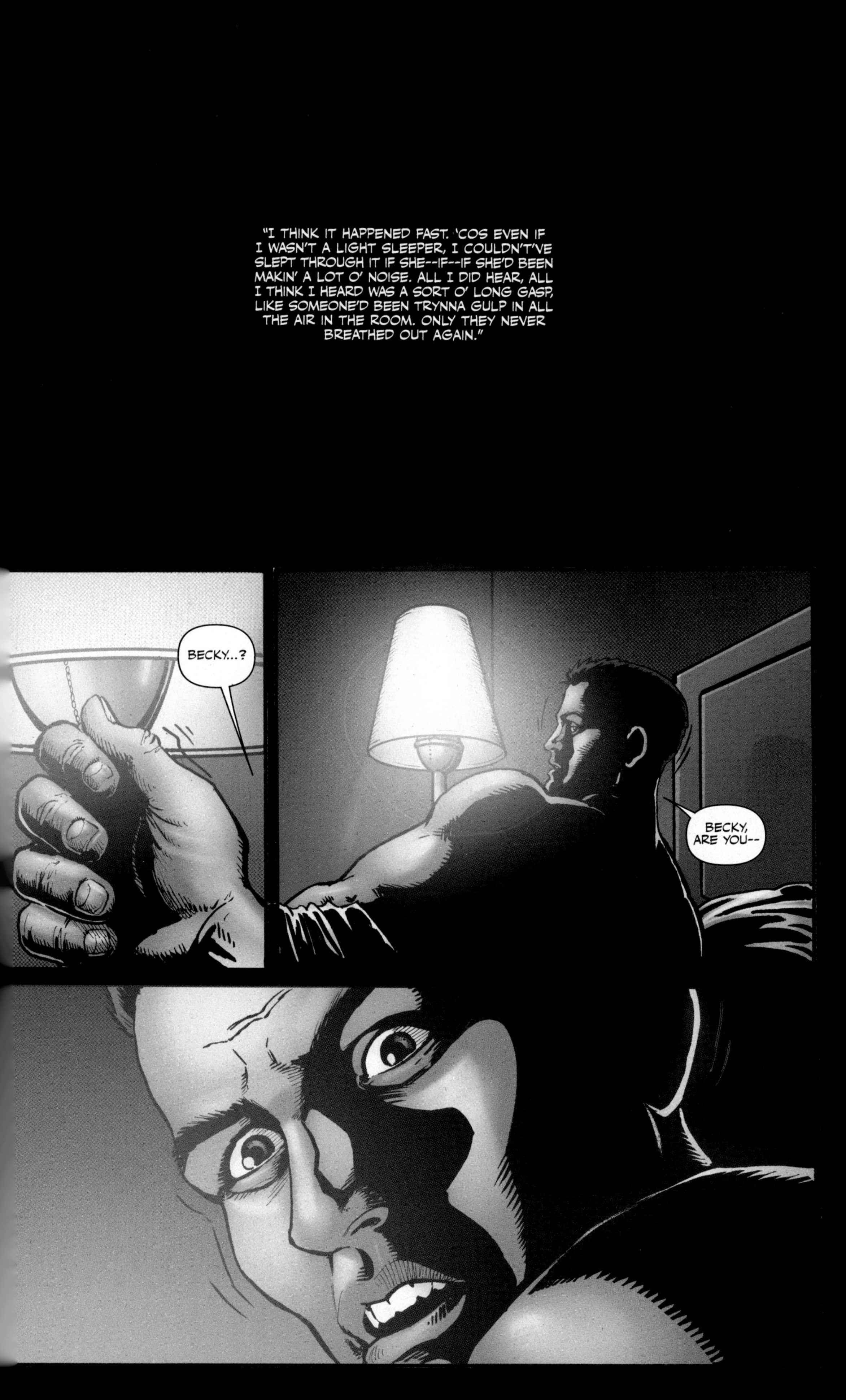
"I THINK IT HAPPENED FAST. 'COS EVEN IF I WASN'T A LIGHT SLEEPER, I COULDN'T'VE SLEPT THROUGH IT IF SHE--IF--IF SHE'D BEEN MAKIN' A LOT O' NOISE. ALL I DID HEAR, ALL I THINK I HEARD WAS A SORT O' LONG GASP, LIKE SOMEONE'D BEEN TRYNNA GULP IN ALL THE AIR IN THE ROOM. ONLY THEY NEVER BREATHED OUT AGAIN."
BECKY...?
BECKY, ARE YOU--

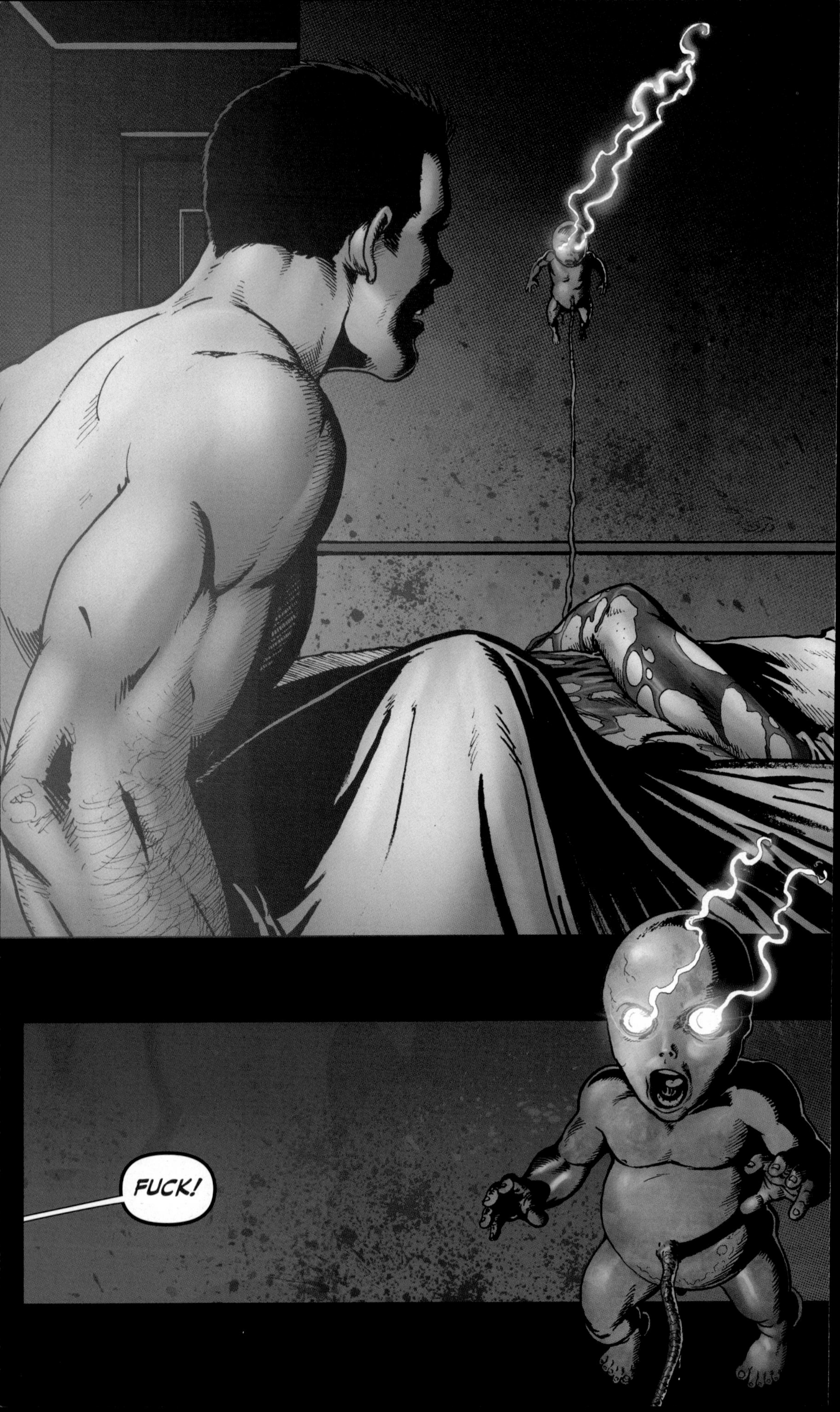
FUCK!

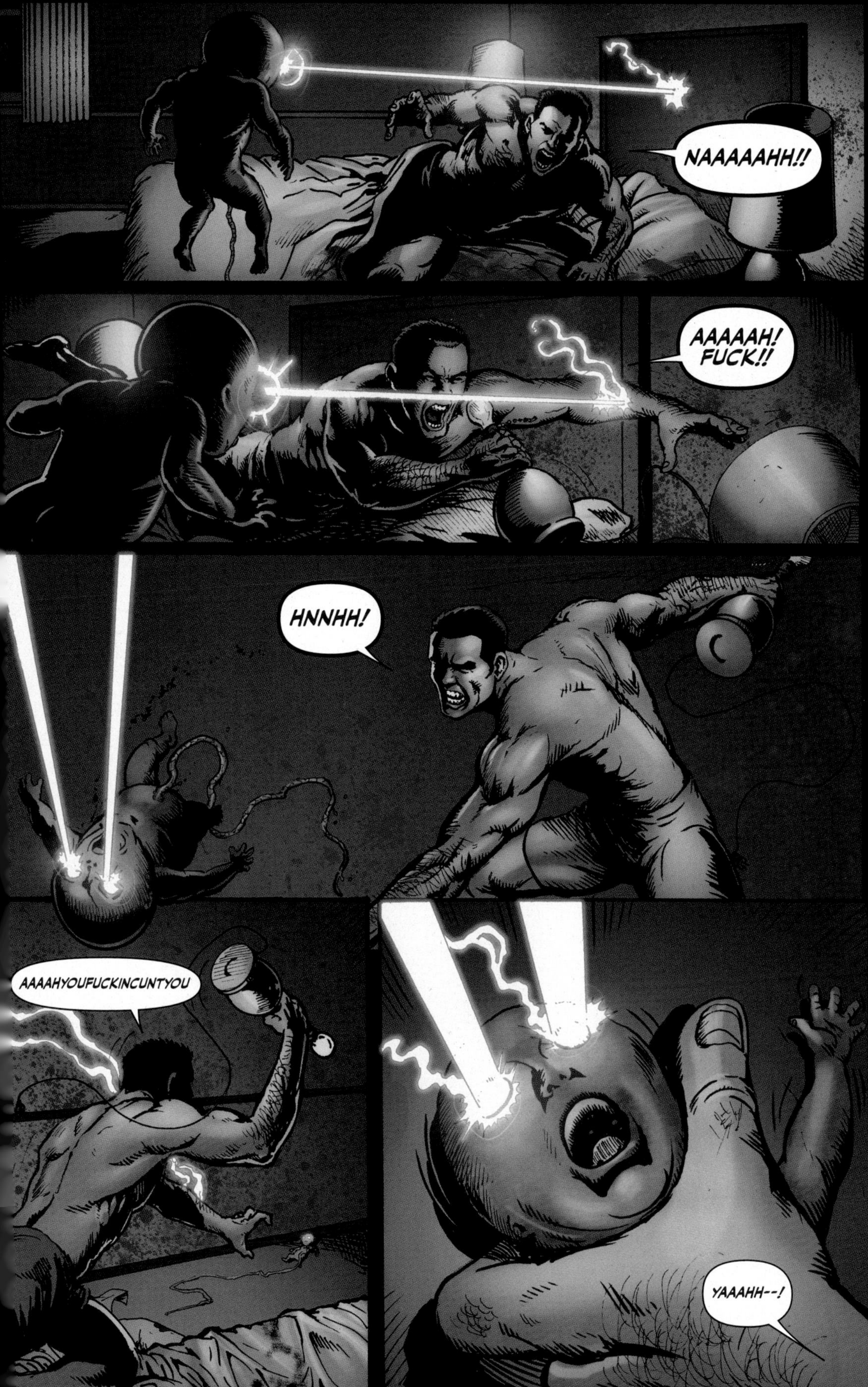
NAAAAAHH!!
AAAAAH! FUCK!!
HNNHH!
AAAAHYOUFUCKINCUNTYOU
YAAAHH--!

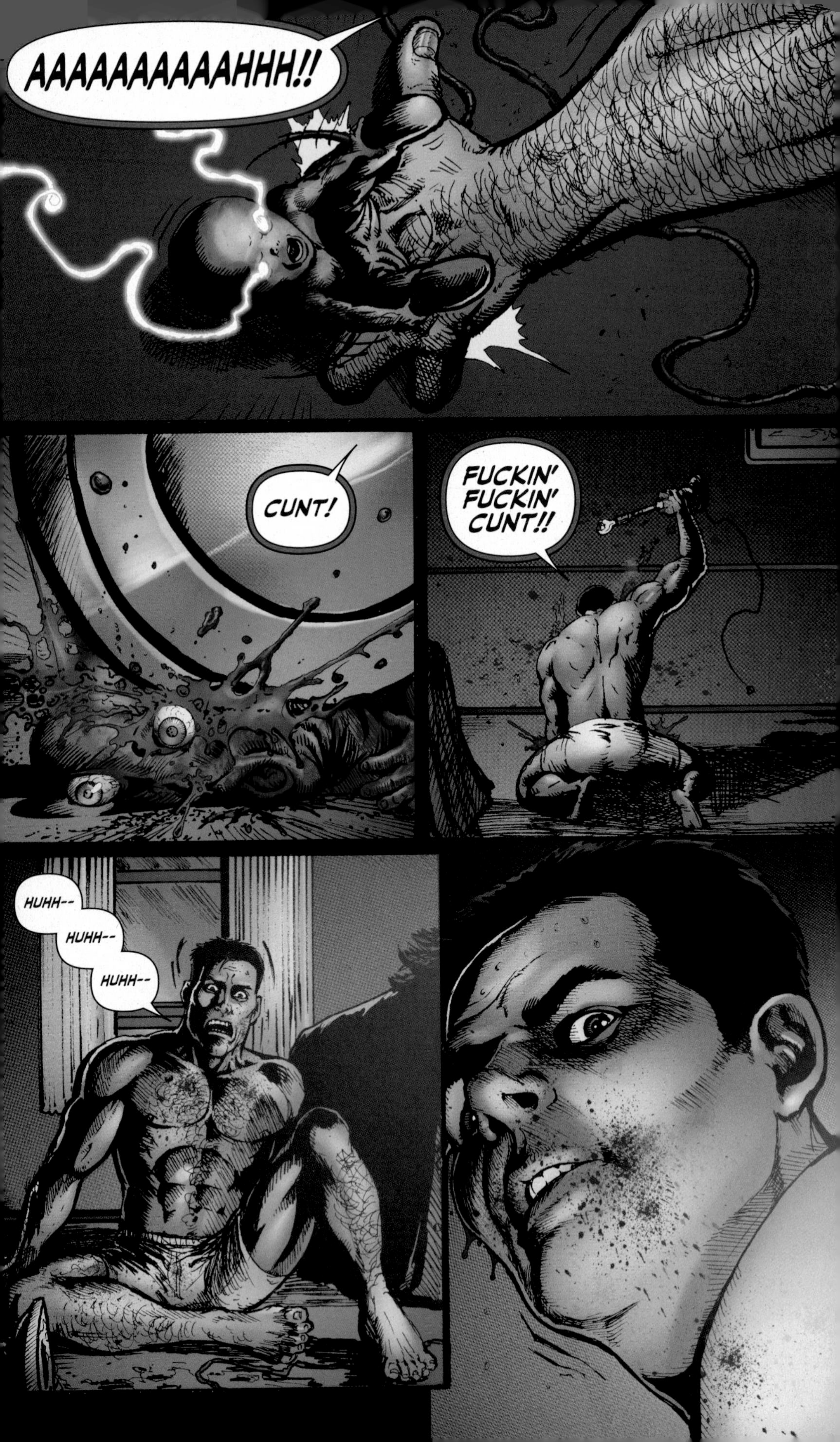
AAAAAAAAAAHHH!!
CUNT!
FUCKIN' FUCKIN' CUNT!!
HUHH--
HUHH--
HUHH--

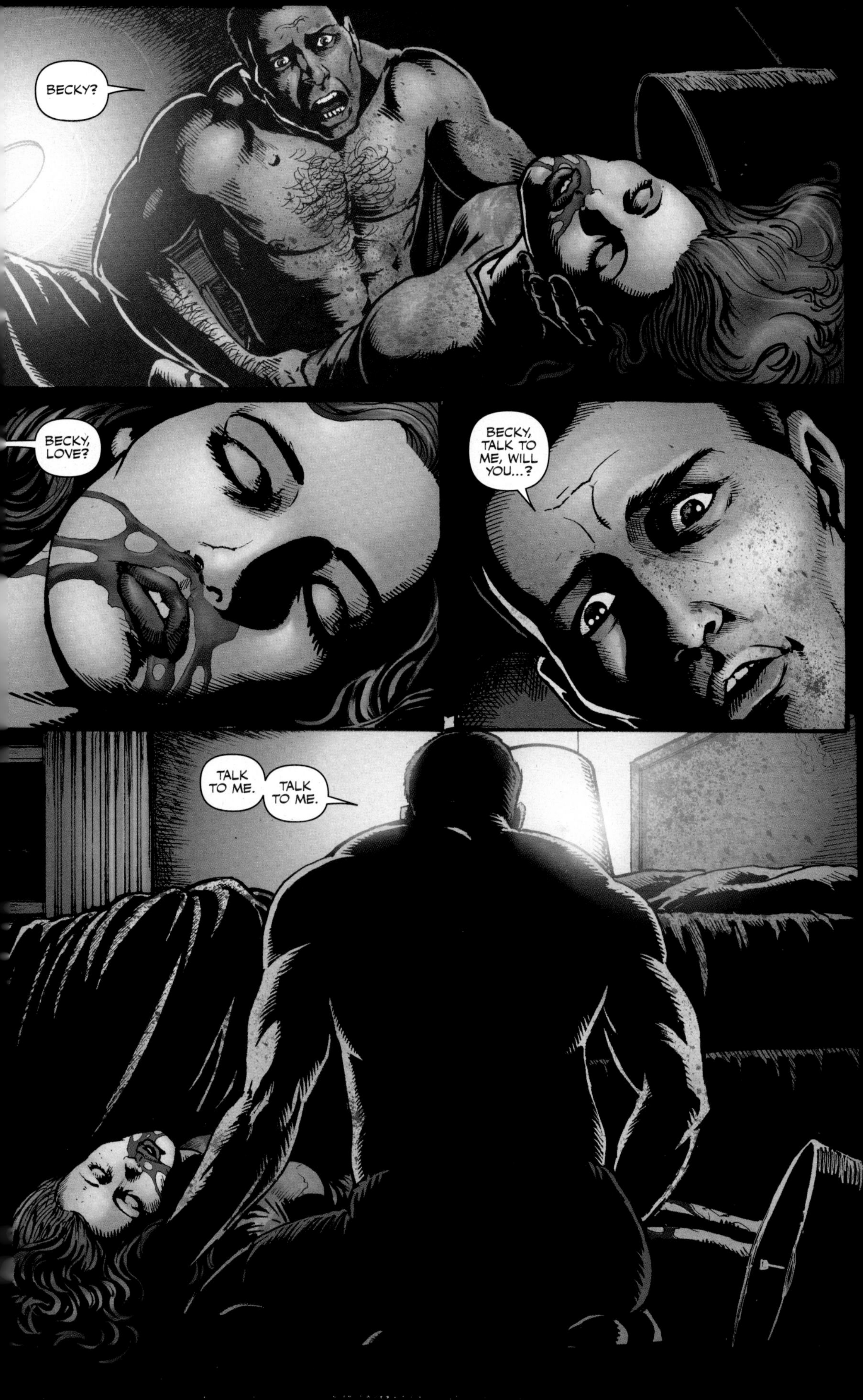
BECKY?
BECKY, LOVE?
BECKY, TALK TO ME, WILL YOU...?
TALK TO ME.
TALK TO ME.

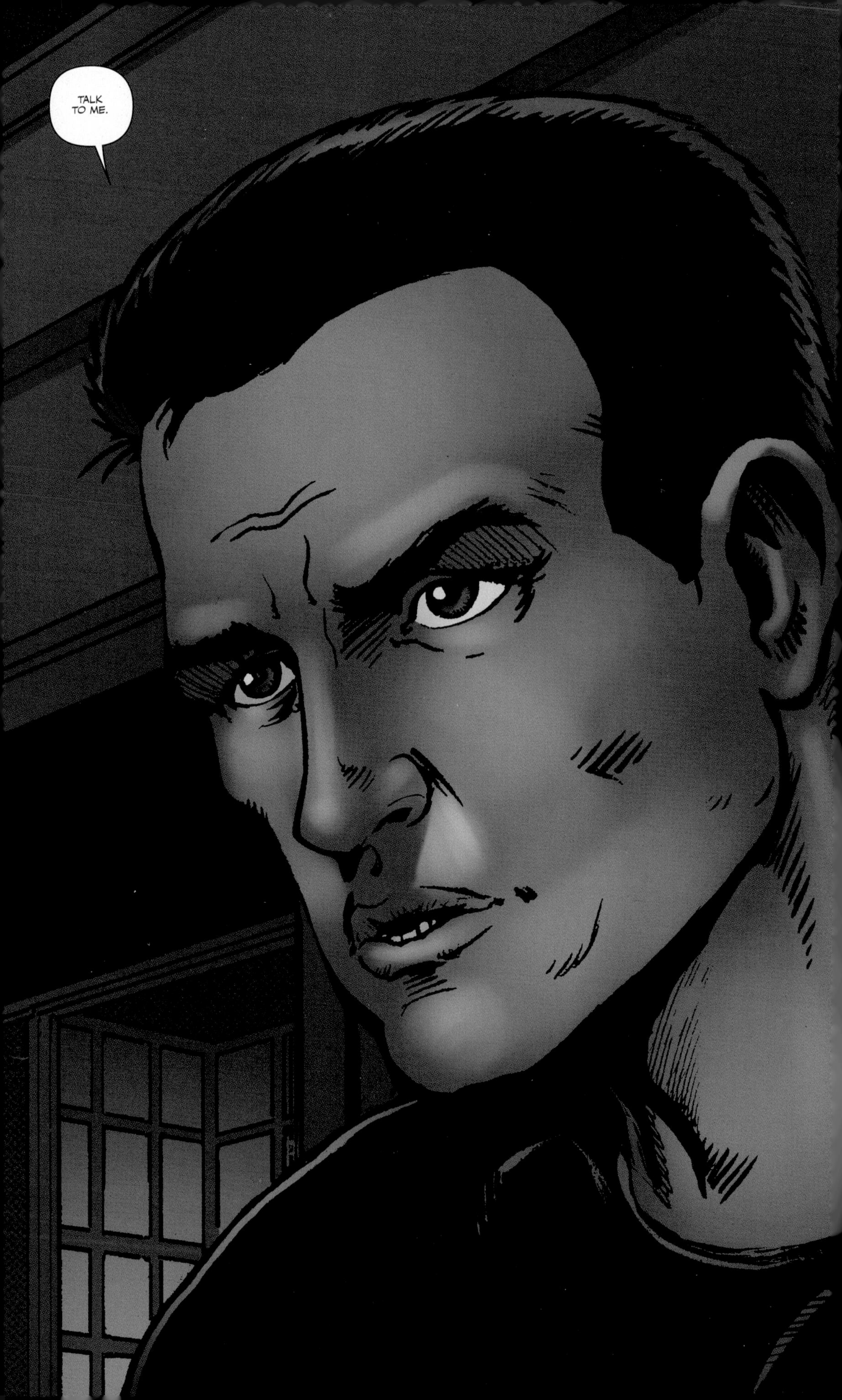
TALK TO ME.

five

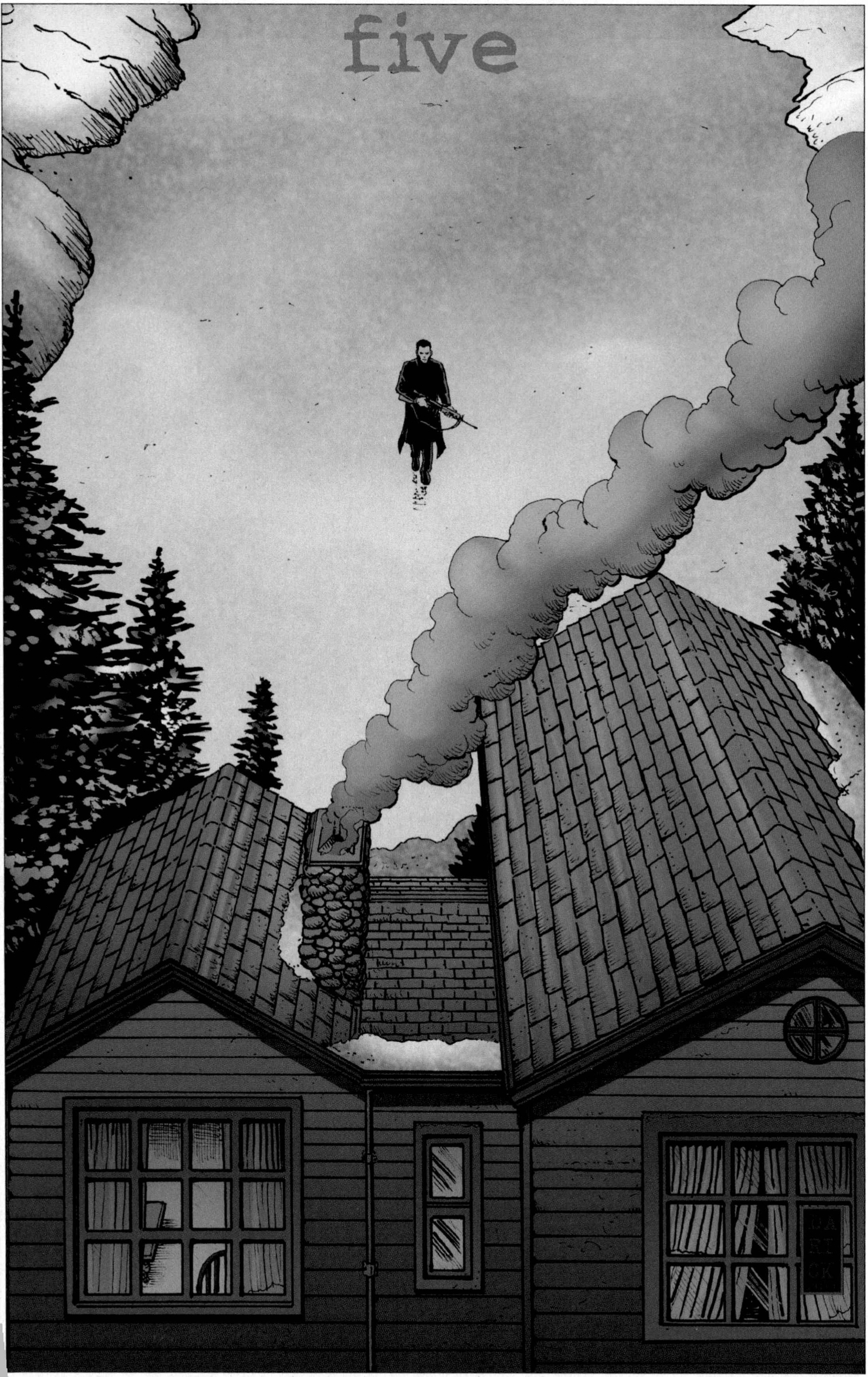

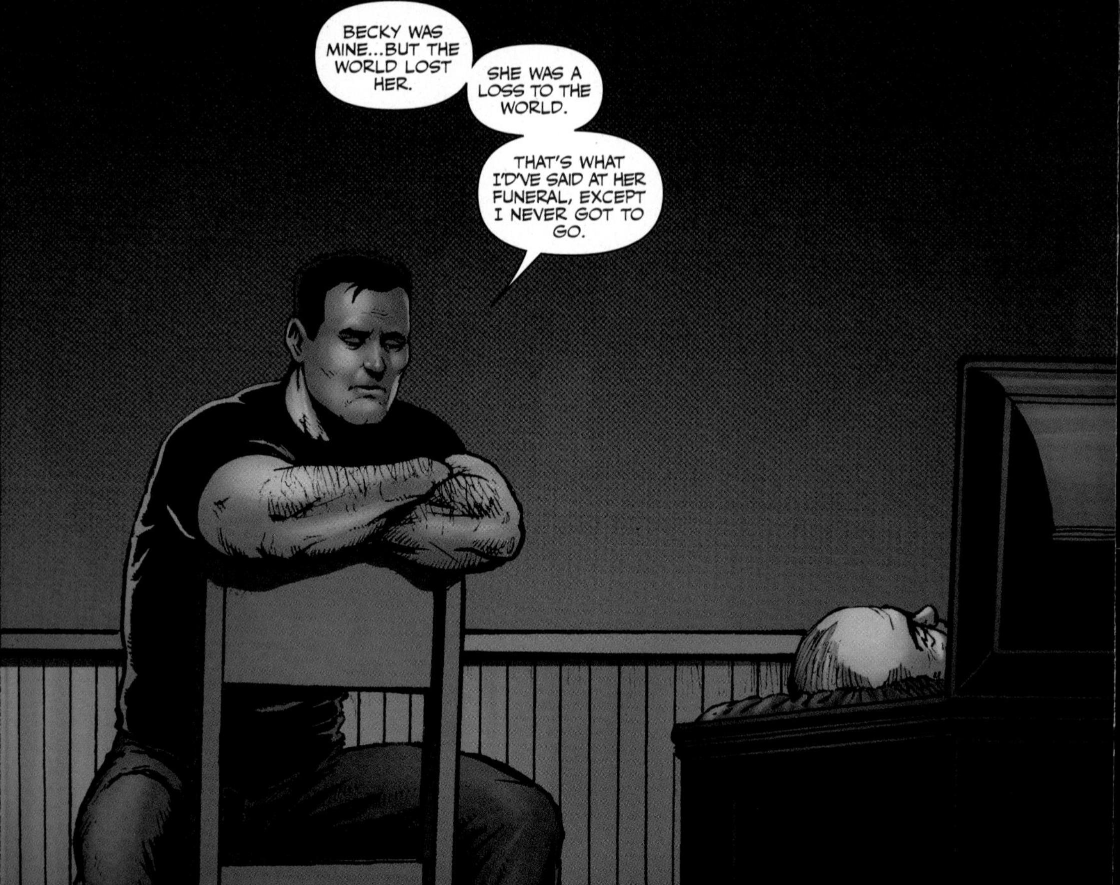
BECKY WAS MINE...BUT THE WORLD LOST HER.
SHE WAS A LOSS TO THE WORLD.
THAT'S WHAT I'D'VE SAID AT HER FUNERAL, EXCEPT I NEVER GOT TO GO.

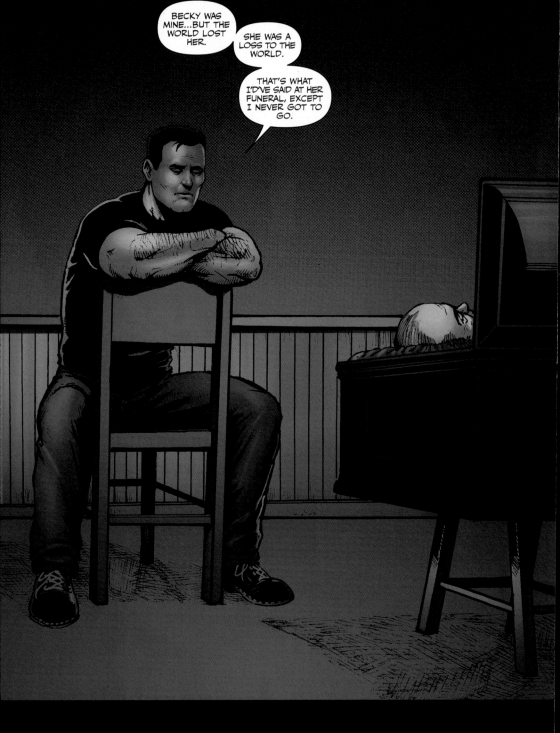

5: HERE COMES A CANDLE TO LIGHT YOU TO BED

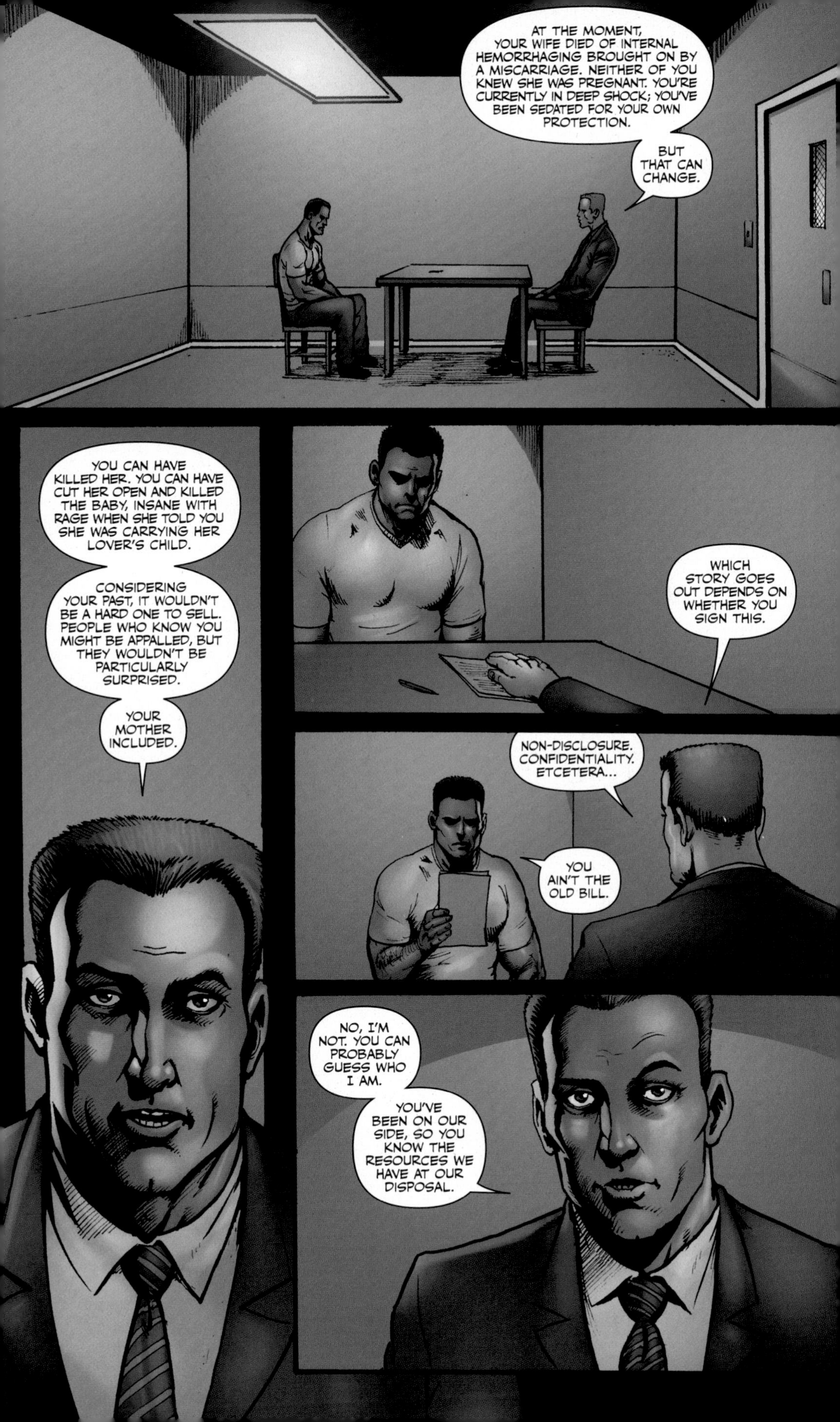
AT THE MOMENT, YOUR WIFE DIED OF INTERNAL HEMORRHAGING BROUGHT ON BY A MISCARRIAGE. NEITHER OF YOU KNEW SHE WAS PREGNANT. YOU'RE CURRENTLY IN DEEP SHOCK; YOU'VE BEEN SEDATED FOR YOUR OWN PROTECTION.
BUT THAT CAN CHANGE.
YOU CAN HAVE KILLED HER. YOU CAN HAVE CUT HER OPEN AND KILLED THE BABY, INSANE WITH RAGE WHEN SHE TOLD YOU SHE WAS CARRYING HER LOVER'S CHILD.
CONSIDERING YOUR PAST, IT WOULDN'T BE A HARD ONE TO SELL. PEOPLE WHO KNOW YOU MIGHT BE APPALLED, BUT THEY WOULDN'T BE PARTICULARLY SURPRISED.
YOUR MOTHER INCLUDED.
WHICH STORY GOES OUT DEPENDS ON WHETHER YOU SIGN THIS.
NON-DISCLOSURE. CONFIDENTIALITY. ETCETERA...
YOU AIN'T THE OLD BILL.
NO, I'M NOT. YOU CAN PROBABLY GUESS WHO I AM.
YOU'VE BEEN ON OUR SIDE, SO YOU KNOW THE RESOURCES WE HAVE AT OUR DISPOSAL.

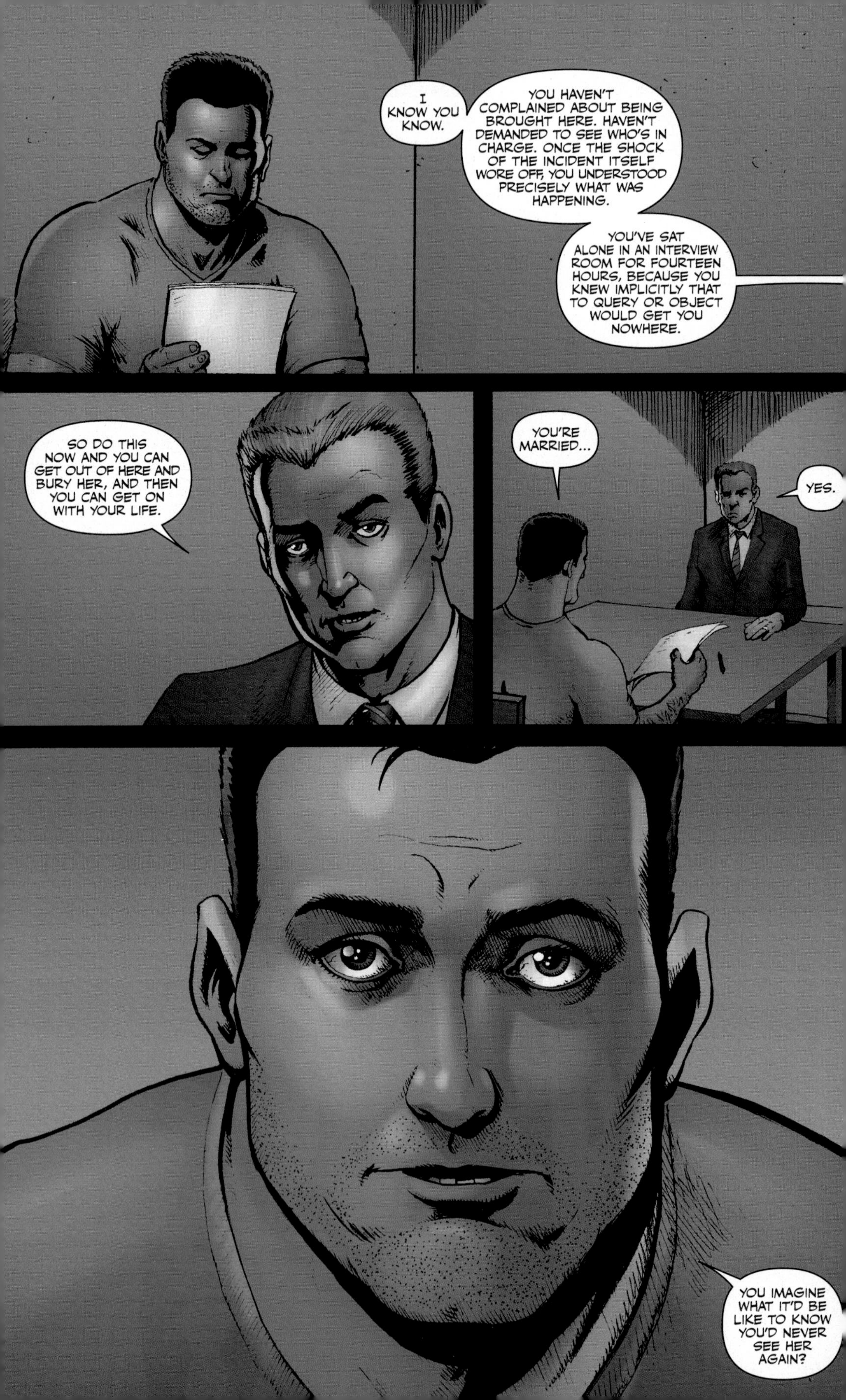
I KNOW YOU KNOW.
YOU HAVEN'T COMPLAINED ABOUT BEING BROUGHT HERE. HAVEN'T DEMANDED TO SEE WHO'S IN CHARGE. ONCE THE SHOCK OF THE INCIDENT ITSELF WORE OFF, YOU UNDERSTOOD PRECISELY WHAT WAS HAPPENING.
YOU'VE SAT ALONE IN AN INTERVIEW ROOM FOR FOURTEEN HOURS, BECAUSE YOU KNEW IMPLICITLY THAT TO QUERY OR OBJECT WOULD GET YOU NOWHERE.
SO DO THIS NOW AND YOU CAN GET OUT OF HERE AND BURY HER, AND THEN YOU CAN GET ON WITH YOUR LIFE.
YOU'RE MARRIED...
YES.
YOU IMAGINE WHAT IT'D BE LIKE TO KNOW YOU'D NEVER SEE HER AGAIN?

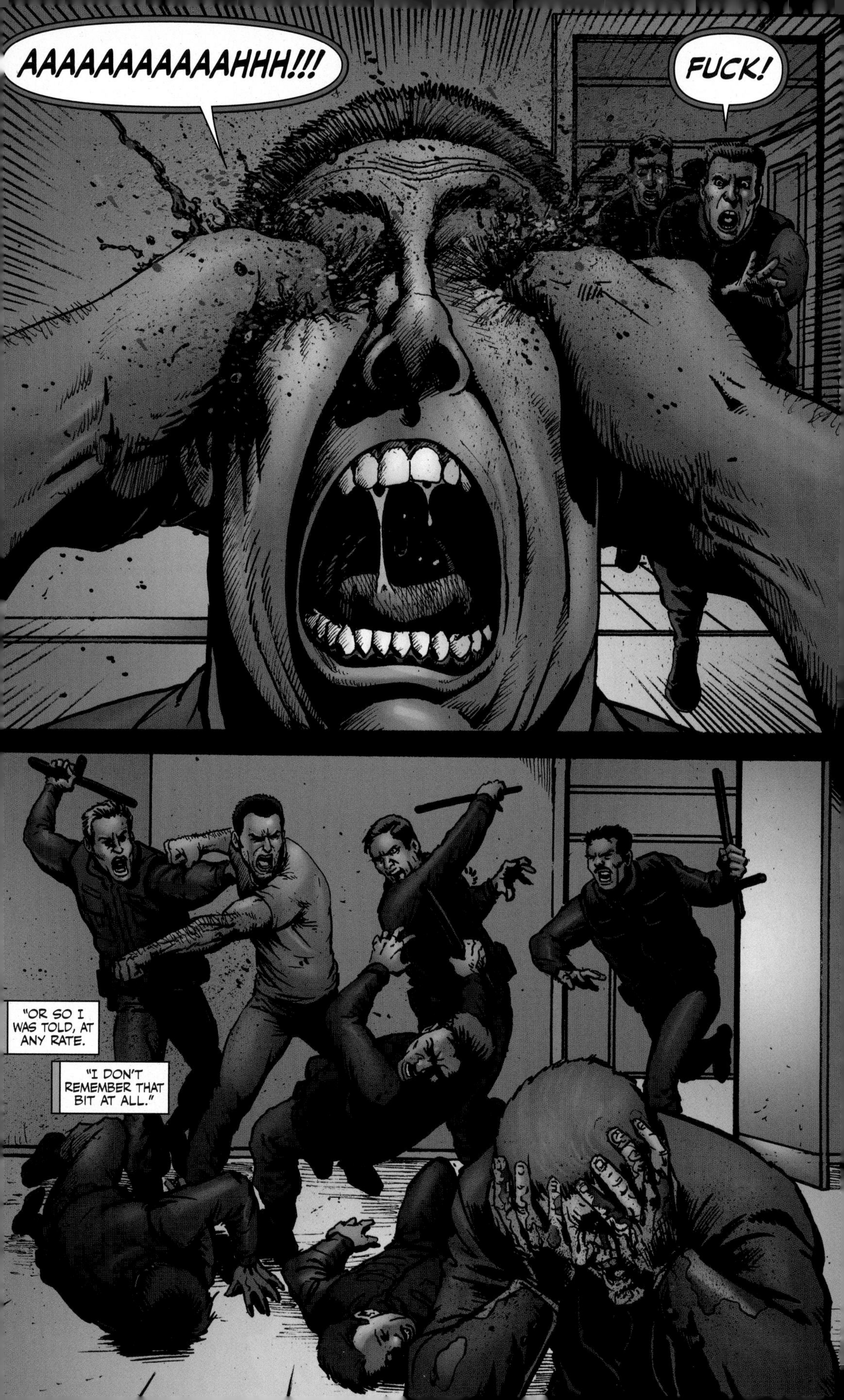
AAAAAAAAAAAAHHH!!!
FUCK!
"OR SO I WAS TOLD, AT ANY RATE.
"I DON'T REMEMBER THAT BIT AT ALL."

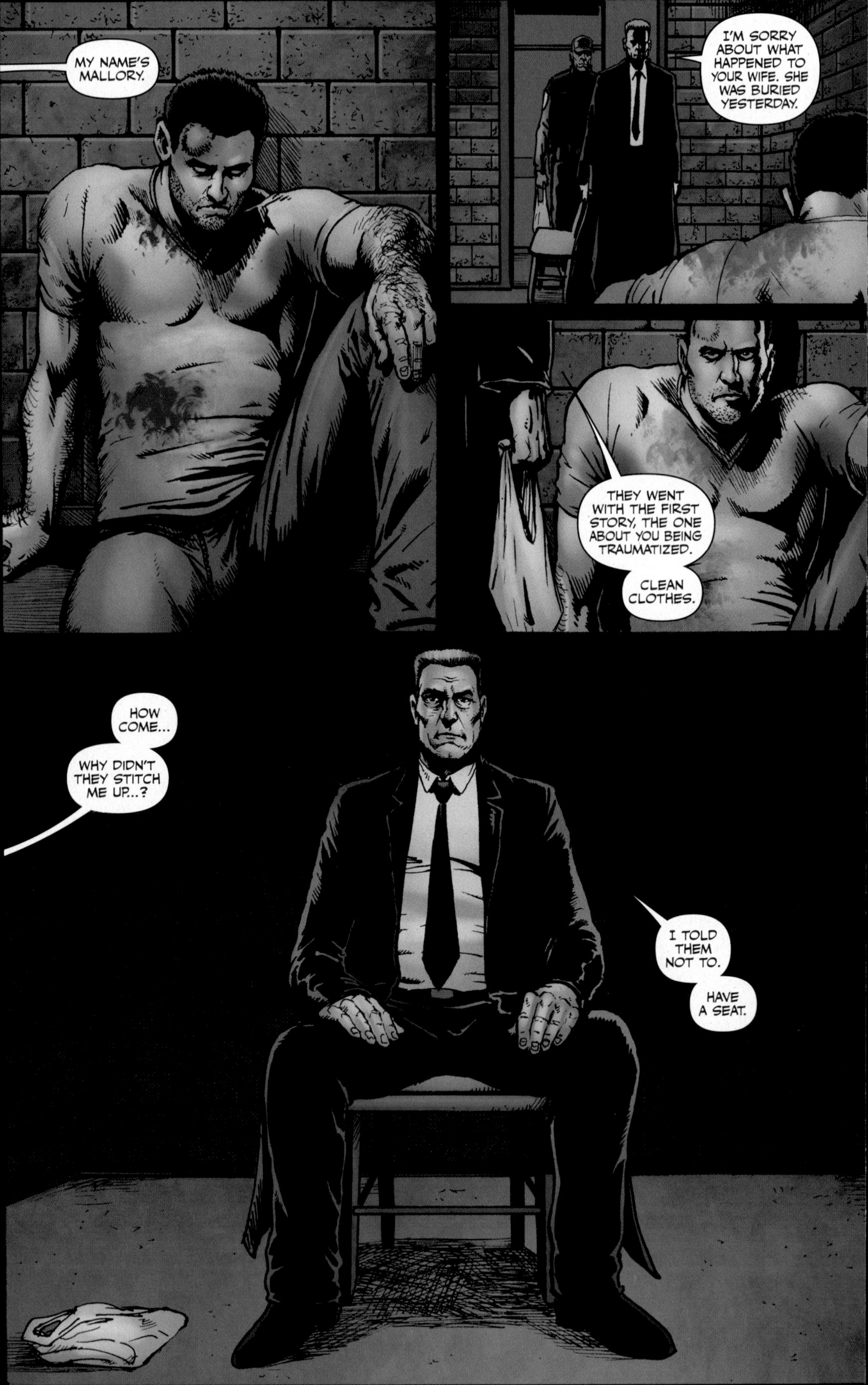

MY NAME'S MALLORY.
I'M SORRY ABOUT WHAT HAPPENED TO YOUR WIFE. SHE WAS BURIED YESTERDAY.
THEY WENT WITH THE FIRST STORY, THE ONE ABOUT YOU BEING TRAUMATIZED.
CLEAN CLOTHES.
HOW COME...
WHY DIDN'T THEY STITCH ME UP...?
I TOLD THEM NOT TO.
HAVE A SEAT.

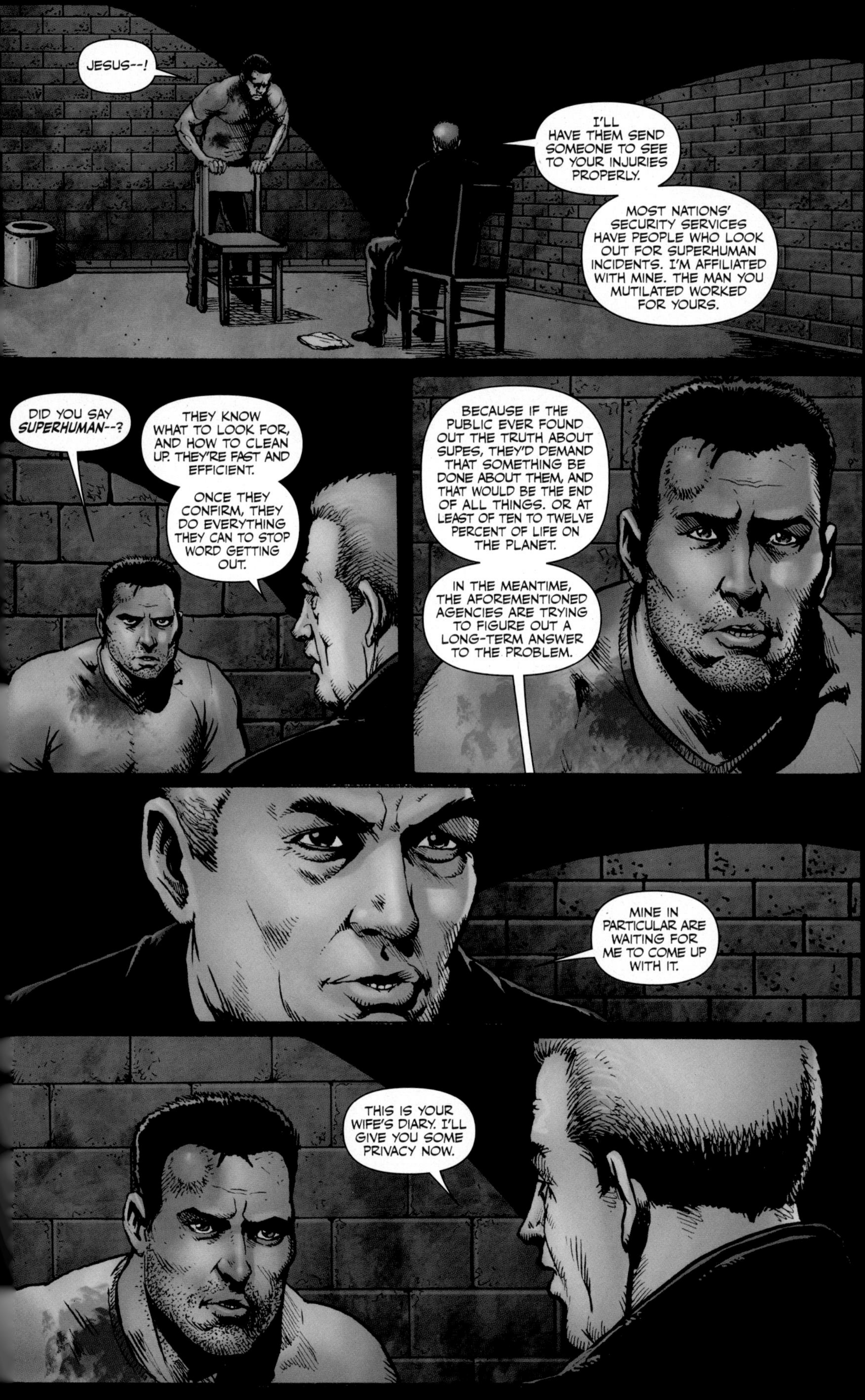
JESUS--!
I'LL HAVE THEM SEND SOMEONE TO SEE TO YOUR INJURIES PROPERLY.
MOST NATIONS' SECURITY SERVICES HAVE PEOPLE WHO LOOK OUT FOR SUPERHUMAN INCIDENTS. I'M AFFILIATED WITH MINE. THE MAN YOU MUTILATED WORKED FOR YOURS.
DID YOU SAY *SUPERHUMAN*--?
THEY KNOW WHAT TO LOOK FOR, AND HOW TO CLEAN UP. THEY'RE FAST AND EFFICIENT.
ONCE THEY CONFIRM, THEY DO EVERYTHING THEY CAN TO STOP WORD GETTING OUT.
BECAUSE IF THE PUBLIC EVER FOUND OUT THE TRUTH ABOUT SUPES, THEY'D DEMAND THAT SOMETHING BE DONE ABOUT THEM, AND THAT WOULD BE THE END OF ALL THINGS. OR AT LEAST OF TEN TO TWELVE PERCENT OF LIFE ON THE PLANET.
IN THE MEANTIME, THE AFOREMENTIONED AGENCIES ARE TRYING TO FIGURE OUT A LONG-TERM ANSWER TO THE PROBLEM.
MINE IN PARTICULAR ARE WAITING FOR ME TO COME UP WITH IT.
THIS IS YOUR WIFE'S DIARY. I'LL GIVE YOU SOME PRIVACY NOW.

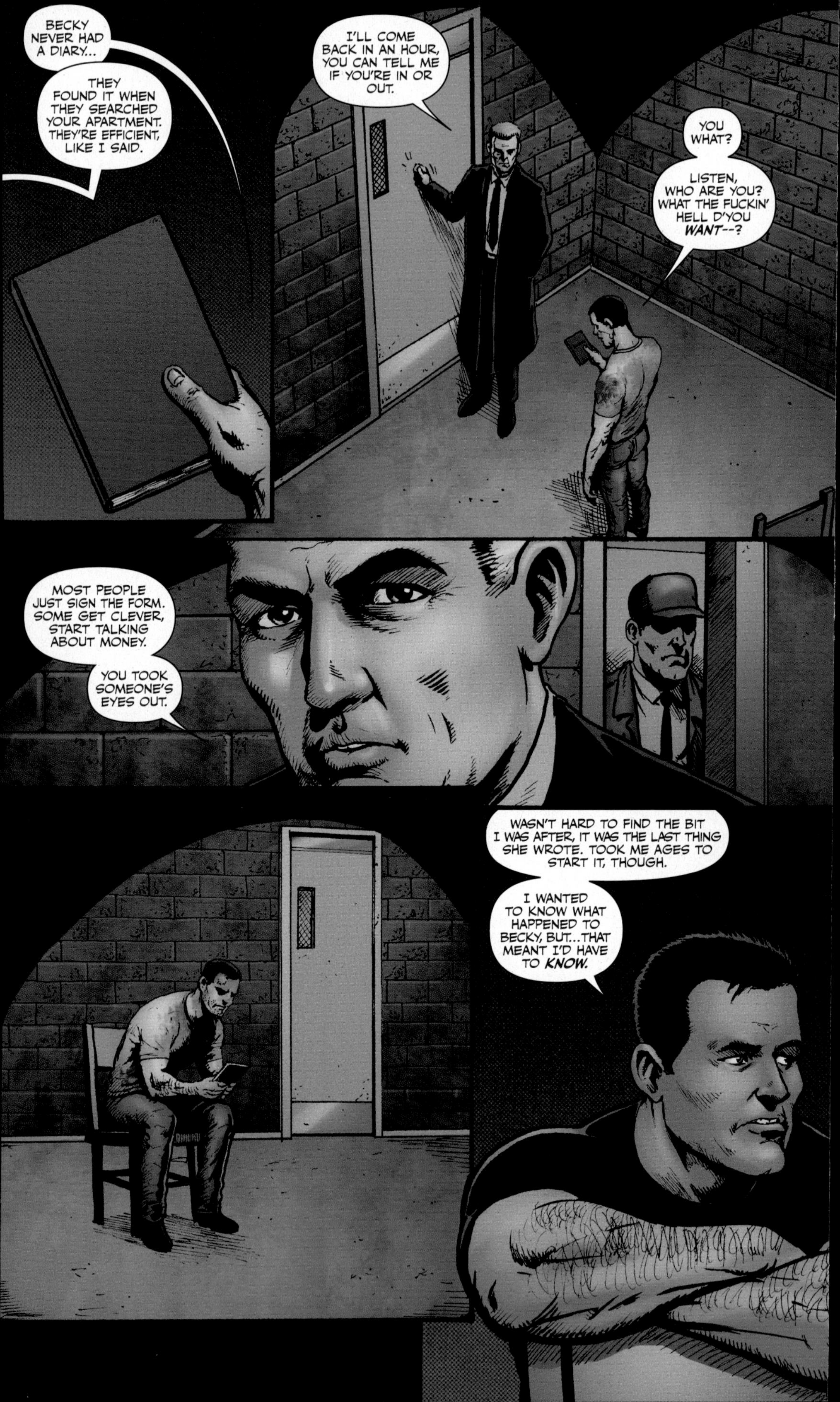

BECKY NEVER HAD A DIARY...
THEY FOUND IT WHEN THEY SEARCHED YOUR APARTMENT. THEY'RE EFFICIENT, LIKE I SAID.
I'LL COME BACK IN AN HOUR, YOU CAN TELL ME IF YOU'RE IN OR OUT.
YOU WHAT?
LISTEN, WHO ARE YOU? WHAT THE FUCKIN' HELL D'YOU WANT--?
MOST PEOPLE JUST SIGN THE FORM. SOME GET CLEVER, START TALKING ABOUT MONEY.
YOU TOOK SOMEONE'S EYES OUT.
WASN'T HARD TO FIND THE BIT I WAS AFTER, IT WAS THE LAST THING SHE WROTE. TOOK ME AGES TO START IT, THOUGH.
I WANTED TO KNOW WHAT HAPPENED TO BECKY, BUT...THAT MEANT I'D HAVE TO KNOW.

I knew it would be hard to write this down but it feels like I have to force the words out of the pen. Making myself remember the details makes me start shaking, I want to scream and be sick and throw a chair through the window and curl up in a ball and die. But I have to do it, I have to get it out or I really will go mad, I know I will.

It has to be this way because I can't tell anyone. If I do they'll think I've lost my mind, they'll never believe a word of it. I'll be locked up and the worst thing of all will be that Billy will find out. And the terrible thing is that he would believe me, he's the only one who could because he thinks I'd never do anything bad, never lie or whatever - and he'd believe me and he'd try to do something about it, he'd try and get the guy, and that would be the worst thing that could ever possibly happen.

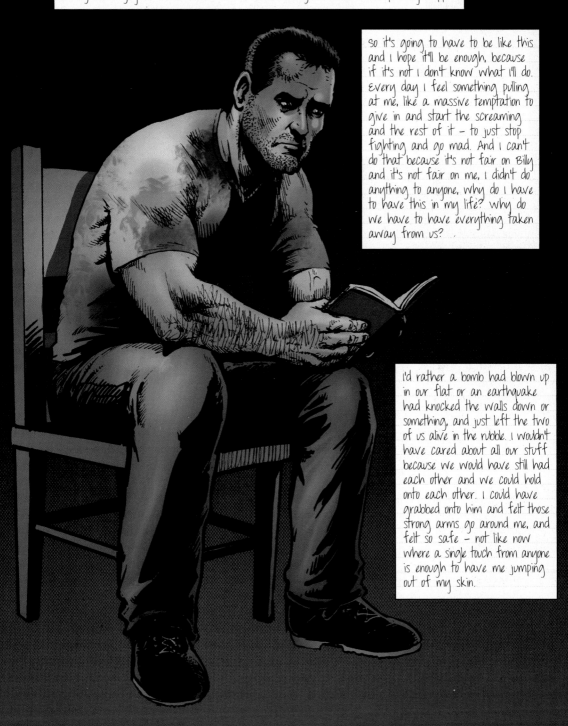

So it's going to have to be like this and I hope it'll be enough, because if it's not I don't know what I'll do. Every day I feel something pulling at me, like a massive temptation to give in and start the screaming and the rest of it - to just stop fighting and go mad. And I can't do that because it's not fair on Billy and it's not fair on me. I didn't do anything to anyone, why do I have to have this in my life? Why do we have to have everything taken away from us?

I'd rather a bomb had blown up in our flat or an earthquake had knocked the walls down or something, and just left the two of us alive in the rubble. I wouldn't have cared about all our stuff because we would have still had each other and we could hold onto each other. I could have grabbed onto him and felt those strong arms go around me, and felt so safe - not like now where a single touch from anyone is enough to have me jumping out of my skin.

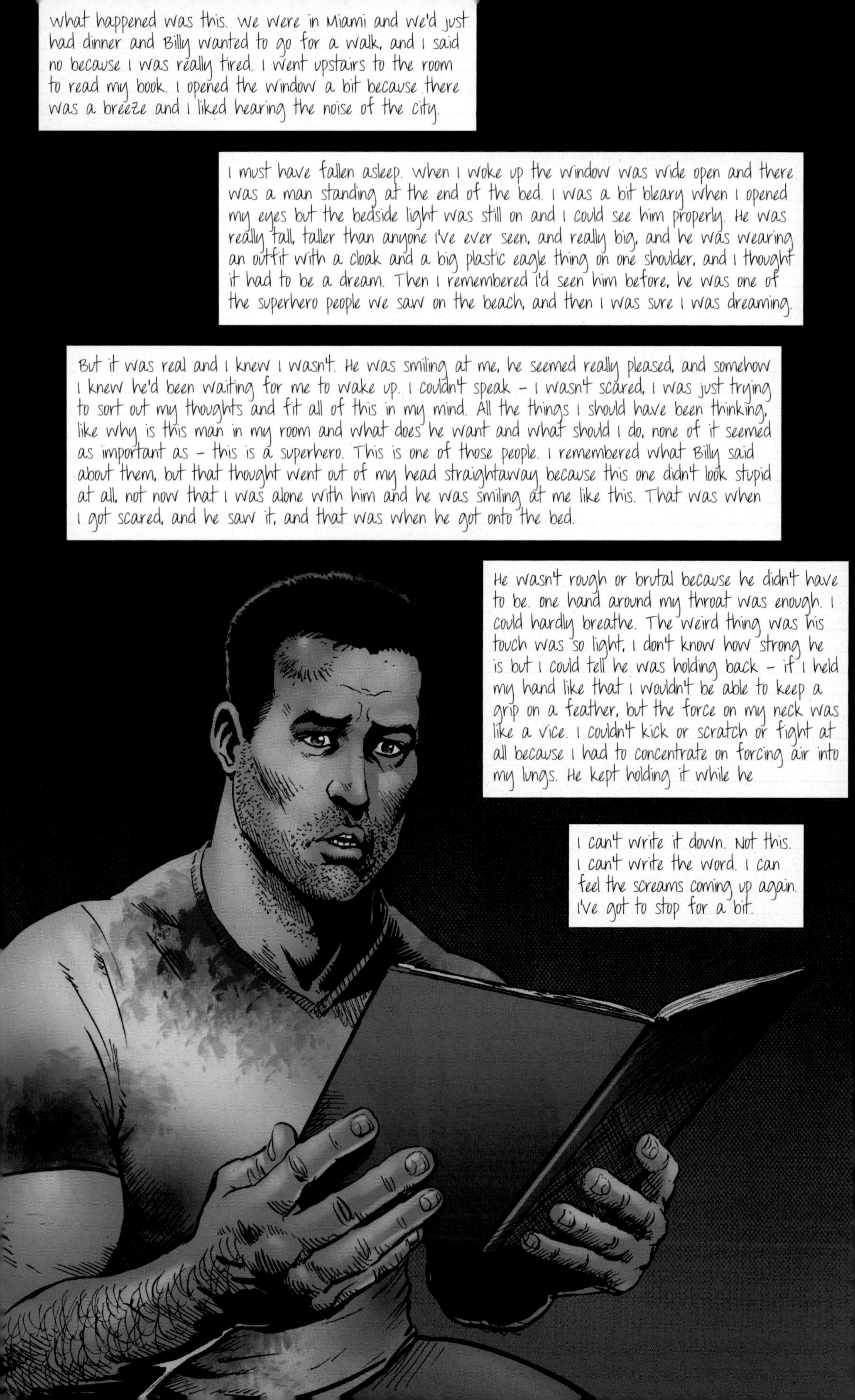
what happened was this. we were in Miami and we'd just had dinner and Billy wanted to go for a walk, and I said no because I was really tired. I went upstairs to the room to read my book. I opened the window a bit because there was a breeze and I liked hearing the noise of the city.
I must have fallen asleep. when I woke up the window was wide open and there was a man standing at the end of the bed. I was a bit bleary when I opened my eyes but the bedside light was still on and I could see him properly. He was really tall, taller than anyone I've ever seen, and really big, and he was wearing an outfit with a cloak and a big plastic eagle thing on one shoulder, and I thought it had to be a dream. Then I remembered I'd seen him before, he was one of the superhero people we saw on the beach, and then I was sure I was dreaming.
But it was real and I knew I wasn't. He was smiling at me, he seemed really pleased, and somehow I knew he'd been waiting for me to wake up. I couldn't speak – I wasn't scared, I was just trying to sort out my thoughts and fit all of this in my mind. All the things I should have been thinking, like why is this man in my room and what does he want and what should I do, none of it seemed as important as – this is a superhero. This is one of those people. I remembered what Billy said about them, but that thought went out of my head straightaway because this one didn't look stupid at all, not now that I was alone with him and he was smiling at me like this. That was when I got scared, and he saw it, and that was when he got onto the bed.
He wasn't rough or brutal because he didn't have to be. one hand around my throat was enough. I could hardly breathe. The weird thing was his touch was so light, I don't know how strong he is but I could tell he was holding back – if I held my hand like that I wouldn't be able to keep a grip on a feather, but the force on my neck was like a vice. I couldn't kick or scratch or fight at all because I had to concentrate on forcing air into my lungs. He kept holding it while he
I can't write it down. Not this. I can't write the word. I can feel the screams coming up again. I've got to stop for a bit.

As soon as he'd gone and I could breathe again I jumped up and closed the window and got in the shower. I was terrified Billy would come back in the middle of it. I was terrified he'd find out. The rest of the holiday and the trip home were awful and I felt so bad for him — God help him, he couldn't work out what was wrong and I couldn't tell him. I had to just shut up and keep going as best as I could, which is what I've been doing ever since.

When I got home I tried not to think about it, which was a bit like holding your breath — all you can think about is what you're concentrating on doing. One day at work I asked Sheila about superheroes, God knows what I told her but I knew her brother was into collecting comics and she told me about a shop in the west end that he goes to. I went in and asked, I remembered Billy found out this particular lot were called the seven. I bought a few issues and I ripped up the first one as soon as I saw his face, even the stupid little pictures were enough to set me off. But I made myself carry on. I had to know.

He's called the Homelander. He's supposed to be the greatest superhero of all, the strongest man in the whole world — and sort of a saint at the same time, he only uses his powers for good. Like a knight in shining armor crossed with Jesus Christ, into helping people and being honest and doing the right thing. It said at the back of the comic that the real life seven are just like they are in it, and you could come back and read about them every month. The only thing is that I know the real life Homelander is completely and totally insane, because I looked up into his eyes while he was doing the thing he did to me, and I could see it there, and now I'm scared every second of every day.

So where does that leave me, and what does it leave for me and Billy? I don't know. I suppose that one day, maybe, just maybe, I might be able to let someone touch me again — I might be able to trust someone enough just to relax with them, and feel safe, and maybe even forget what happened. But at the moment, all I can see is this awful thing that my life has turned into stretching out forever, and I know deep down that something was stolen that night that I'm not getting back. Something was murdered, that's all there is to it.

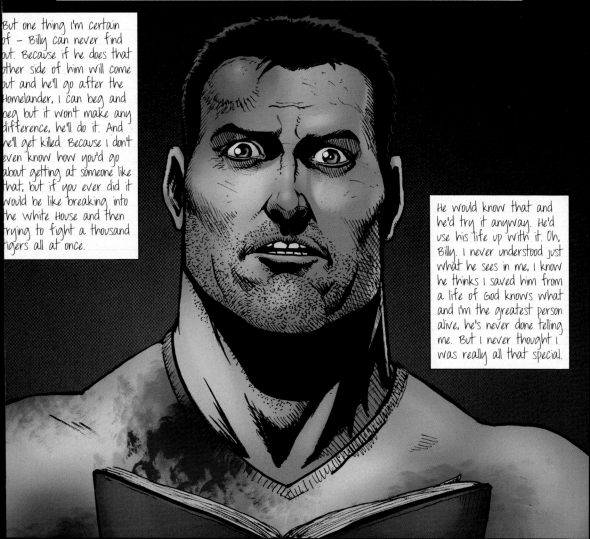

But one thing I'm certain of — Billy can never find out. Because if he does that other side of him will come out and he'll go after the Homelander, I can beg and beg but it won't make any difference, he'll do it. And he'll get killed. Because I don't even know how you'd go about getting at someone like that, but if you ever did it would be like breaking into the White House and then trying to fight a thousand tigers all at once.

He would know that and he'd try it anyway. He'd use his life up with it. Oh, Billy. I never understood just what he sees in me, I know he thinks I saved him from a life of God knows what and I'm the greatest person alive, he's never done telling me. But I never thought I was really all that special.

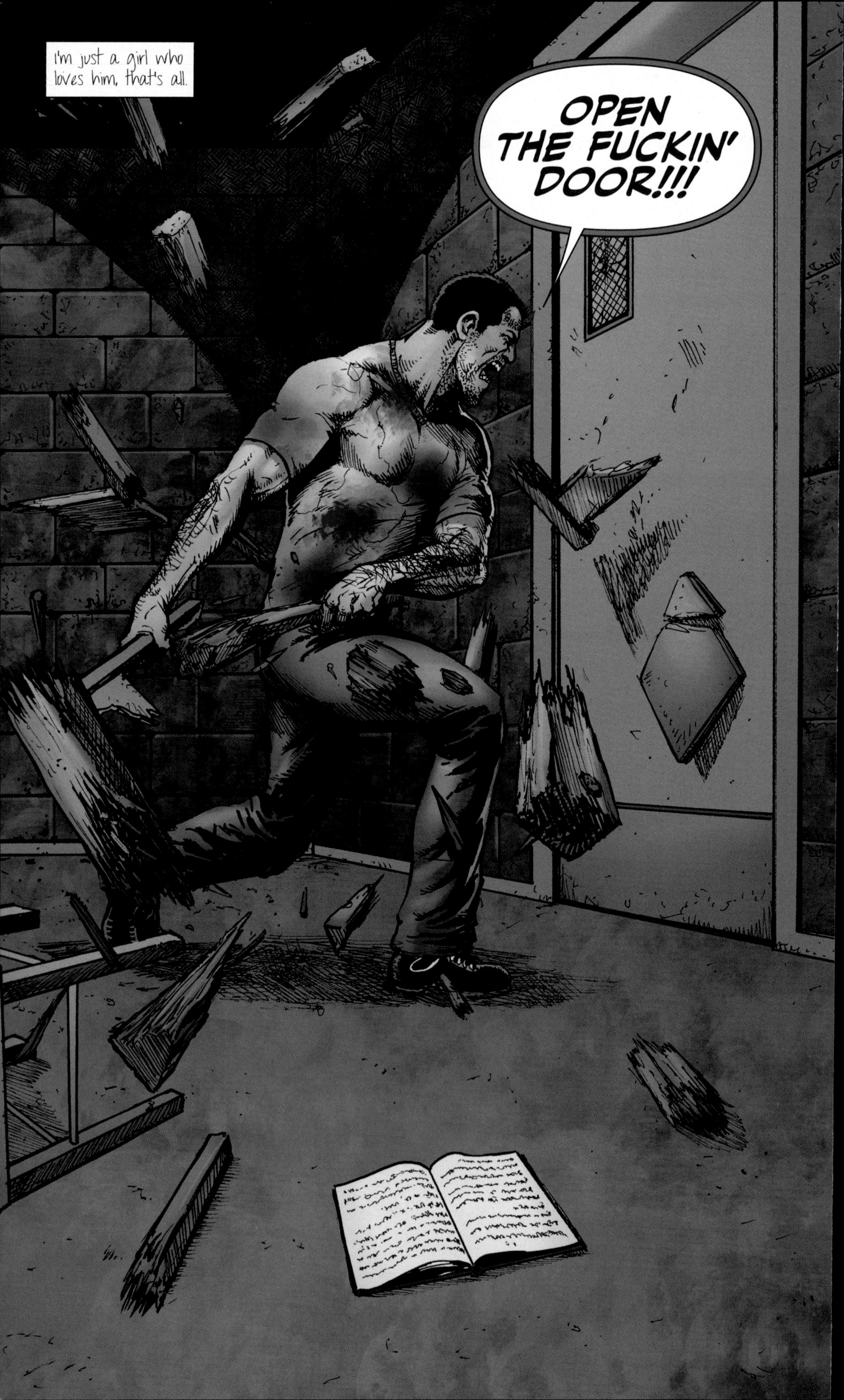
I'm just a girl who loves him, that's all.
OPEN THE FUCKIN' DOOR!!!

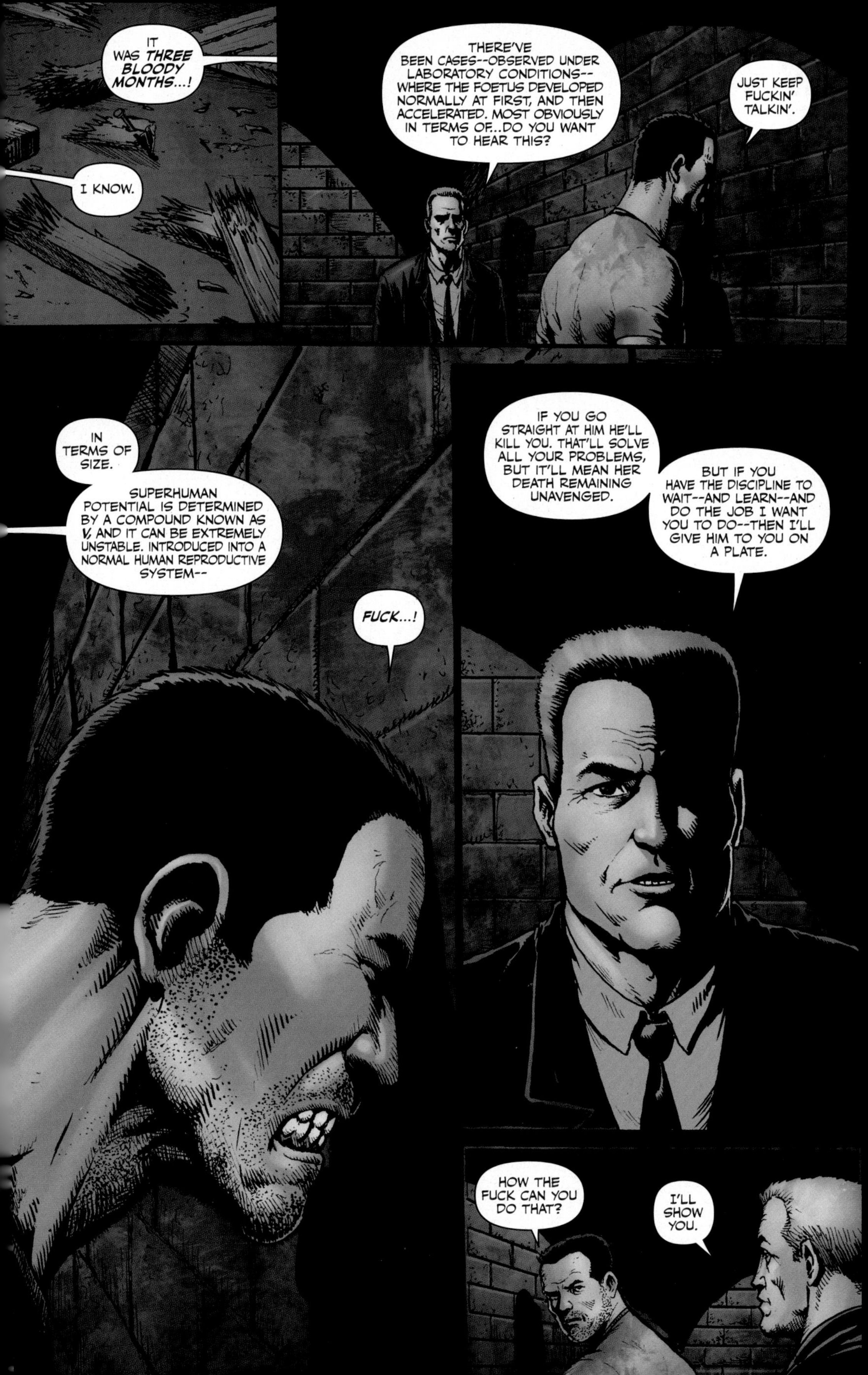
IT WAS THREE BLOODY MONTHS...!
I KNOW.
THERE'VE BEEN CASES--OBSERVED UNDER LABORATORY CONDITIONS--WHERE THE FOETUS DEVELOPED NORMALLY AT FIRST, AND THEN ACCELERATED. MOST OBVIOUSLY IN TERMS OF...DO YOU WANT TO HEAR THIS?
JUST KEEP FUCKIN' TALKIN'.
IN TERMS OF SIZE.
SUPERHUMAN POTENTIAL IS DETERMINED BY A COMPOUND KNOWN AS V, AND IT CAN BE EXTREMELY UNSTABLE. INTRODUCED INTO A NORMAL HUMAN REPRODUCTIVE SYSTEM--
FUCK...!
IF YOU GO STRAIGHT AT HIM HE'LL KILL YOU. THAT'LL SOLVE ALL YOUR PROBLEMS, BUT IT'LL MEAN HER DEATH REMAINING UNAVENGED.
BUT IF YOU HAVE THE DISCIPLINE TO WAIT--AND LEARN--AND DO THE JOB I WANT YOU TO DO--THEN I'LL GIVE HIM TO YOU ON A PLATE.
HOW THE FUCK CAN YOU DO THAT?
I'LL SHOW YOU.

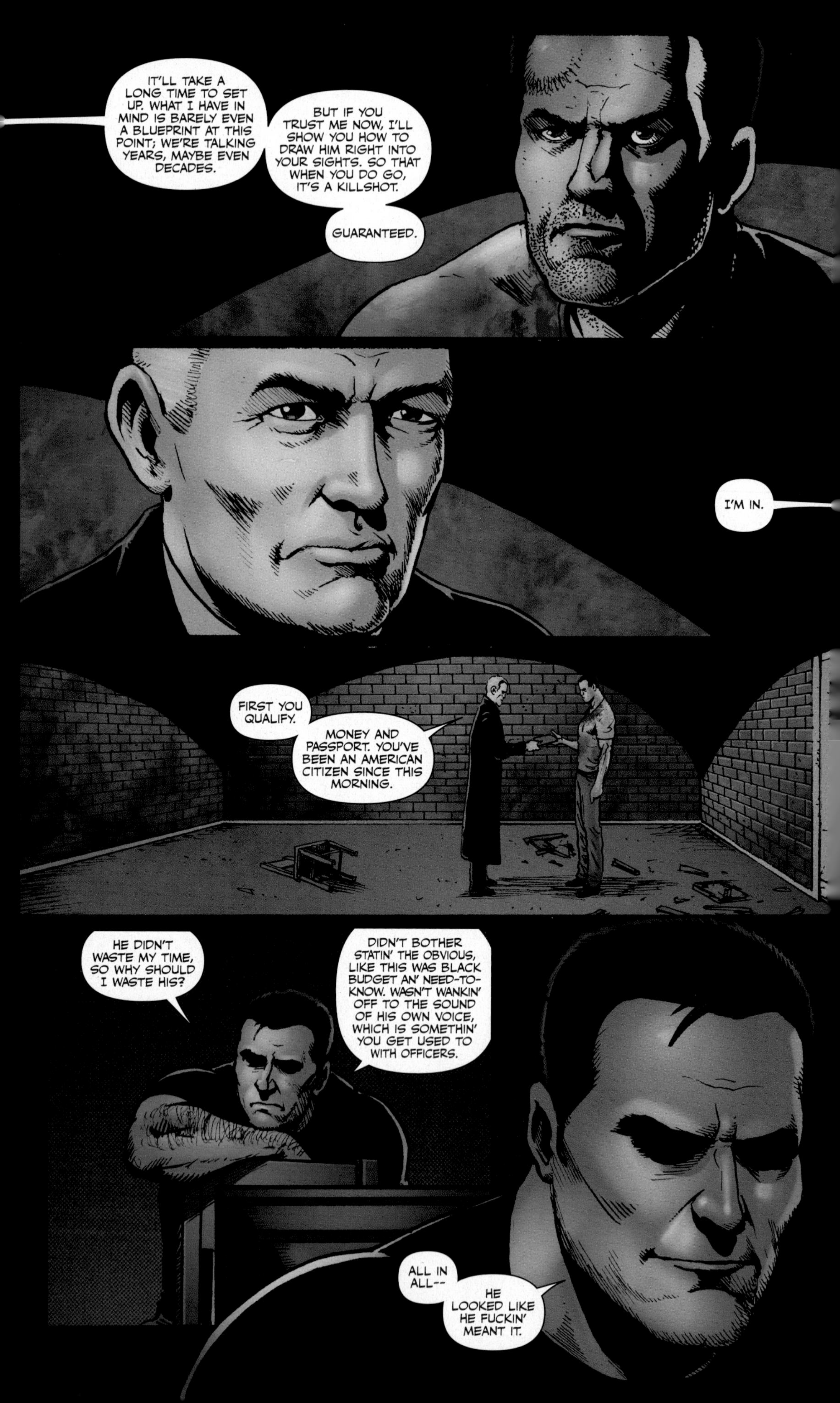
IT'LL TAKE A LONG TIME TO SET UP. WHAT I HAVE IN MIND IS BARELY EVEN A BLUEPRINT AT THIS POINT; WE'RE TALKING YEARS, MAYBE EVEN DECADES.
BUT IF YOU TRUST ME NOW, I'LL SHOW YOU HOW TO DRAW HIM RIGHT INTO YOUR SIGHTS. SO THAT WHEN YOU DO GO, IT'S A KILLSHOT.
GUARANTEED.
I'M IN.
FIRST YOU QUALIFY.
MONEY AND PASSPORT. YOU'VE BEEN AN AMERICAN CITIZEN SINCE THIS MORNING.
HE DIDN'T WASTE MY TIME, SO WHY SHOULD I WASTE HIS?
DIDN'T BOTHER STATIN' THE OBVIOUS, LIKE THIS WAS BLACK BUDGET AN' NEED-TO-KNOW. WASN'T WANKIN' OFF TO THE SOUND OF HIS OWN VOICE, WHICH IS SOMETHIN' YOU GET USED TO WITH OFFICERS.
ALL IN ALL--
HE LOOKED LIKE HE FUCKIN' MEANT IT.

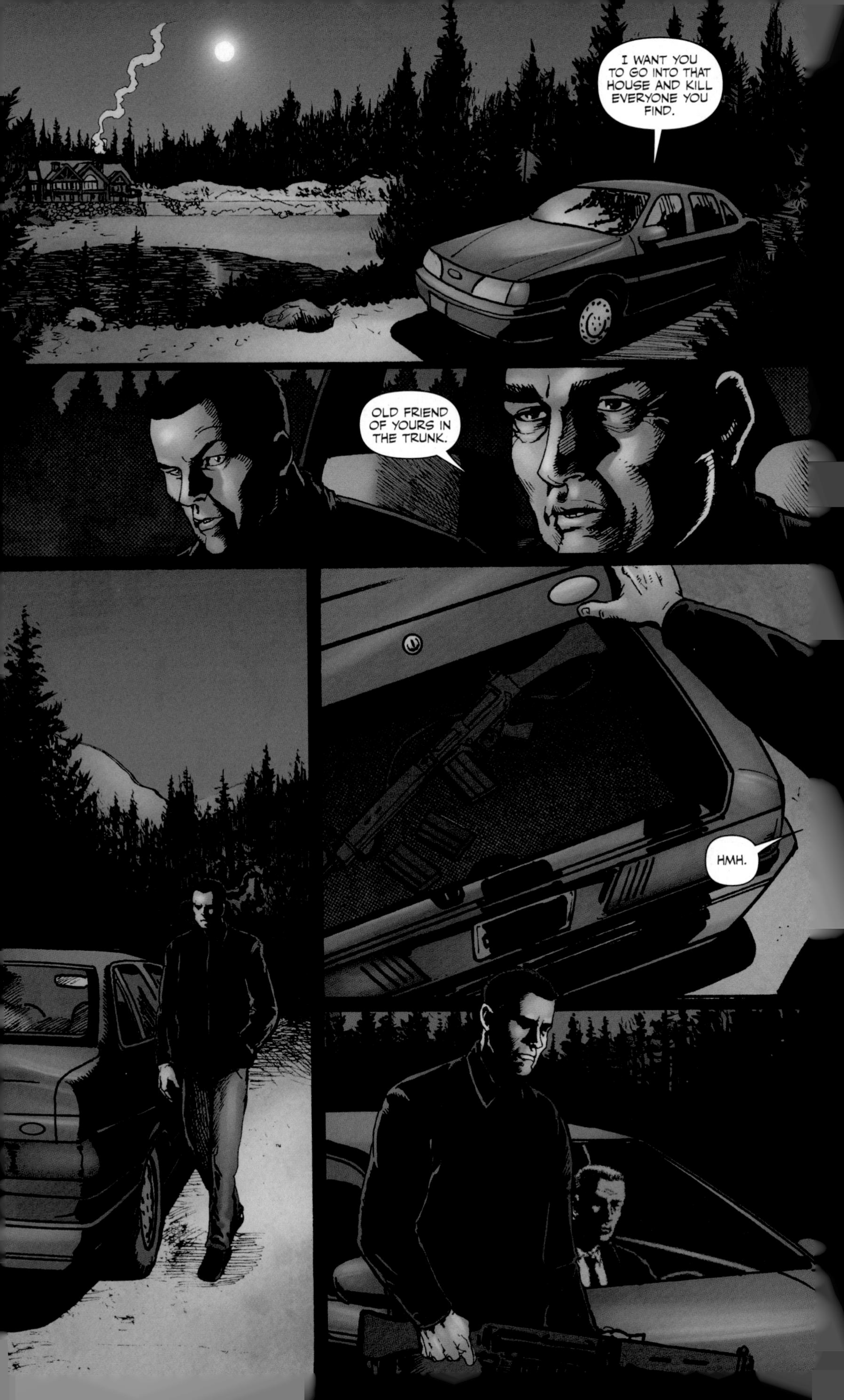
I WANT YOU TO GO INTO THAT HOUSE AND KILL EVERYONE YOU FIND.
OLD FRIEND OF YOURS IN THE TRUNK.
HMH.

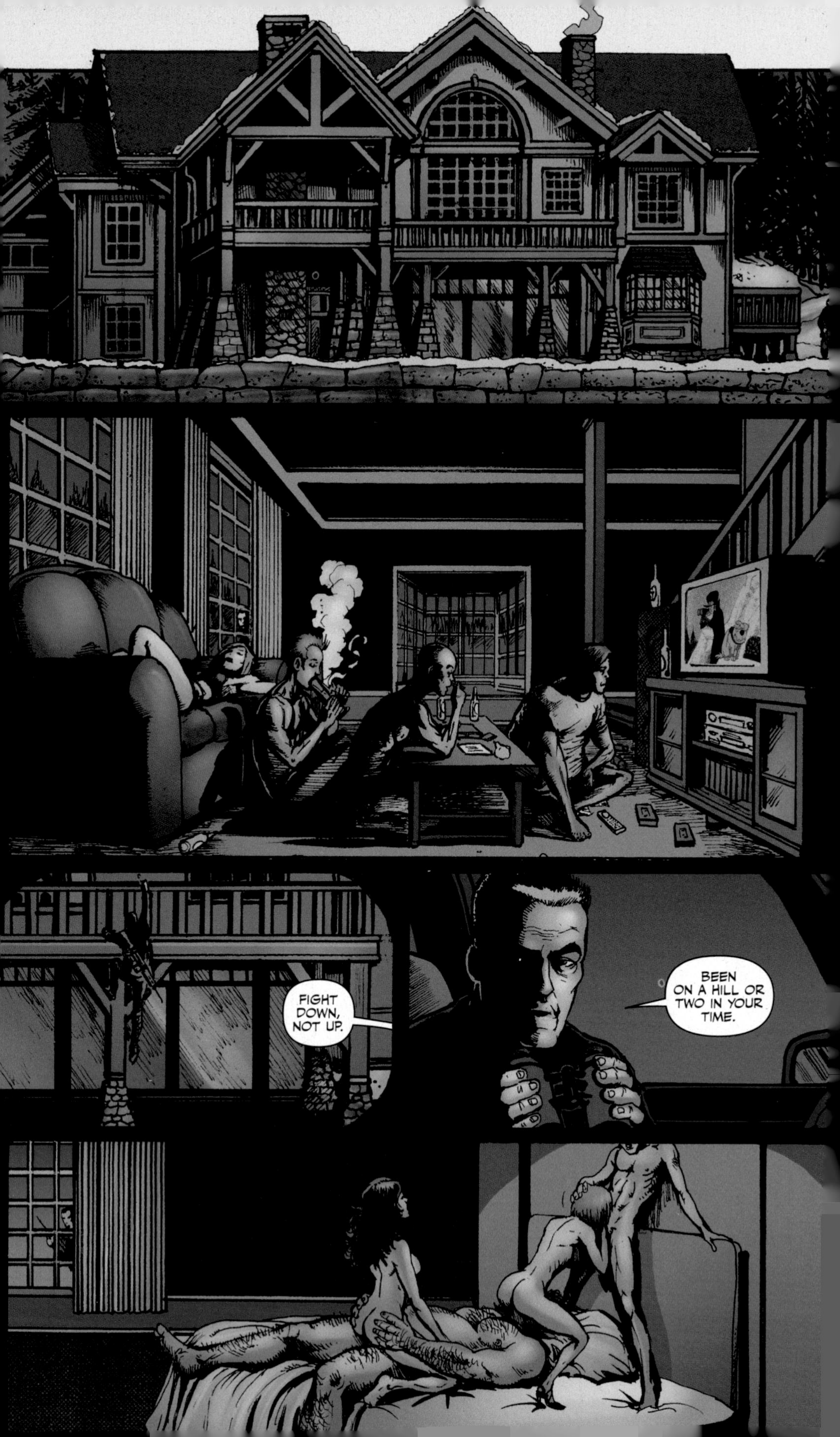
FIGHT DOWN, NOT UP.
BEEN ON A HILL OR TWO IN YOUR TIME.

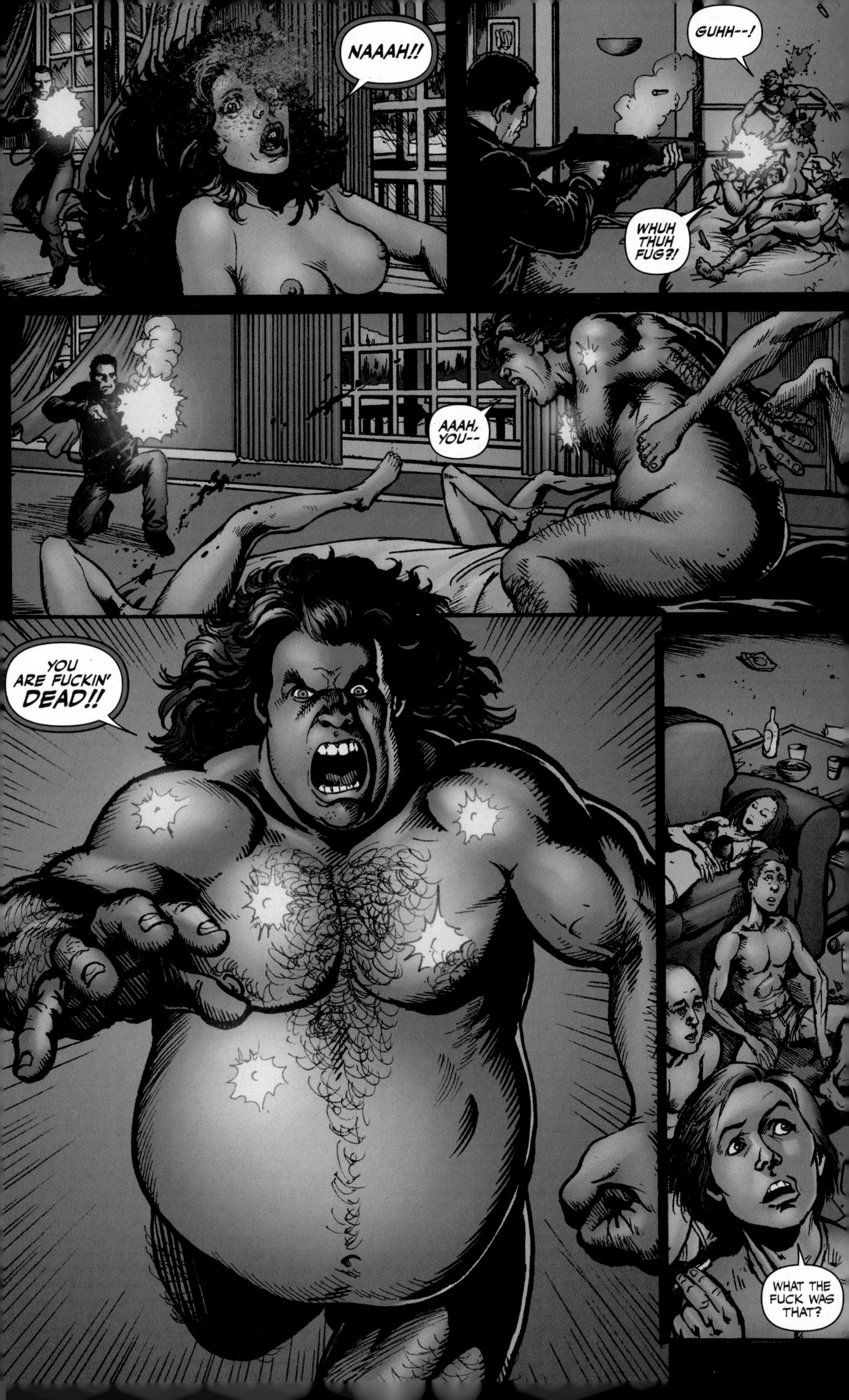
NAAAH!!
GUHH--!
WHUH THUH FUG?!
AAAH, YOU--
YOU ARE FUCKIN' DEAD!!
WHAT THE FUCK WAS THAT?

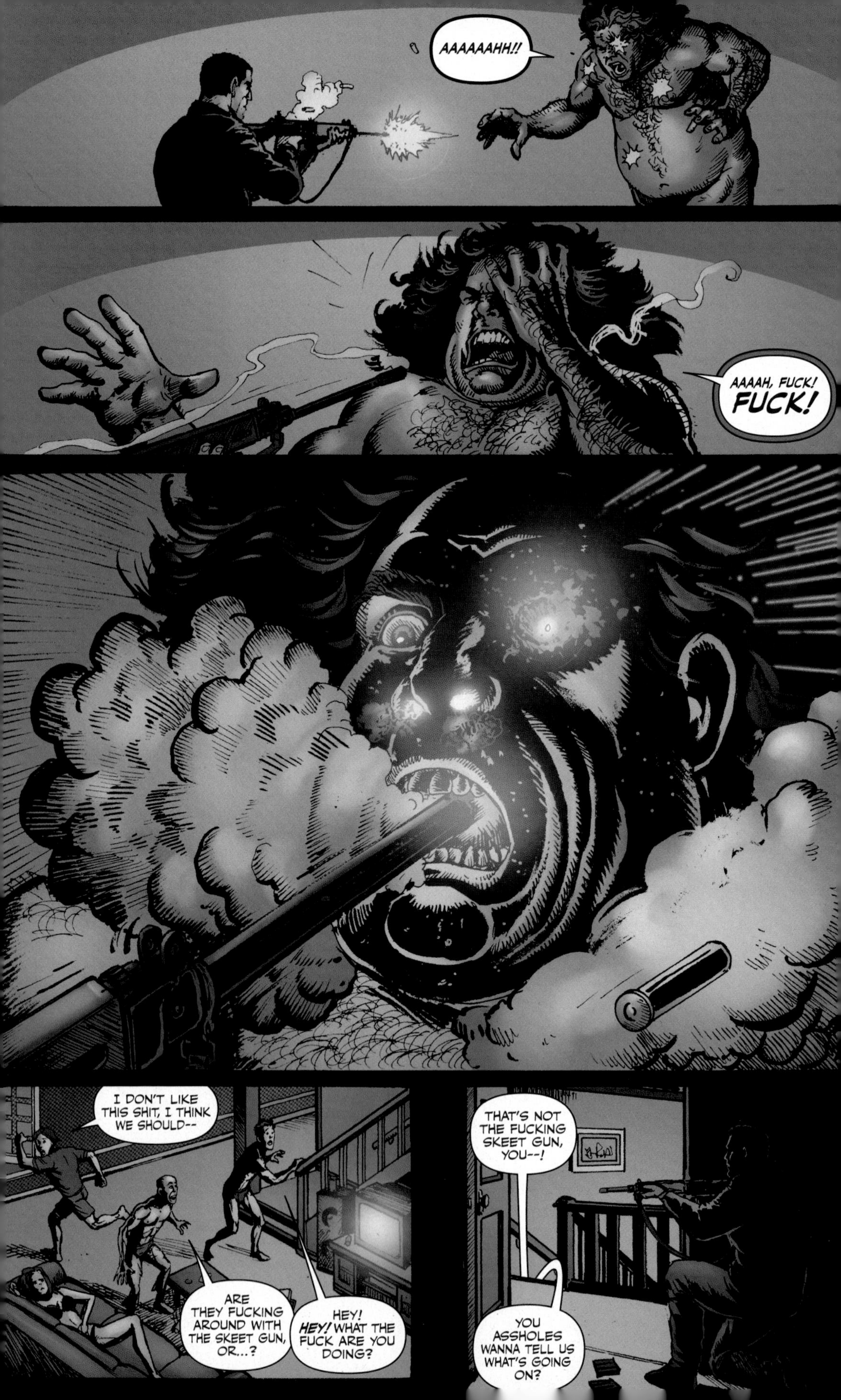
AAAAAAHH!!
AAAAH, FUCK! FUCK!
I DON'T LIKE THIS SHIT, I THINK WE SHOULD--
ARE THEY FUCKING AROUND WITH THE SKEET GUN, OR...?
HEY! HEY! WHAT THE FUCK ARE YOU DOING?
THAT'S NOT THE FUCKING SKEET GUN, YOU--!
YOU ASSHOLES WANNA TELL US WHAT'S GOING ON?

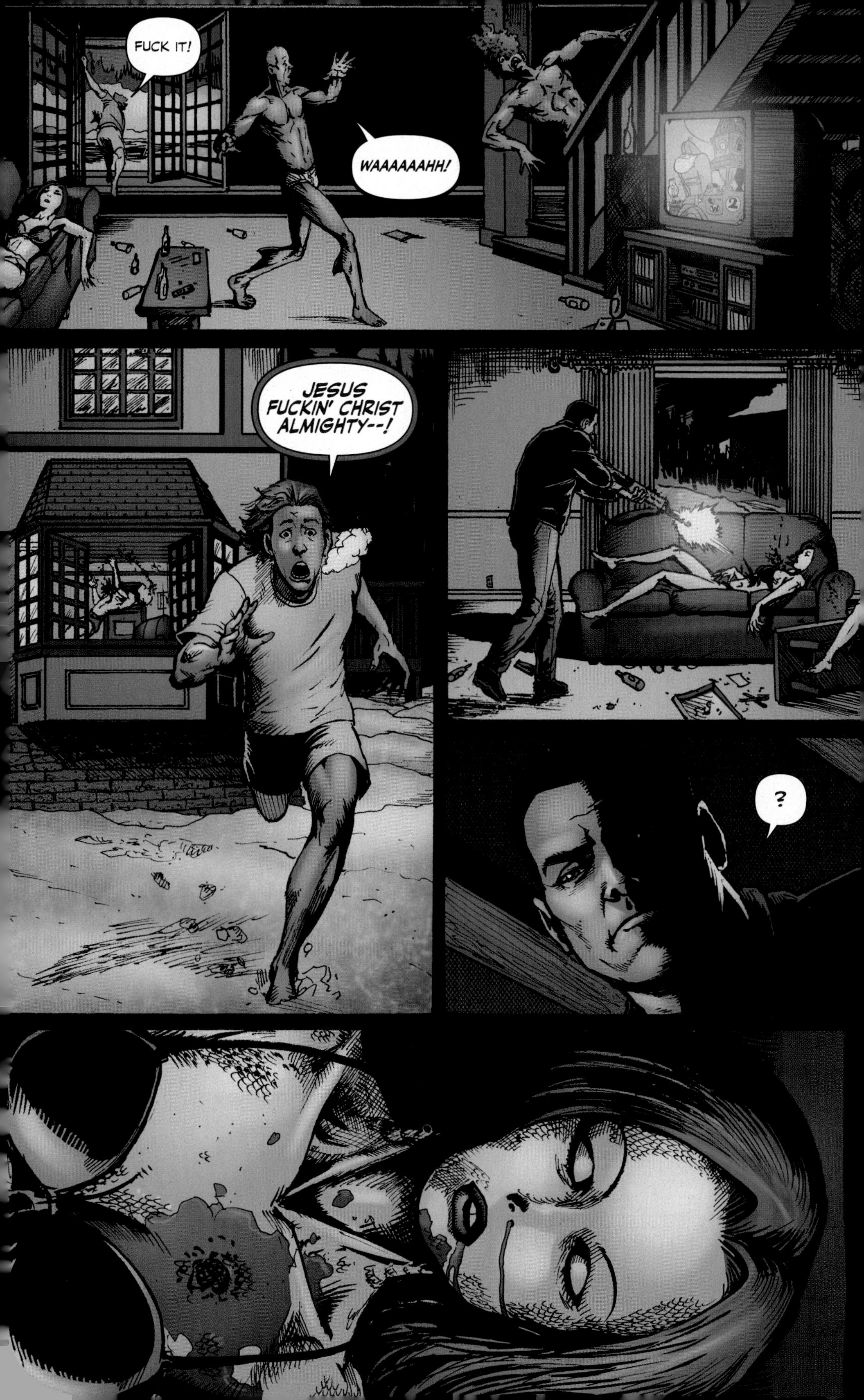
FUCK IT!
WAAAAAAHH!
JESUS FUCKIN' CHRIST ALMIGHTY--!
?

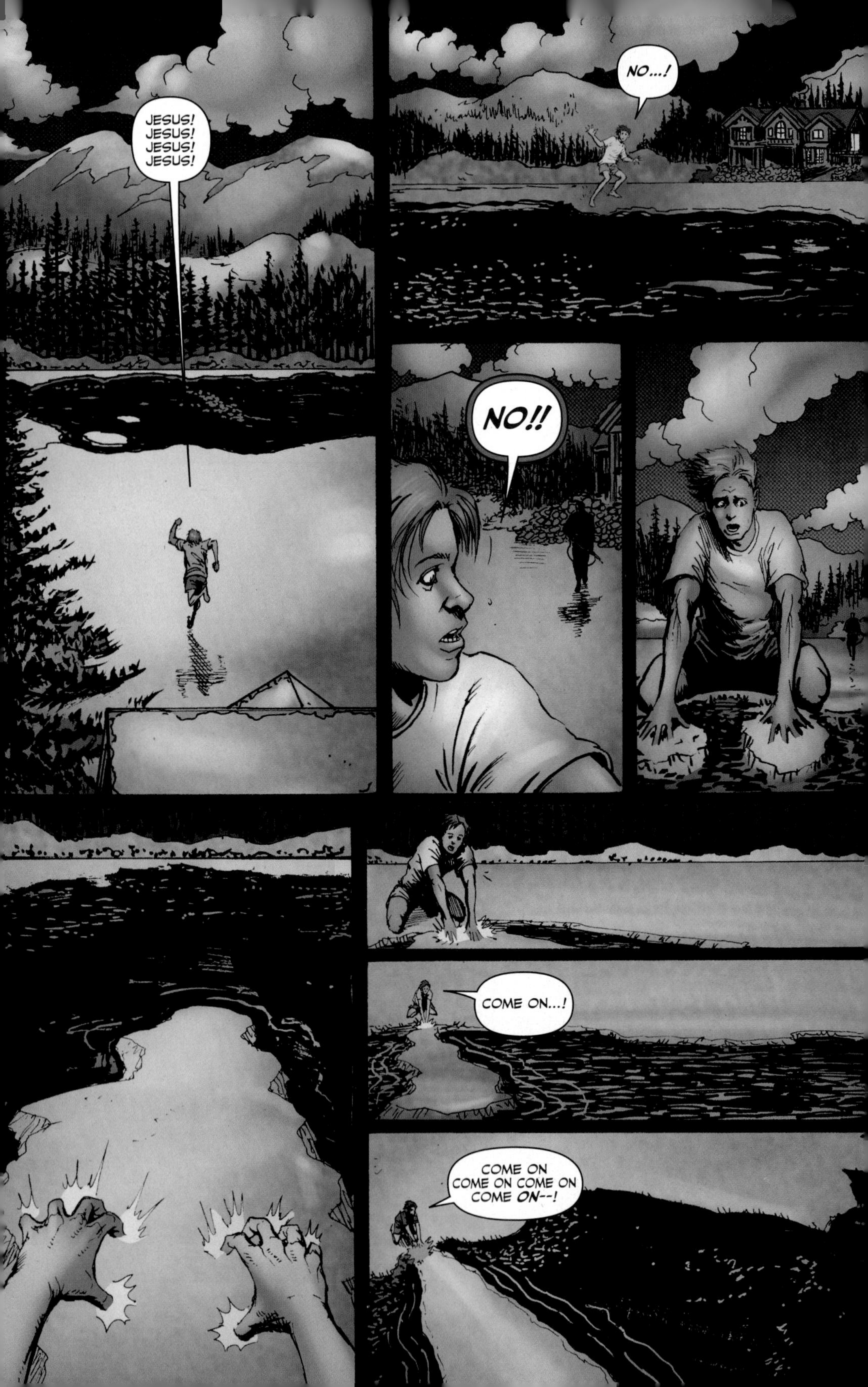
JESUS!
JESUS!
JESUS!
JESUS!
NO...!
NO!!
COME ON...!
COME ON
COME ON COME ON
COME ON--!

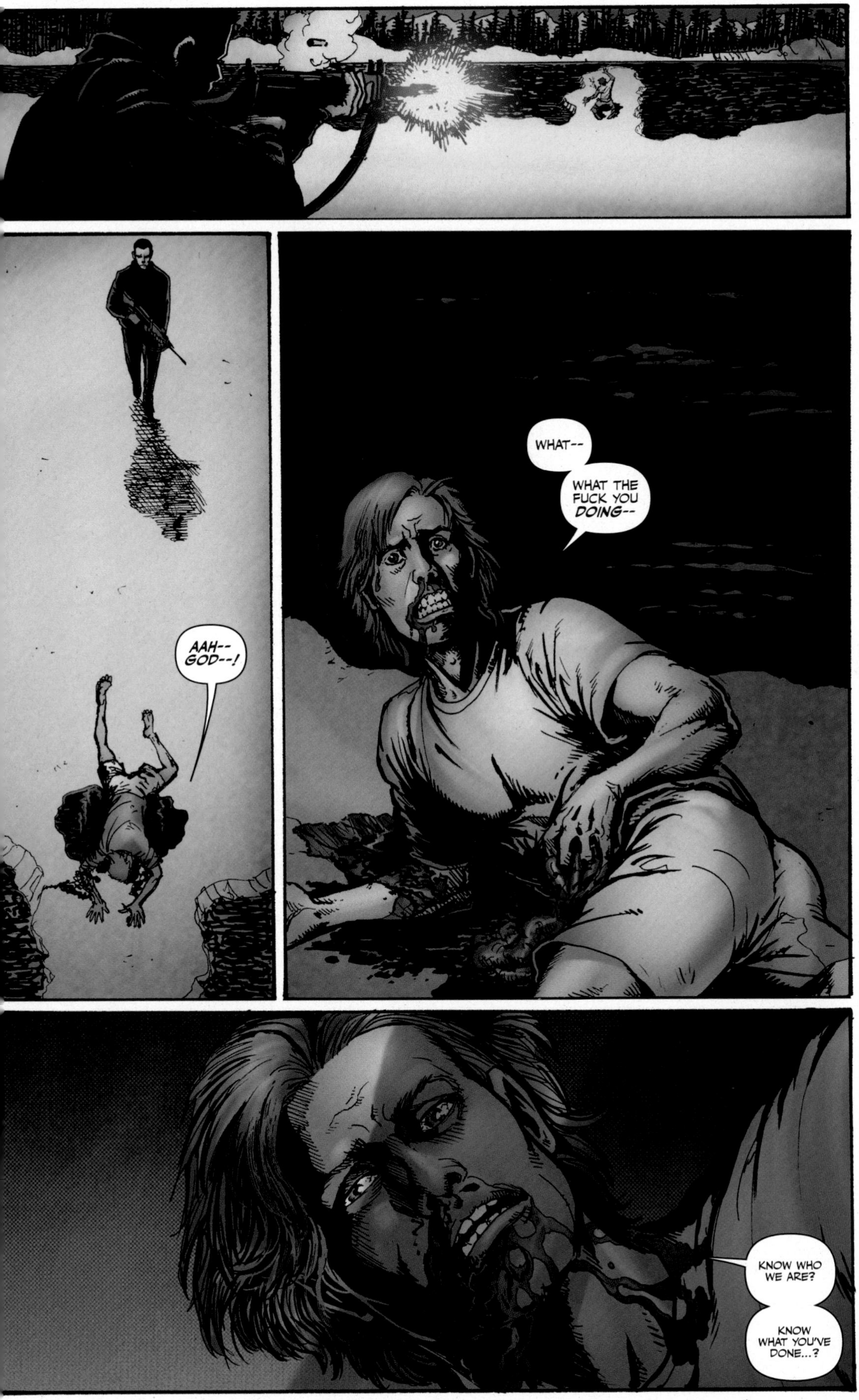
AAH--
GOD--!
WHAT--
WHAT THE FUCK YOU *DOING*--
KNOW WHO WE ARE?
KNOW WHAT YOU'VE DONE...?

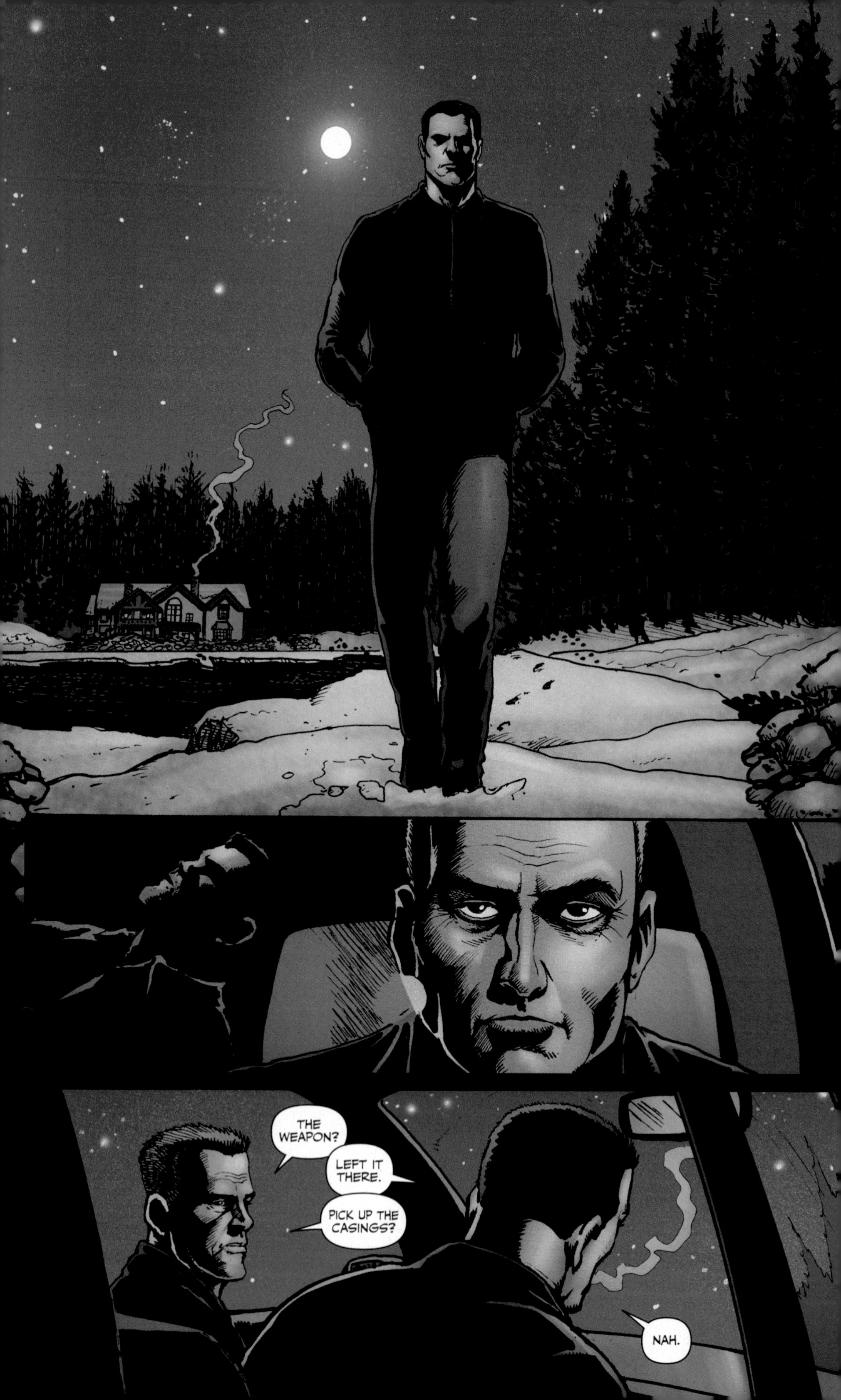
THE WEAPON?
LEFT IT THERE.
PICK UP THE CASINGS?
NAH.

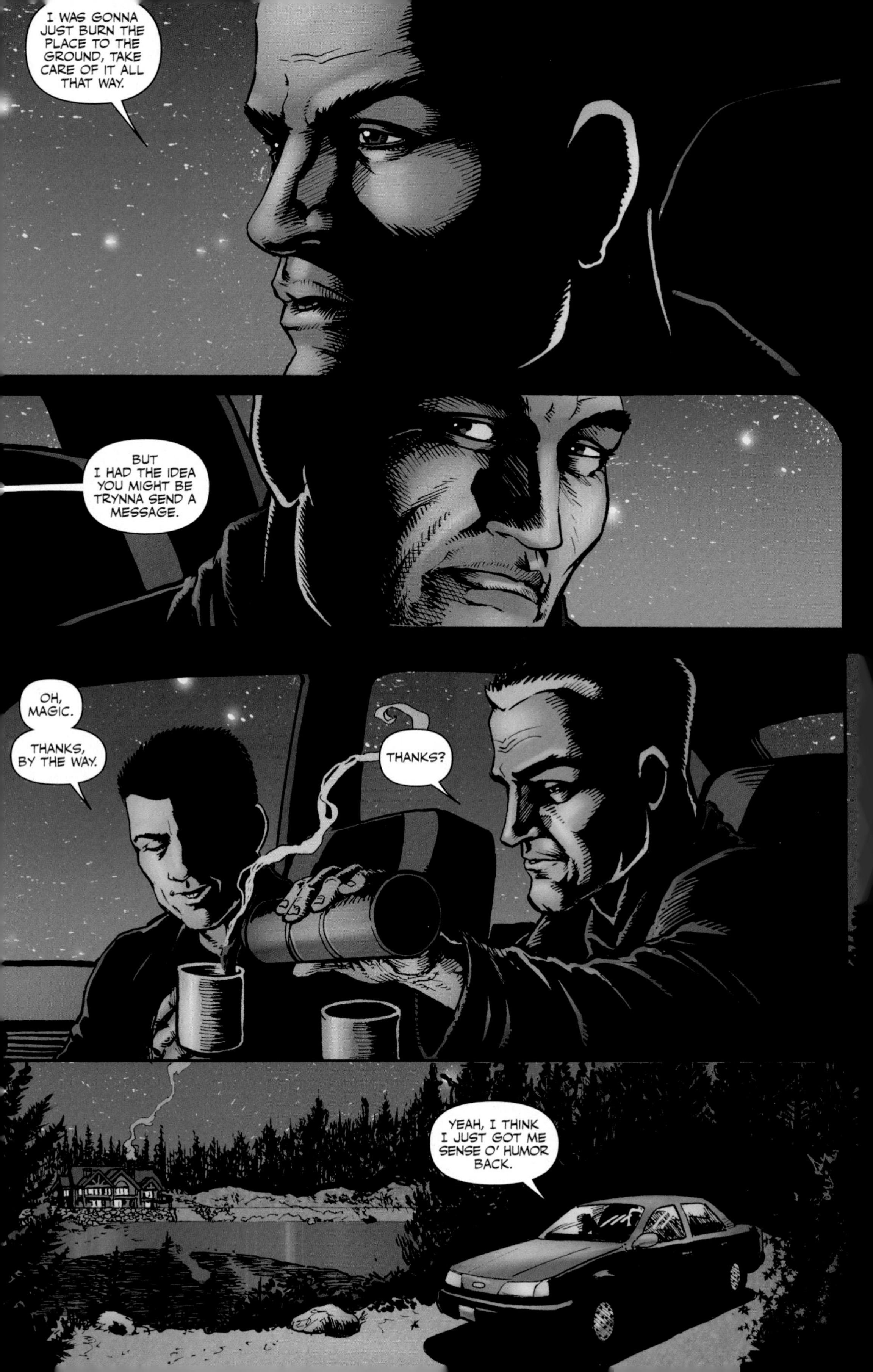
I WAS GONNA JUST BURN THE PLACE TO THE GROUND, TAKE CARE OF IT ALL THAT WAY.
BUT I HAD THE IDEA YOU MIGHT BE TRYNNA SEND A MESSAGE.
OH, MAGIC.
THANKS, BY THE WAY.
THANKS?
YEAH, I THINK I JUST GOT ME SENSE O' HUMOR BACK.

six

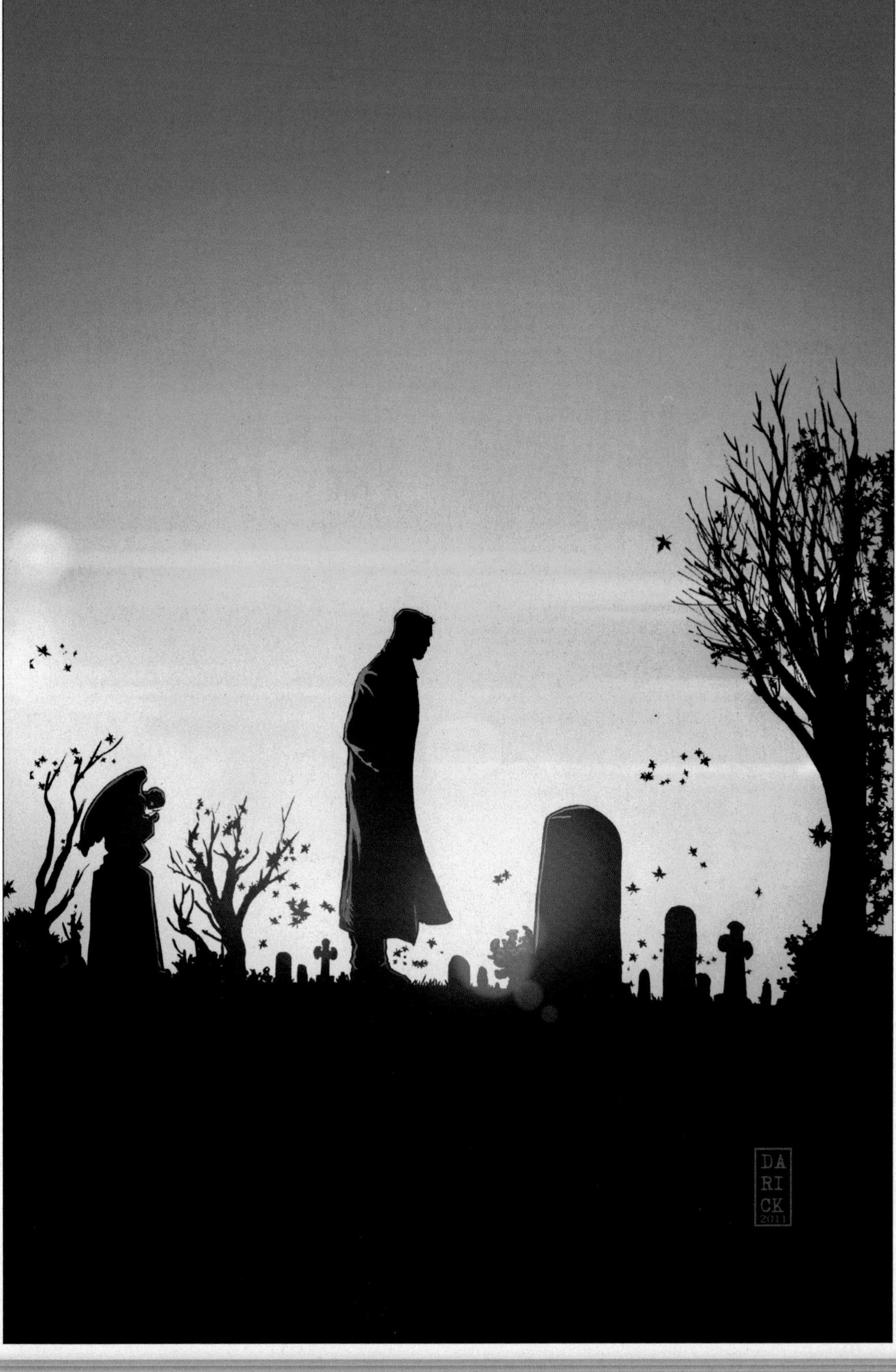
DA
RI
CK
2011

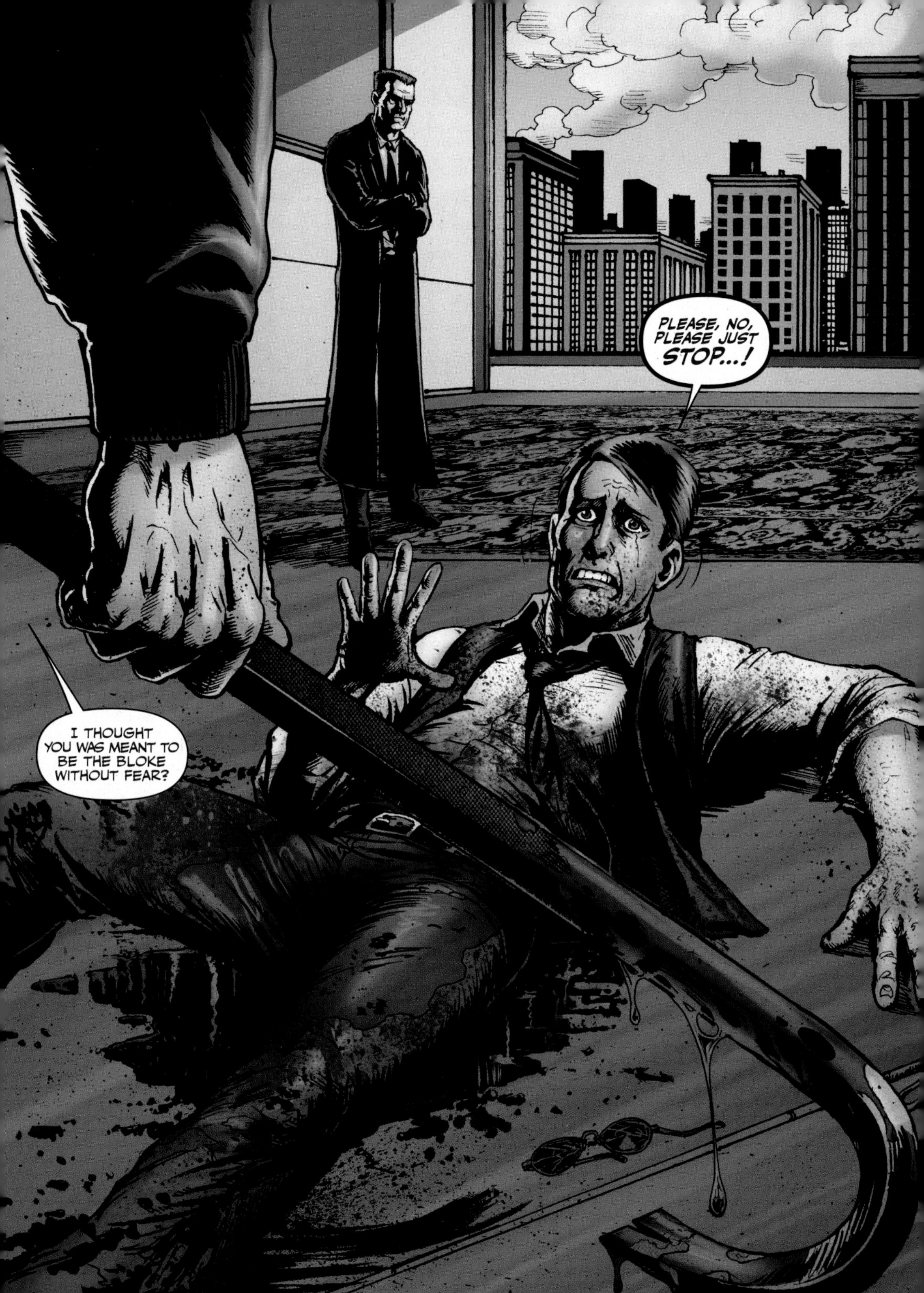
PLEASE, NO, PLEASE JUST STOP...!
I THOUGHT YOU WAS MEANT TO BE THE BLOKE WITHOUT FEAR?

6: EVERY ONE OF YOU SONS OF BITCHES

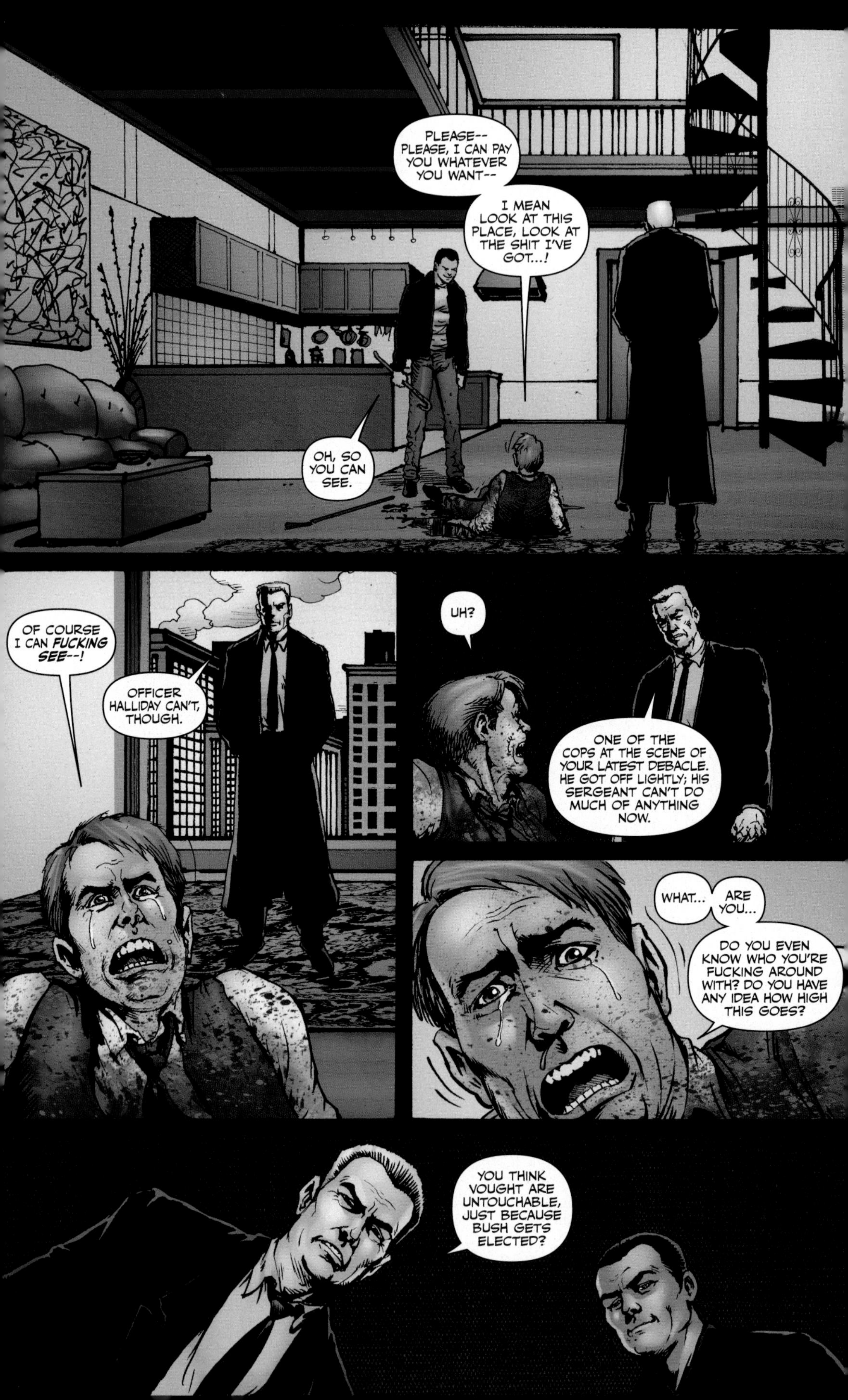
PLEASE-- PLEASE, I CAN PAY YOU WHATEVER YOU WANT--
I MEAN LOOK AT THIS PLACE, LOOK AT THE SHIT I'VE GOT...!
OH, SO YOU CAN SEE.
OF COURSE I CAN *FUCKING SEE*--!
OFFICER HALLIDAY CAN'T, THOUGH.
UH?
ONE OF THE COPS AT THE SCENE OF YOUR LATEST DEBACLE. HE GOT OFF LIGHTLY; HIS SERGEANT CAN'T DO MUCH OF ANYTHING NOW.
WHAT...
ARE YOU...
DO YOU EVEN KNOW WHO YOU'RE FUCKING AROUND WITH? DO YOU HAVE ANY IDEA HOW HIGH THIS GOES?
YOU THINK VOUGHT ARE UNTOUCHABLE, JUST BECAUSE BUSH GETS ELECTED?

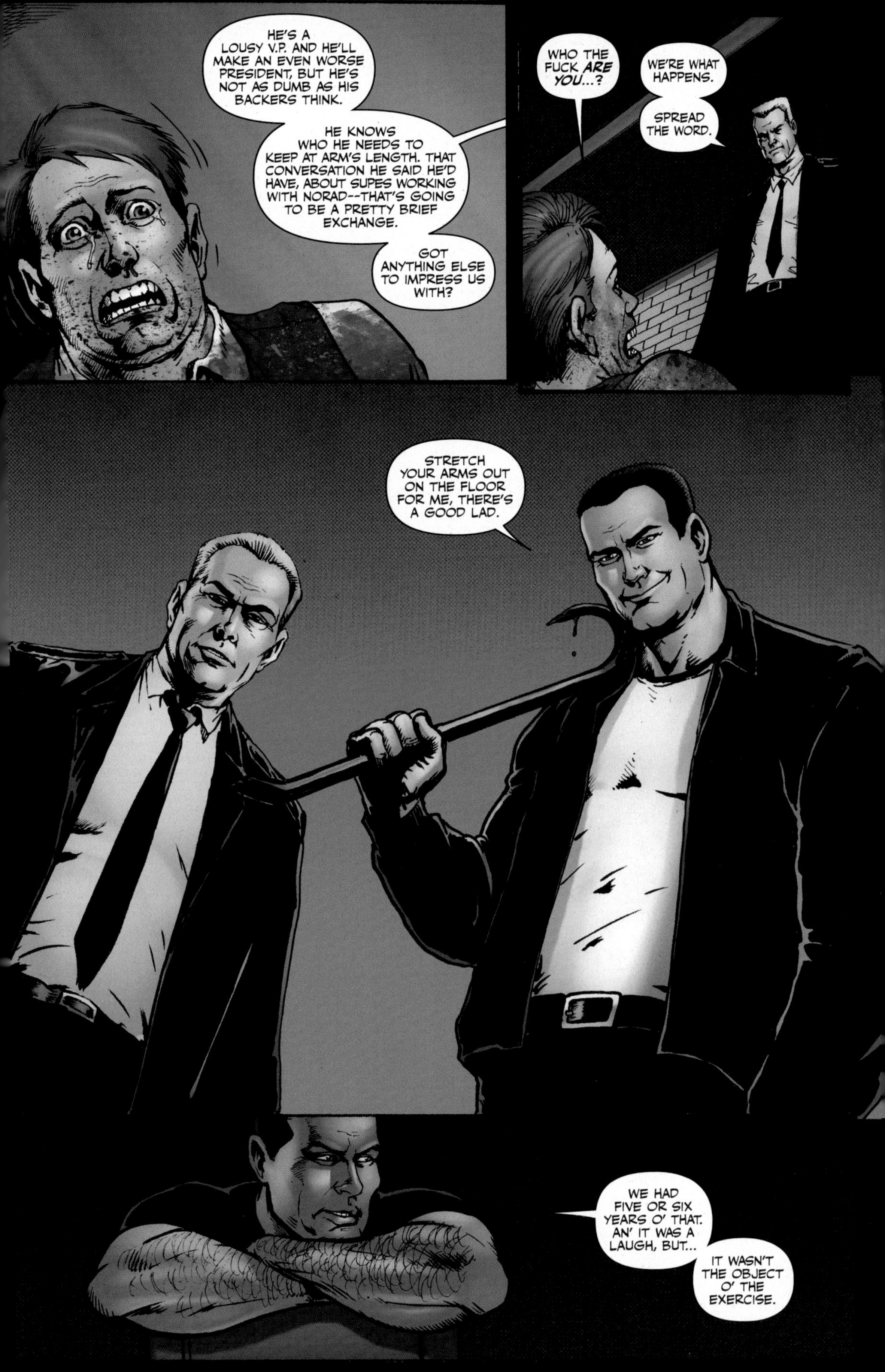
HE'S A LOUSY V.P. AND HE'LL MAKE AN EVEN WORSE PRESIDENT, BUT HE'S NOT AS DUMB AS HIS BACKERS THINK.
HE KNOWS WHO HE NEEDS TO KEEP AT ARM'S LENGTH. THAT CONVERSATION HE SAID HE'D HAVE, ABOUT SUPES WORKING WITH NORAD--THAT'S GOING TO BE A PRETTY BRIEF EXCHANGE.
GOT ANYTHING ELSE TO IMPRESS US WITH?
WHO THE FUCK *ARE YOU*...?
WE'RE WHAT HAPPENS.
SPREAD THE WORD.
STRETCH YOUR ARMS OUT ON THE FLOOR FOR ME, THERE'S A GOOD LAD.
WE HAD FIVE OR SIX YEARS O' THAT. AN' IT WAS A LAUGH, BUT...
IT WASN'T THE OBJECT O' THE EXERCISE.

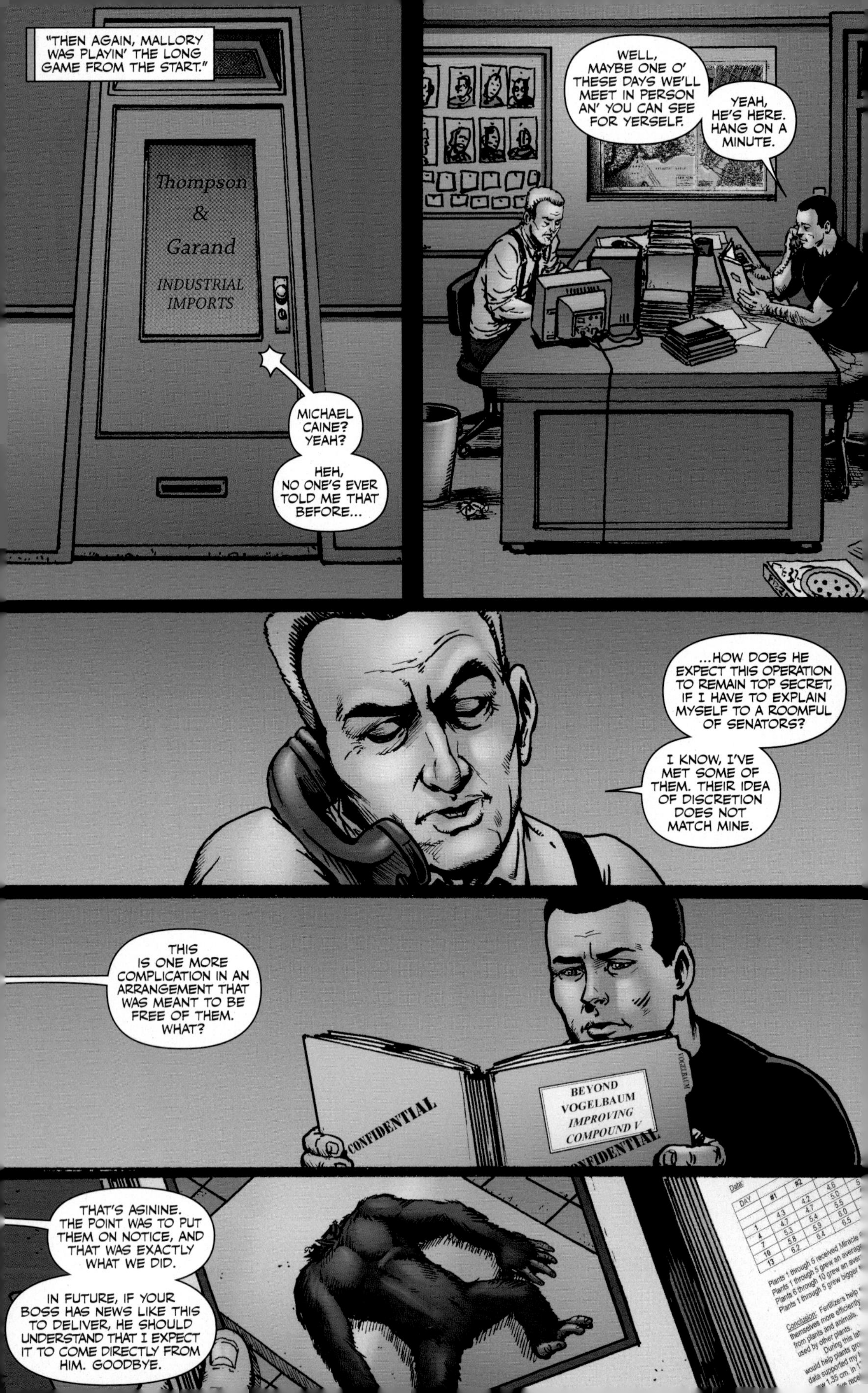
"THEN AGAIN, MALLORY WAS PLAYIN' THE LONG GAME FROM THE START."
Thompson & Garand INDUSTRIAL IMPORTS
MICHAEL CAINE? YEAH?
HEH, NO ONE'S EVER TOLD ME THAT BEFORE...
WELL, MAYBE ONE O' THESE DAYS WE'LL MEET IN PERSON AN' YOU CAN SEE FOR YERSELF.
YEAH, HE'S HERE. HANG ON A MINUTE.
...HOW DOES HE EXPECT THIS OPERATION TO REMAIN TOP SECRET, IF I HAVE TO EXPLAIN MYSELF TO A ROOMFUL OF SENATORS?
I KNOW, I'VE MET SOME OF THEM. THEIR IDEA OF DISCRETION DOES NOT MATCH MINE.
THIS IS ONE MORE COMPLICATION IN AN ARRANGEMENT THAT WAS MEANT TO BE FREE OF THEM. WHAT?
CONFIDENTIAL
BEYOND VOGELBAUM IMPROVING COMPOUND V
VOGELBAUM
THAT'S ASININE. THE POINT WAS TO PUT THEM ON NOTICE, AND THAT WAS EXACTLY WHAT WE DID.
IN FUTURE, IF YOUR BOSS HAS NEWS LIKE THIS TO DELIVER, HE SHOULD UNDERSTAND THAT I EXPECT IT TO COME DIRECTLY FROM HIM. GOODBYE.

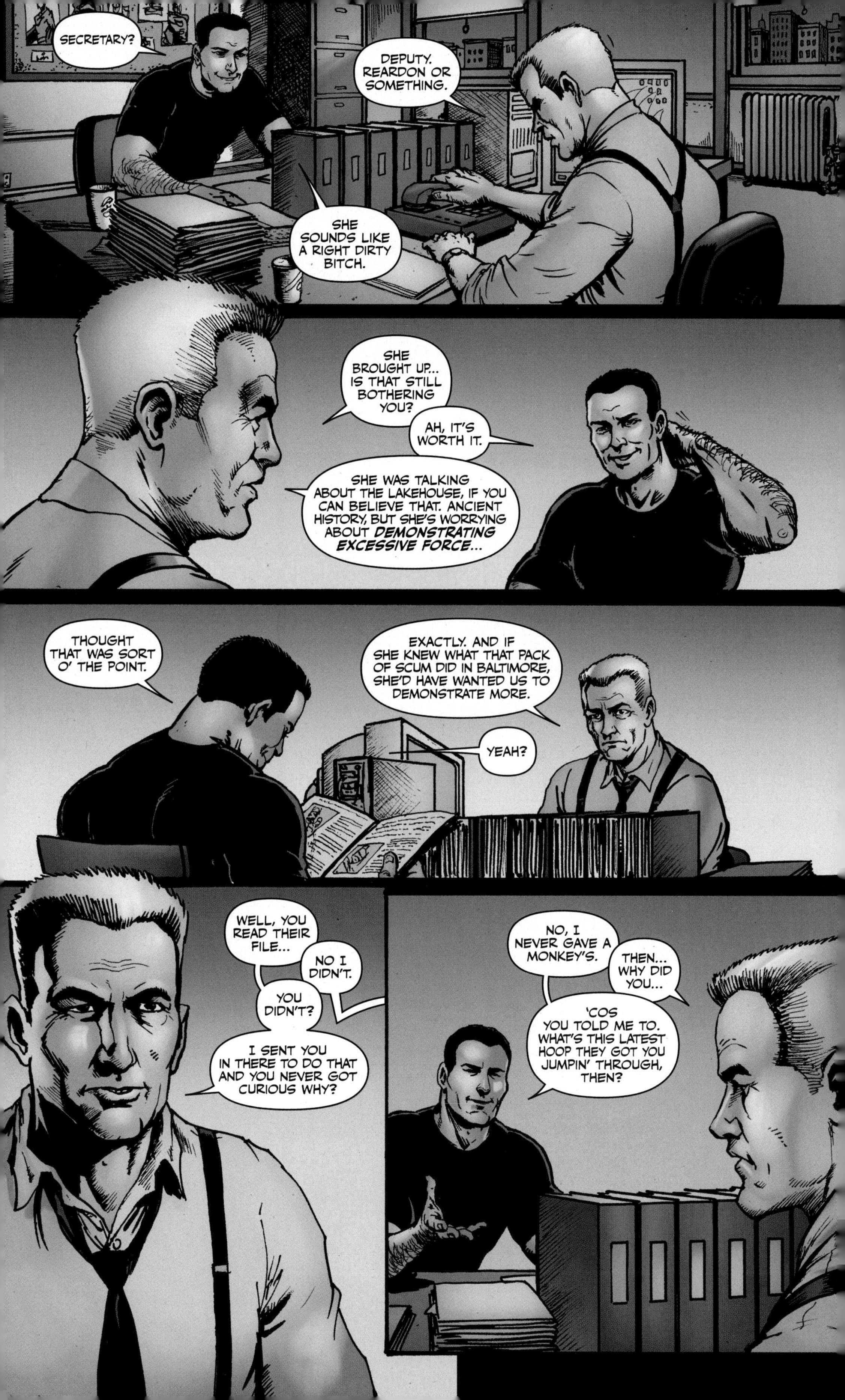
SECRETARY?
DEPUTY. REARDON OR SOMETHING.
SHE SOUNDS LIKE A RIGHT DIRTY BITCH.
SHE BROUGHT UP... IS THAT STILL BOTHERING YOU?
AH, IT'S WORTH IT.
SHE WAS TALKING ABOUT THE LAKEHOUSE, IF YOU CAN BELIEVE THAT. ANCIENT HISTORY, BUT SHE'S WORRYING ABOUT *DEMONSTRATING EXCESSIVE FORCE*...
THOUGHT THAT WAS SORT O' THE POINT.
EXACTLY. AND IF SHE KNEW WHAT THAT PACK OF SCUM DID IN BALTIMORE, SHE'D HAVE WANTED US TO DEMONSTRATE MORE.
YEAH?
WELL, YOU READ THEIR FILE...
NO I DIDN'T.
YOU DIDN'T?
I SENT YOU IN THERE TO DO THAT AND YOU NEVER GOT CURIOUS WHY?
NO, I NEVER GAVE A MONKEY'S.
THEN... WHY DID YOU...
'COS YOU TOLD ME TO. WHAT'S THIS LATEST HOOP THEY GOT YOU JUMPIN' THROUGH, THEN?

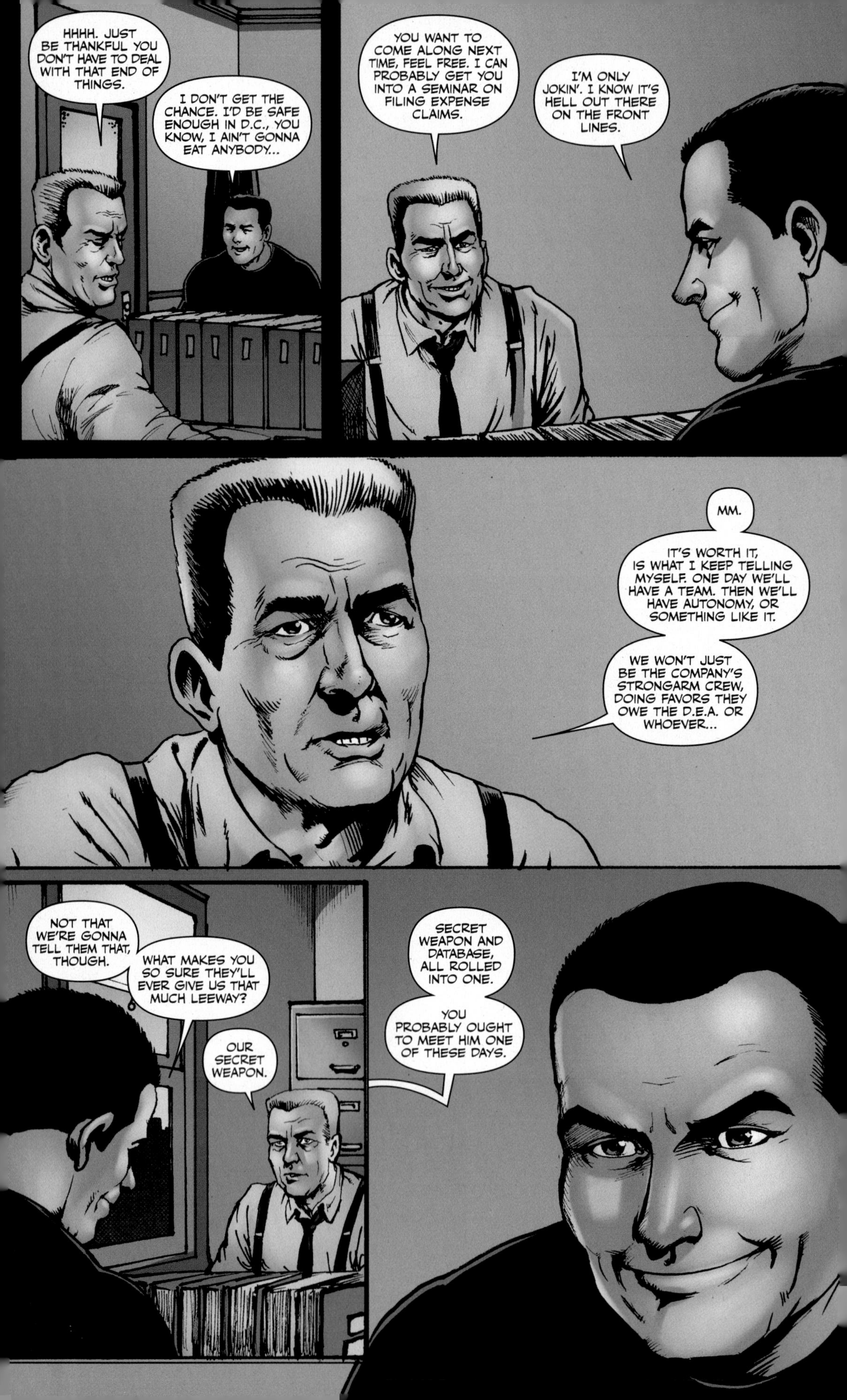
HHHH. JUST BE THANKFUL YOU DON'T HAVE TO DEAL WITH THAT END OF THINGS.
I DON'T GET THE CHANCE. I'D BE SAFE ENOUGH IN D.C., YOU KNOW, I AIN'T GONNA EAT ANYBODY...
YOU WANT TO COME ALONG NEXT TIME, FEEL FREE. I CAN PROBABLY GET YOU INTO A SEMINAR ON FILING EXPENSE CLAIMS.
I'M ONLY JOKIN'. I KNOW IT'S HELL OUT THERE ON THE FRONT LINES.
MM.
IT'S WORTH IT, IS WHAT I KEEP TELLING MYSELF. ONE DAY WE'LL HAVE A TEAM. THEN WE'LL HAVE AUTONOMY, OR SOMETHING LIKE IT.
WE WON'T JUST BE THE COMPANY'S STRONGARM CREW, DOING FAVORS THEY OWE THE D.E.A. OR WHOEVER...
NOT THAT WE'RE GONNA TELL THEM THAT, THOUGH.
WHAT MAKES YOU SO SURE THEY'LL EVER GIVE US THAT MUCH LEEWAY?
OUR SECRET WEAPON.
SECRET WEAPON AND DATABASE, ALL ROLLED INTO ONE.
YOU PROBABLY OUGHT TO MEET HIM ONE OF THESE DAYS.

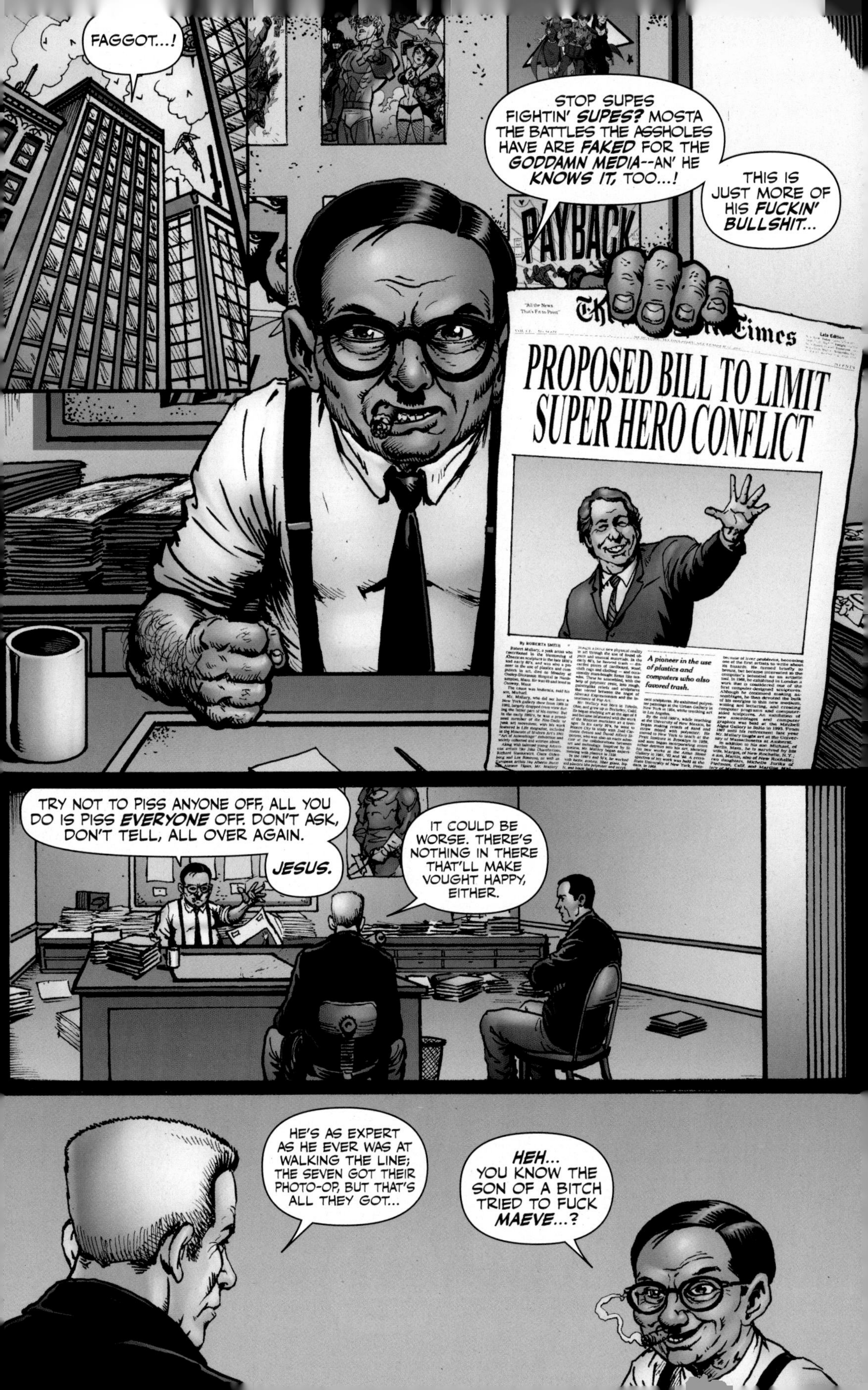
FAGGOT...!
STOP SUPES FIGHTIN' SUPES? MOSTA THE BATTLES THE ASSHOLES HAVE ARE FAKED FOR THE GODDAMN MEDIA--AN' HE KNOWS IT, TOO...!
PAYBACK
THIS IS JUST MORE OF HIS FUCKIN' BULLSHIT...
"All the News That's Fit to Print"
PROPOSED BILL TO LIMIT SUPER HERO CONFLICT
A pioneer in the use of plastics and computers who also favored trash.
TRY NOT TO PISS ANYONE OFF, ALL YOU DO IS PISS EVERYONE OFF. DON'T ASK, DON'T TELL, ALL OVER AGAIN.
JESUS.
IT COULD BE WORSE. THERE'S NOTHING IN THERE THAT'LL MAKE VOUGHT HAPPY, EITHER.
HE'S AS EXPERT AS HE EVER WAS AT WALKING THE LINE; THE SEVEN GOT THEIR PHOTO-OP, BUT THAT'S ALL THEY GOT...
HEH... YOU KNOW THE SON OF A BITCH TRIED TO FUCK MAEVE...?

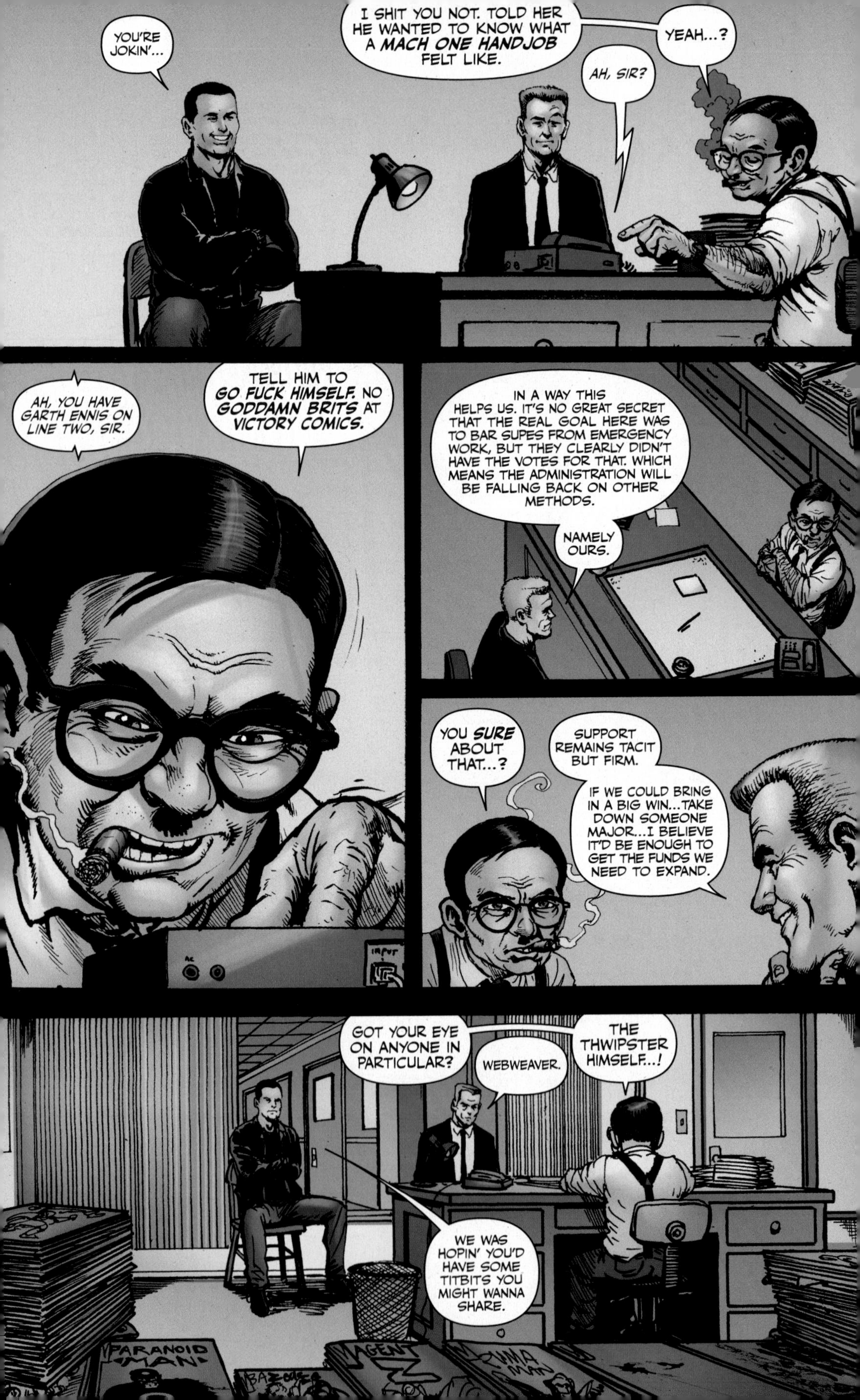
YOU'RE JOKIN'...
I SHIT YOU NOT. TOLD HER HE WANTED TO KNOW WHAT A *MACH ONE HANDJOB* FELT LIKE.
YEAH...?
AH, SIR?
AH, YOU HAVE GARTH ENNIS ON LINE TWO, SIR.
TELL HIM TO *GO FUCK HIMSELF.* NO *GODDAMN BRITS* AT *VICTORY COMICS.*
IN A WAY THIS HELPS US. IT'S NO GREAT SECRET THAT THE REAL GOAL HERE WAS TO BAR SUPES FROM EMERGENCY WORK, BUT THEY CLEARLY DIDN'T HAVE THE VOTES FOR THAT. WHICH MEANS THE ADMINISTRATION WILL BE FALLING BACK ON OTHER METHODS.
NAMELY OURS.
YOU *SURE* ABOUT THAT...?
SUPPORT REMAINS TACIT BUT FIRM.
IF WE COULD BRING IN A BIG WIN...TAKE DOWN SOMEONE MAJOR...I BELIEVE IT'D BE ENOUGH TO GET THE FUNDS WE NEED TO EXPAND.
GOT YOUR EYE ON ANYONE IN PARTICULAR?
THE THWIPSTER HIMSELF...!
WEBWEAVER.
WE WAS HOPIN' YOU'D HAVE SOME TITBITS YOU MIGHT WANNA SHARE.
PARANOID MAN

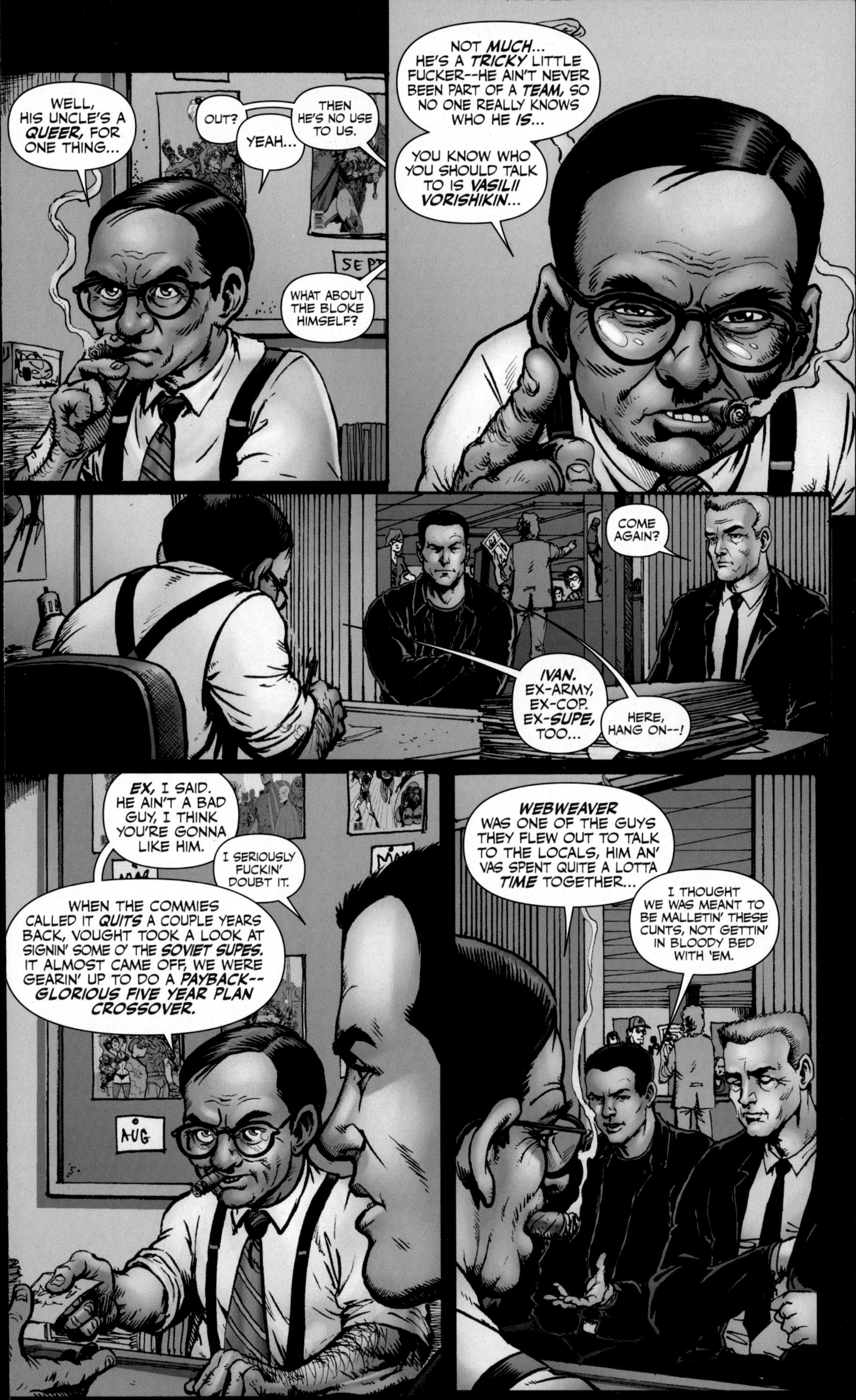

WELL, HIS UNCLE'S A QUEER, FOR ONE THING...
OUT?
YEAH...
THEN HE'S NO USE TO US.
WHAT ABOUT THE BLOKE HIMSELF?
NOT MUCH... HE'S A TRICKY LITTLE FUCKER--HE AIN'T NEVER BEEN PART OF A TEAM, SO NO ONE REALLY KNOWS WHO HE IS...
YOU KNOW WHO YOU SHOULD TALK TO IS VASILII VORISHIKIN...
COME AGAIN?
IVAN. EX-ARMY, EX-COP. EX-SUPE, TOO...
HERE, HANG ON--!
EX, I SAID. HE AIN'T A BAD GUY, I THINK YOU'RE GONNA LIKE HIM.
I SERIOUSLY FUCKIN' DOUBT IT.
WHEN THE COMMIES CALLED IT QUITS A COUPLE YEARS BACK, VOUGHT TOOK A LOOK AT SIGNIN' SOME O' THE SOVIET SUPES. IT ALMOST CAME OFF, WE WERE GEARIN' UP TO DO A PAYBACK--GLORIOUS FIVE YEAR PLAN CROSSOVER.
WEBWEAVER WAS ONE OF THE GUYS THEY FLEW OUT TO TALK TO THE LOCALS, HIM AN' VAS SPENT QUITE A LOTTA TIME TOGETHER...
I THOUGHT WE WAS MEANT TO BE MALLETIN' THESE CUNTS, NOT GETTIN' IN BLOODY BED WITH 'EM.

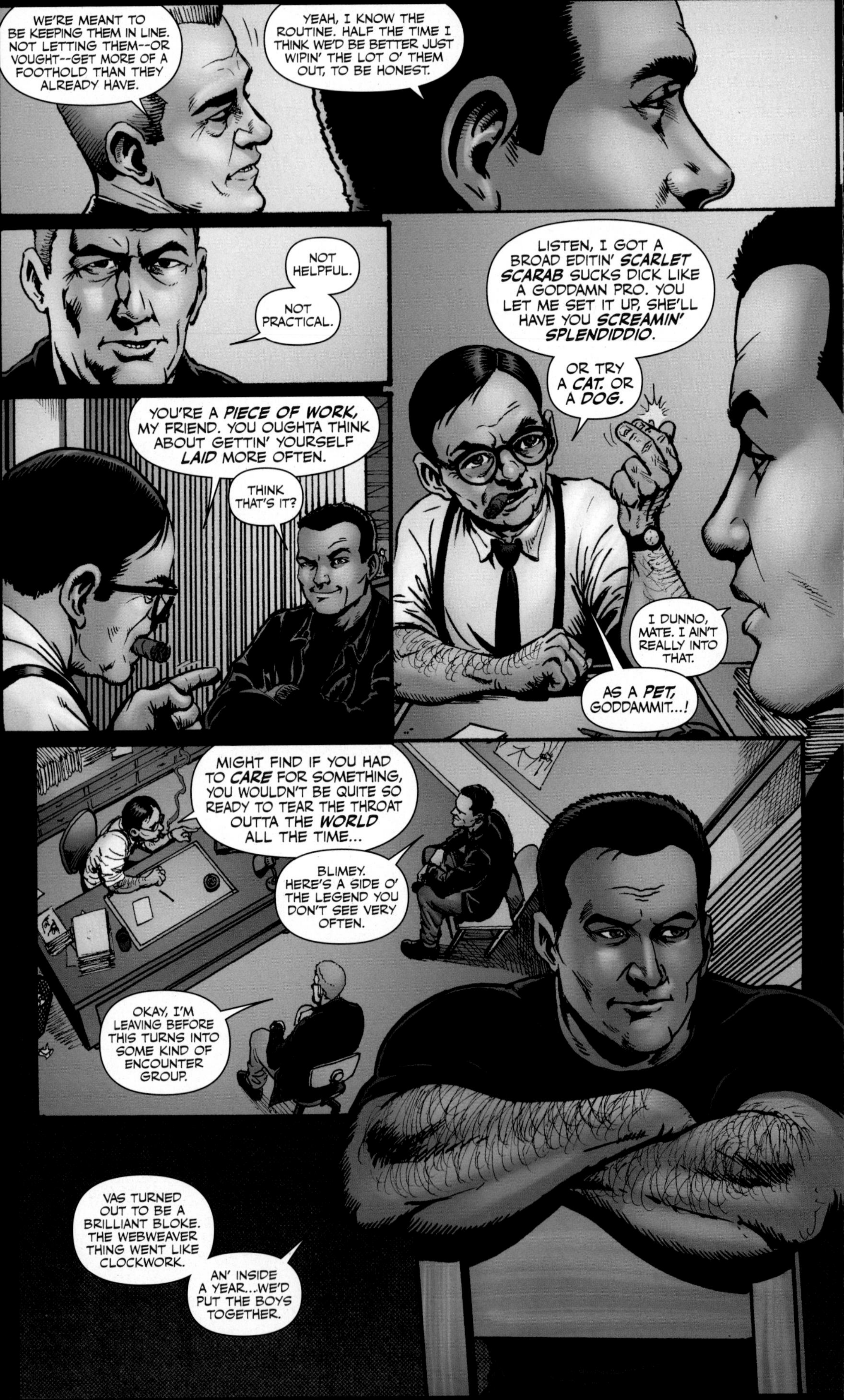
WE'RE MEANT TO BE KEEPING THEM IN LINE. NOT LETTING THEM--OR VOUGHT--GET MORE OF A FOOTHOLD THAN THEY ALREADY HAVE.
YEAH, I KNOW THE ROUTINE. HALF THE TIME I THINK WE'D BE BETTER JUST WIPIN' THE LOT O' THEM OUT, TO BE HONEST.
NOT HELPFUL.
NOT PRACTICAL.
LISTEN, I GOT A BROAD EDITIN' SCARLET SCARAB SUCKS DICK LIKE A GODDAMN PRO. YOU LET ME SET IT UP, SHE'LL HAVE YOU SCREAMIN' SPLENDIDDIO.
OR TRY A CAT. OR A DOG.
YOU'RE A PIECE OF WORK, MY FRIEND. YOU OUGHTA THINK ABOUT GETTIN' YOURSELF LAID MORE OFTEN.
THINK THAT'S IT?
I DUNNO, MATE. I AIN'T REALLY INTO THAT.
AS A PET, GODDAMMIT...!
MIGHT FIND IF YOU HAD TO CARE FOR SOMETHING, YOU WOULDN'T BE QUITE SO READY TO TEAR THE THROAT OUTTA THE WORLD ALL THE TIME...
BLIMEY. HERE'S A SIDE O' THE LEGEND YOU DON'T SEE VERY OFTEN.
OKAY, I'M LEAVING BEFORE THIS TURNS INTO SOME KIND OF ENCOUNTER GROUP.
VAS TURNED OUT TO BE A BRILLIANT BLOKE. THE WEBWEAVER THING WENT LIKE CLOCKWORK.
AN' INSIDE A YEAR...WE'D PUT THE BOYS TOGETHER.

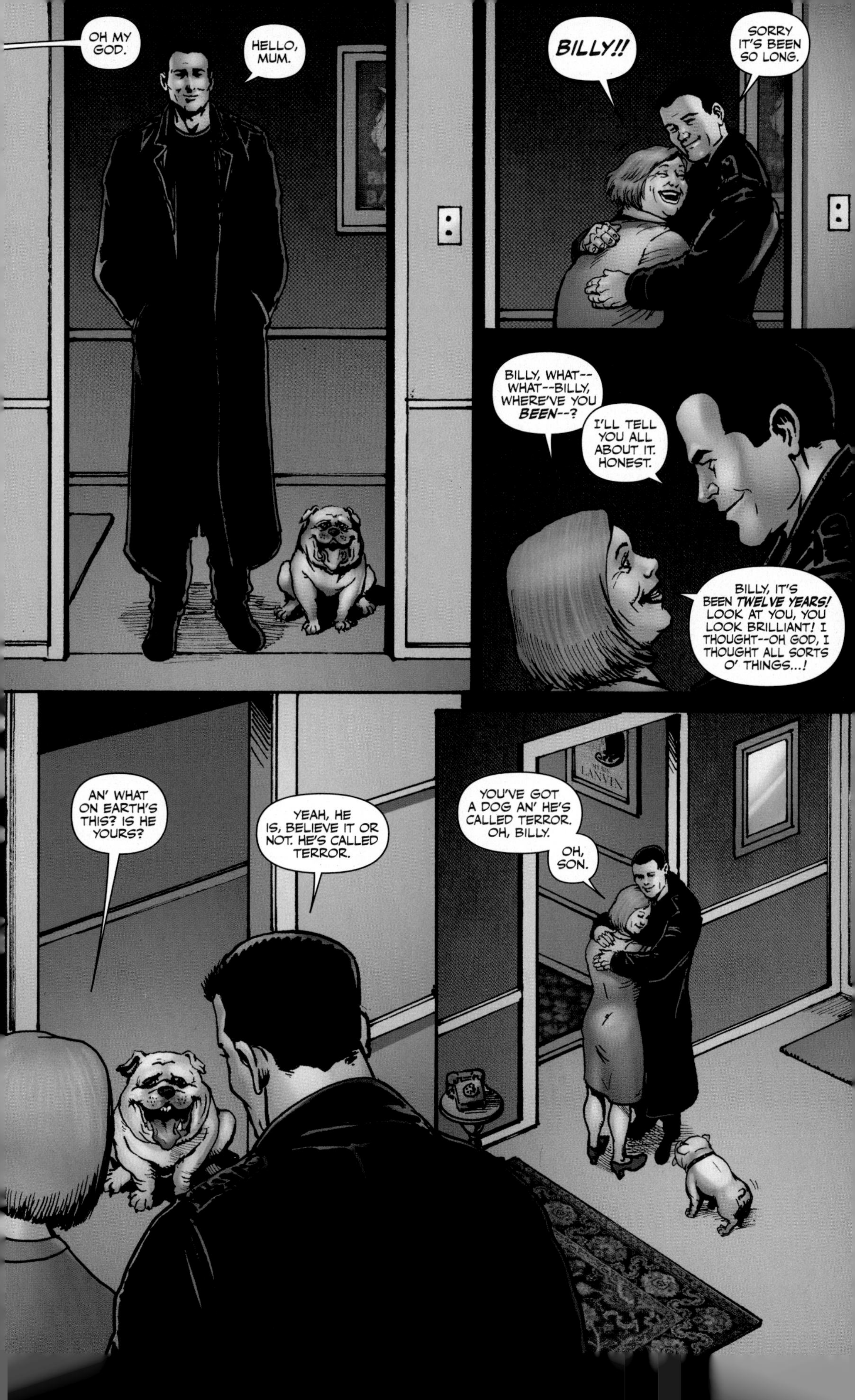
OH MY GOD.
HELLO, MUM.
BILLY!!
SORRY IT'S BEEN SO LONG.
BILLY, WHAT-- WHAT--BILLY, WHERE'VE YOU BEEN--?
I'LL TELL YOU ALL ABOUT IT. HONEST.
BILLY, IT'S BEEN TWELVE YEARS! LOOK AT YOU, YOU LOOK BRILLIANT! I THOUGHT--OH GOD, I THOUGHT ALL SORTS O' THINGS...!
AN' WHAT ON EARTH'S THIS? IS HE YOURS?
YEAH, HE IS, BELIEVE IT OR NOT. HE'S CALLED TERROR.
LANVIN
YOU'VE GOT A DOG AN' HE'S CALLED TERROR. OH, BILLY.
OH, SON.

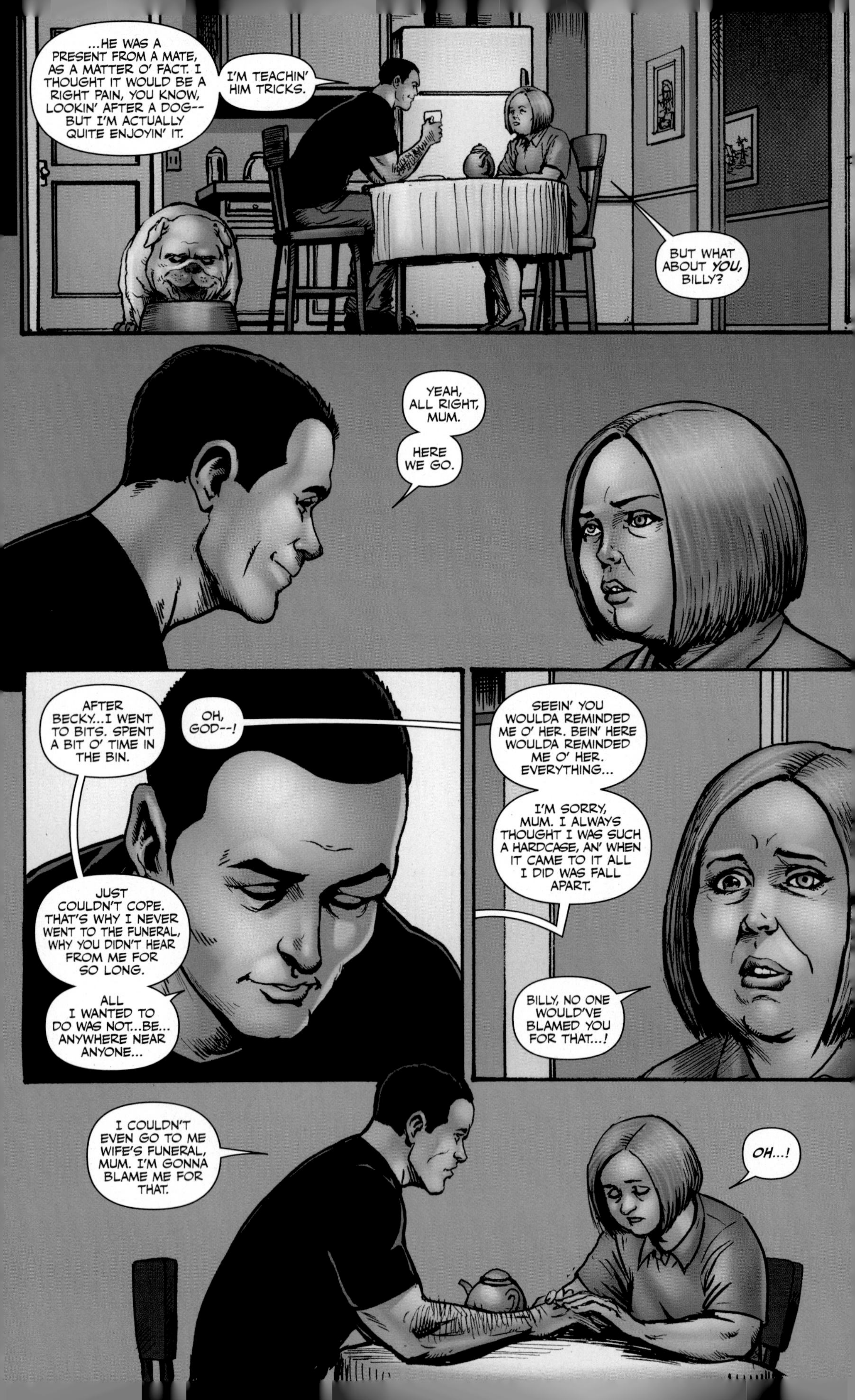
...HE WAS A PRESENT FROM A MATE, AS A MATTER O' FACT. I THOUGHT IT WOULD BE A RIGHT PAIN, YOU KNOW, LOOKIN' AFTER A DOG-- BUT I'M ACTUALLY QUITE ENJOYIN' IT.
I'M TEACHIN' HIM TRICKS.
BUT WHAT ABOUT *YOU,* BILLY?
YEAH, ALL RIGHT, MUM.
HERE WE GO.
AFTER BECKY...I WENT TO BITS. SPENT A BIT O' TIME IN THE BIN.
OH, GOD--!
JUST COULDN'T COPE. THAT'S WHY I NEVER WENT TO THE FUNERAL, WHY YOU DIDN'T HEAR FROM ME FOR SO LONG.
ALL I WANTED TO DO WAS NOT...BE... ANYWHERE NEAR ANYONE...
SEEIN' YOU WOULDA REMINDED ME O' HER. BEIN' HERE WOULDA REMINDED ME O' HER. EVERYTHING...
I'M SORRY, MUM. I ALWAYS THOUGHT I WAS SUCH A HARDCASE, AN' WHEN IT CAME TO IT ALL I DID WAS FALL APART.
BILLY, NO ONE WOULD'VE BLAMED YOU FOR THAT...!
I COULDN'T EVEN GO TO ME WIFE'S FUNERAL, MUM. I'M GONNA BLAME ME FOR THAT.
OH...!

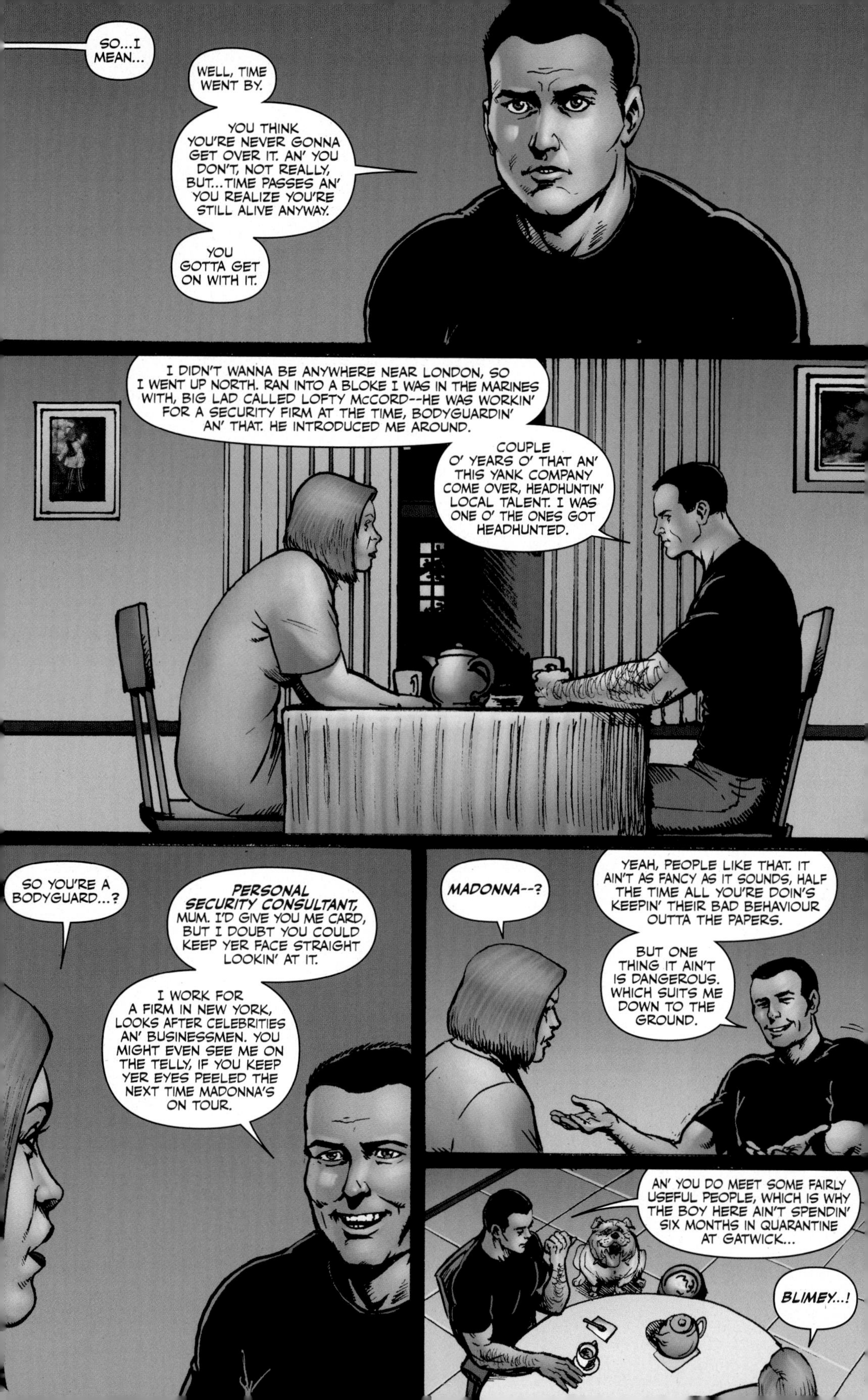
SO...I MEAN...
WELL, TIME WENT BY.
YOU THINK YOU'RE NEVER GONNA GET OVER IT. AN' YOU DON'T, NOT REALLY, BUT...TIME PASSES AN' YOU REALIZE YOU'RE STILL ALIVE ANYWAY.
YOU GOTTA GET ON WITH IT.
I DIDN'T WANNA BE ANYWHERE NEAR LONDON, SO I WENT UP NORTH. RAN INTO A BLOKE I WAS IN THE MARINES WITH, BIG LAD CALLED LOFTY McCORD--HE WAS WORKIN' FOR A SECURITY FIRM AT THE TIME, BODYGUARDIN' AN' THAT. HE INTRODUCED ME AROUND.
COUPLE O' YEARS O' THAT AN' THIS YANK COMPANY COME OVER, HEADHUNTIN' LOCAL TALENT. I WAS ONE O' THE ONES GOT HEADHUNTED.
SO YOU'RE A BODYGUARD...?
PERSONAL SECURITY CONSULTANT, MUM. I'D GIVE YOU ME CARD, BUT I DOUBT YOU COULD KEEP YER FACE STRAIGHT LOOKIN' AT IT.
I WORK FOR A FIRM IN NEW YORK, LOOKS AFTER CELEBRITIES AN' BUSINESSMEN. YOU MIGHT EVEN SEE ME ON THE TELLY, IF YOU KEEP YER EYES PEELED THE NEXT TIME MADONNA'S ON TOUR.
MADONNA--?
YEAH, PEOPLE LIKE THAT. IT AIN'T AS FANCY AS IT SOUNDS, HALF THE TIME ALL YOU'RE DOIN'S KEEPIN' THEIR BAD BEHAVIOUR OUTTA THE PAPERS.
BUT ONE THING IT AIN'T IS DANGEROUS. WHICH SUITS ME DOWN TO THE GROUND.
AN' YOU DO MEET SOME FAIRLY USEFUL PEOPLE, WHICH IS WHY THE BOY HERE AIN'T SPENDIN' SIX MONTHS IN QUARANTINE AT GATWICK...
BLIMEY...!

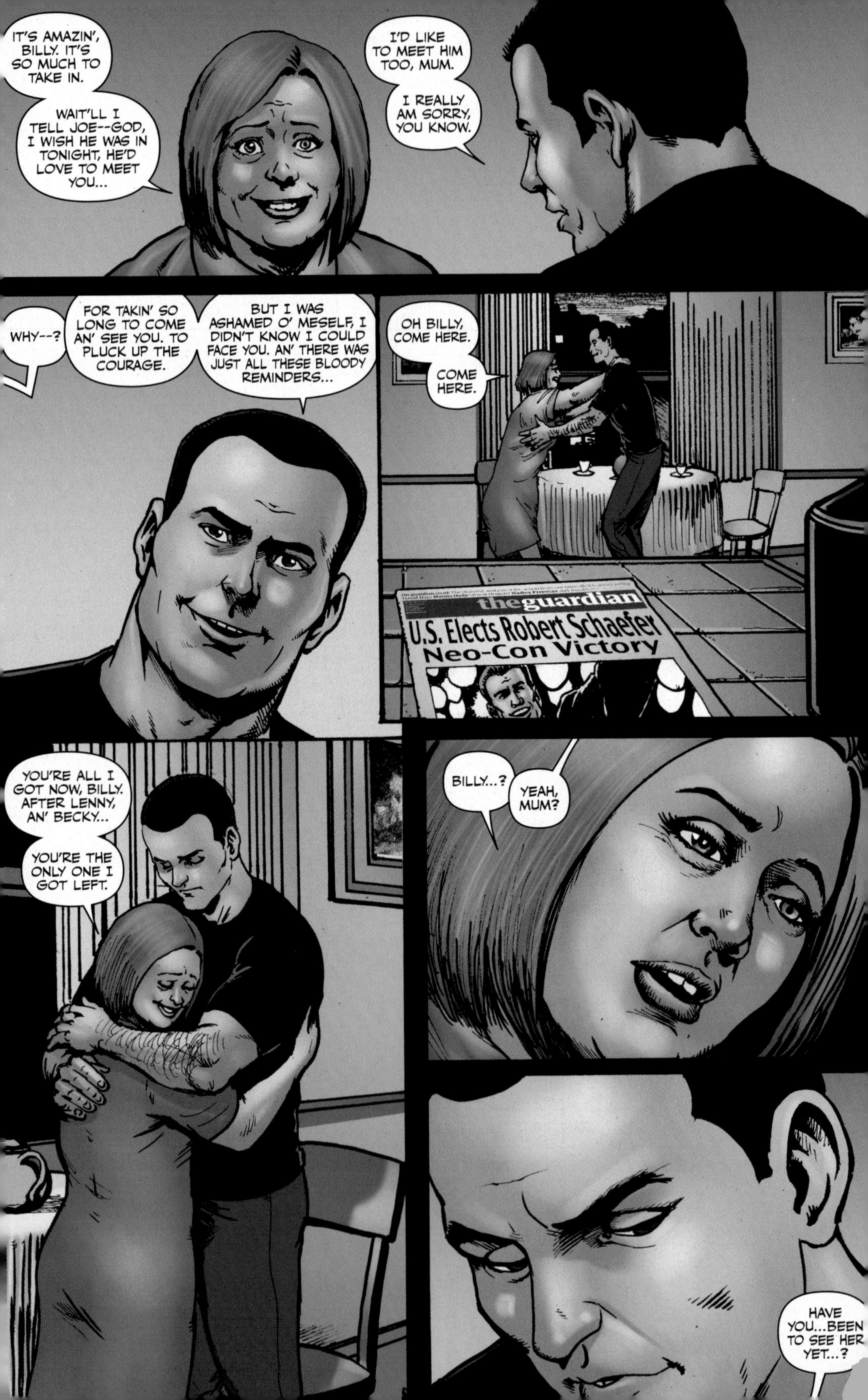
IT'S AMAZIN', BILLY. IT'S SO MUCH TO TAKE IN.
WAIT'LL I TELL JOE--GOD, I WISH HE WAS IN TONIGHT, HE'D LOVE TO MEET YOU...
I'D LIKE TO MEET HIM TOO, MUM.
I REALLY AM SORRY, YOU KNOW.
WHY--?
FOR TAKIN' SO LONG TO COME AN' SEE YOU. TO PLUCK UP THE COURAGE.
BUT I WAS ASHAMED O' MESELF, I DIDN'T KNOW I COULD FACE YOU. AN' THERE WAS JUST ALL THESE BLOODY REMINDERS...
OH BILLY, COME HERE.
COME HERE.
theguardian
U.S. Elects Robert Schaefer
Neo-Con Victory
YOU'RE ALL I GOT NOW, BILLY. AFTER LENNY, AN' BECKY...
YOU'RE THE ONLY ONE I GOT LEFT.
BILLY...?
YEAH, MUM?
HAVE YOU...BEEN TO SEE HER YET...?

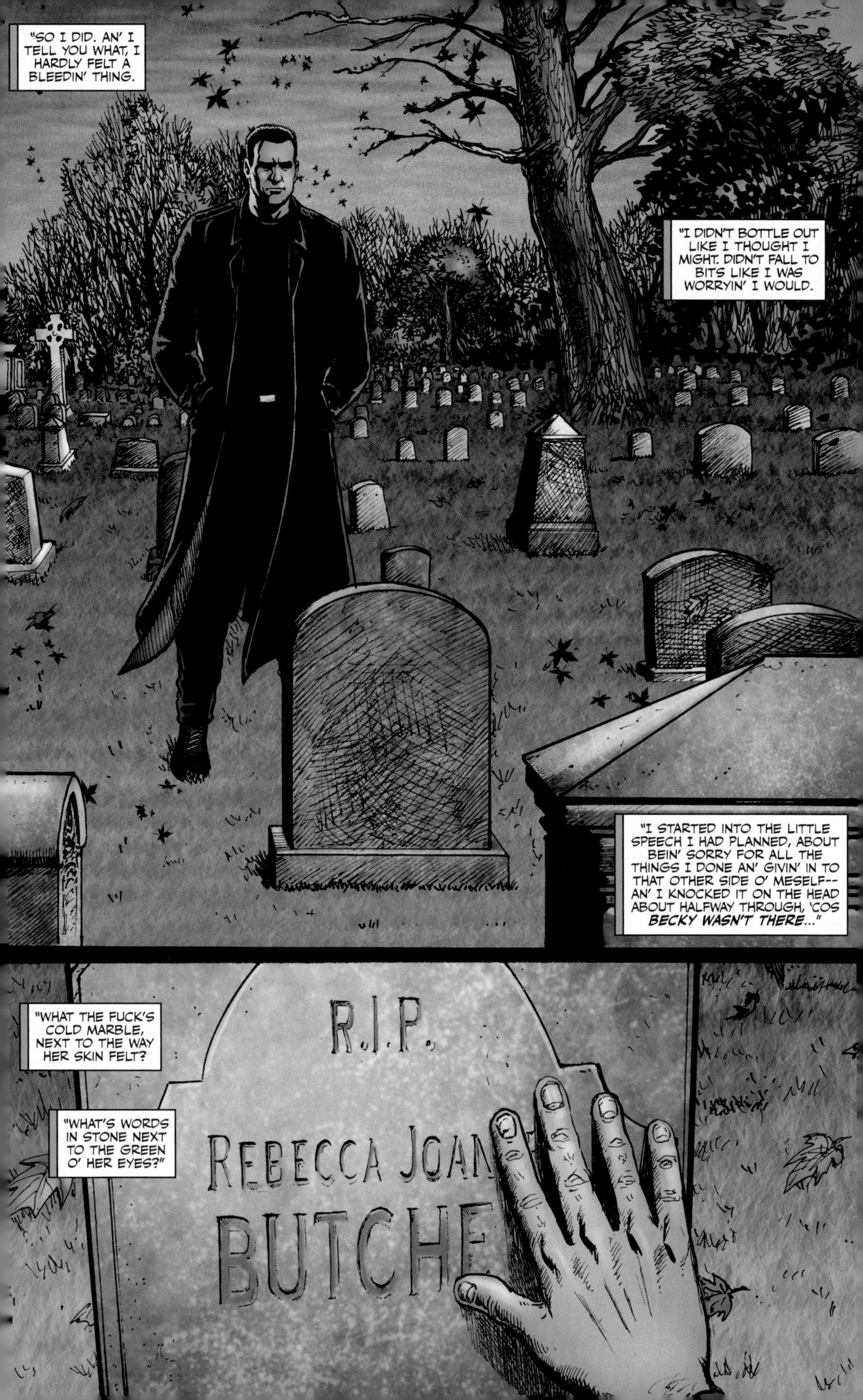
"SO I DID. AN' I TELL YOU WHAT, I HARDLY FELT A BLEEDIN' THING.
"I DIDN'T BOTTLE OUT LIKE I THOUGHT I MIGHT. DIDN'T FALL TO BITS LIKE I WAS WORRYIN' I WOULD.
"I STARTED INTO THE LITTLE SPEECH I HAD PLANNED, ABOUT BEIN' SORRY FOR ALL THE THINGS I DONE AN' GIVIN' IN TO THAT OTHER SIDE O' MESELF-- AN' I KNOCKED IT ON THE HEAD ABOUT HALFWAY THROUGH, 'COS *BECKY WASN'T THERE...*"
"WHAT THE FUCK'S COLD MARBLE, NEXT TO THE WAY HER SKIN FELT?
"WHAT'S WORDS IN STONE NEXT TO THE GREEN O' HER EYES?"
R.I.P.
REBECCA JOAN
BUTCHE

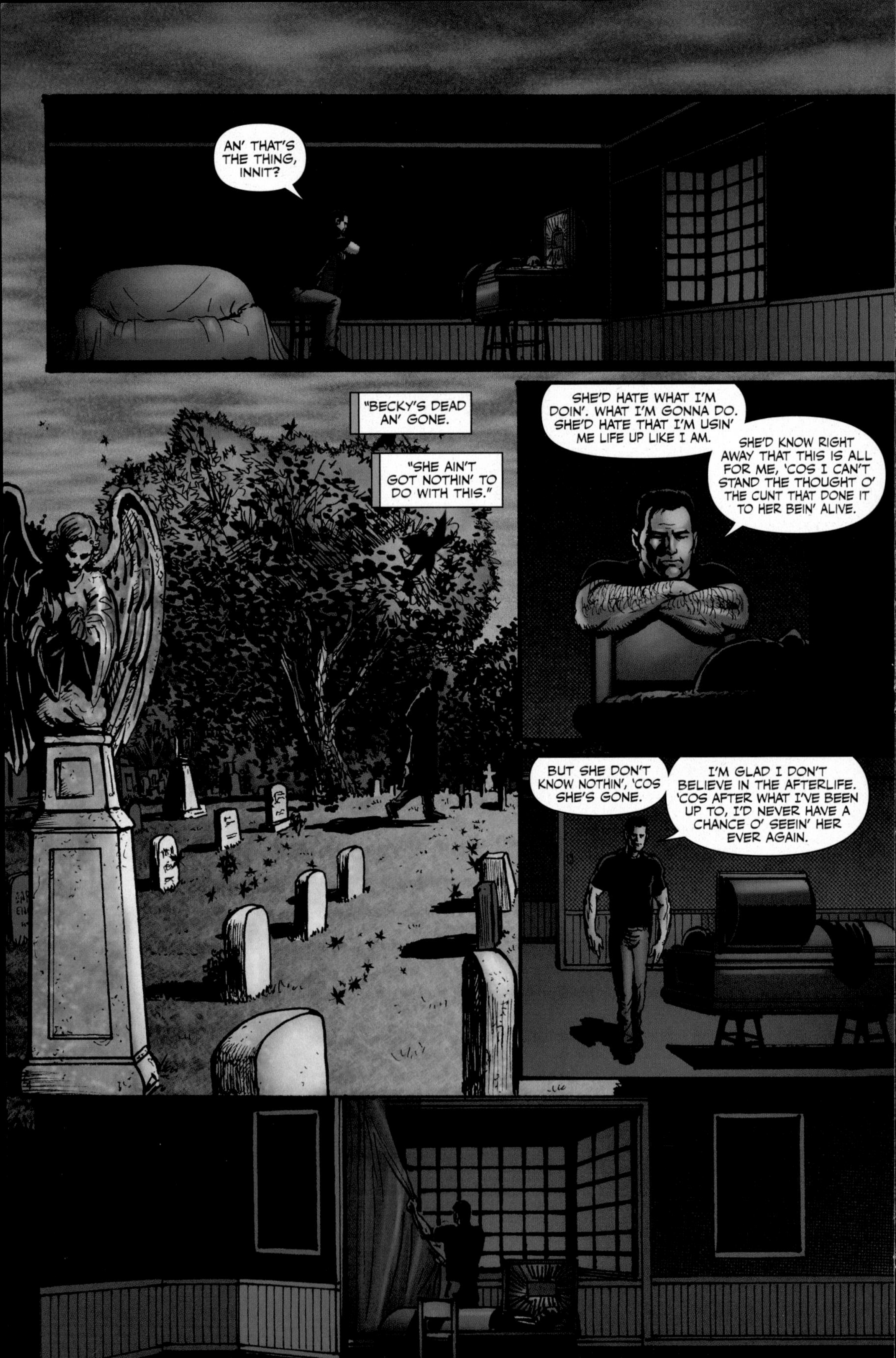
AN' THAT'S THE THING, INNIT?
"BECKY'S DEAD AN' GONE.
"SHE AIN'T GOT NOTHIN' TO DO WITH THIS."
SHE'D HATE WHAT I'M DOIN'. WHAT I'M GONNA DO. SHE'D HATE THAT I'M USIN' ME LIFE UP LIKE I AM.
SHE'D KNOW RIGHT AWAY THAT THIS IS ALL FOR ME, 'COS I CAN'T STAND THE THOUGHT O' THE CUNT THAT DONE IT TO HER BEIN' ALIVE.
BUT SHE DON'T KNOW NOTHIN', 'COS SHE'S GONE.
I'M GLAD I DON'T BELIEVE IN THE AFTERLIFE. 'COS AFTER WHAT I'VE BEEN UP TO, I'D NEVER HAVE A CHANCE O' SEEIN' HER EVER AGAIN.

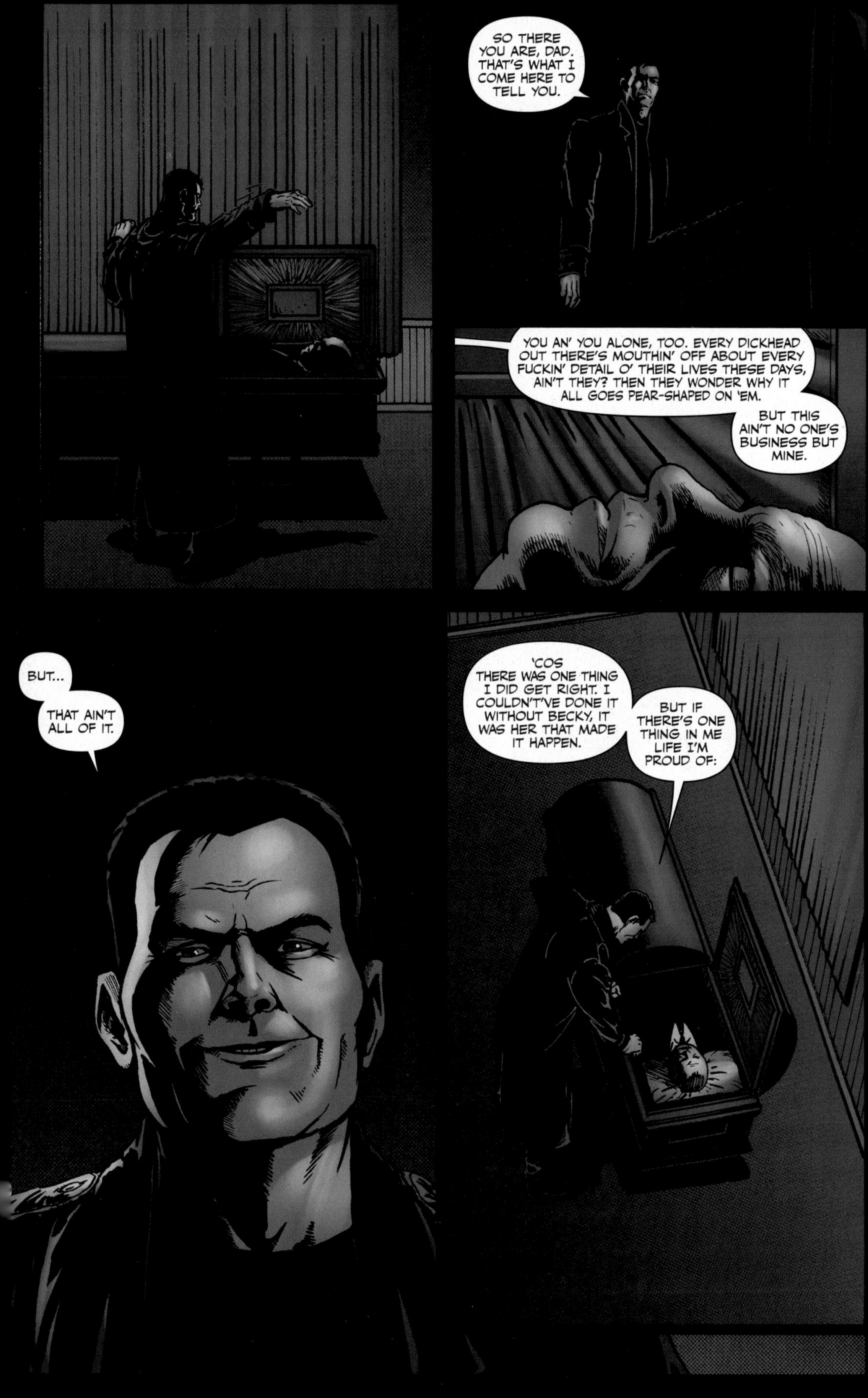
SO THERE YOU ARE, DAD. THAT'S WHAT I COME HERE TO TELL YOU.
YOU AN' YOU ALONE, TOO. EVERY DICKHEAD OUT THERE'S MOUTHIN' OFF ABOUT EVERY FUCKIN' DETAIL O' THEIR LIVES THESE DAYS, AIN'T THEY? THEN THEY WONDER WHY IT ALL GOES PEAR-SHAPED ON 'EM.
BUT THIS AIN'T NO ONE'S BUSINESS BUT MINE.
BUT...
THAT AIN'T ALL OF IT.
'COS THERE WAS ONE THING I DID GET RIGHT. I COULDN'T'VE DONE IT WITHOUT BECKY, IT WAS HER THAT MADE IT HAPPEN.
BUT IF THERE'S ONE THING IN ME LIFE I'M PROUD OF:

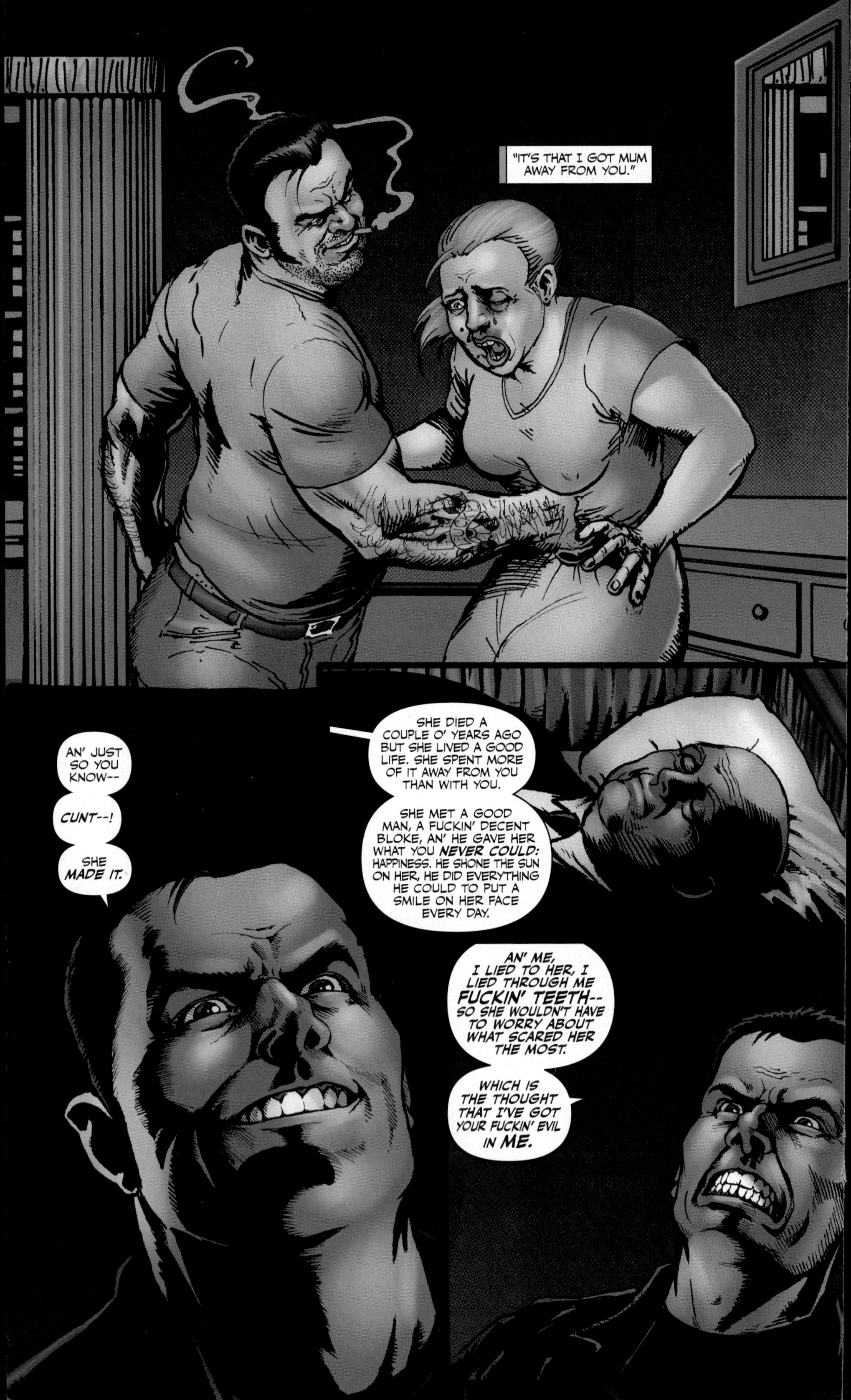
"IT'S THAT I GOT MUM AWAY FROM YOU."
AN' JUST SO YOU KNOW--
CUNT--!
SHE MADE IT.
SHE DIED A COUPLE O' YEARS AGO BUT SHE LIVED A GOOD LIFE. SHE SPENT MORE OF IT AWAY FROM YOU THAN WITH YOU.
SHE MET A GOOD MAN, A FUCKIN' DECENT BLOKE, AN' HE GAVE HER WHAT YOU NEVER COULD: HAPPINESS. HE SHONE THE SUN ON HER, HE DID EVERYTHING HE COULD TO PUT A SMILE ON HER FACE EVERY DAY.
AN' ME, I LIED TO HER, I LIED THROUGH ME FUCKIN' TEETH-- SO SHE WOULDN'T HAVE TO WORRY ABOUT WHAT SCARED HER THE MOST.
WHICH IS THE THOUGHT THAT I'VE GOT YOUR FUCKIN' EVIL IN ME.

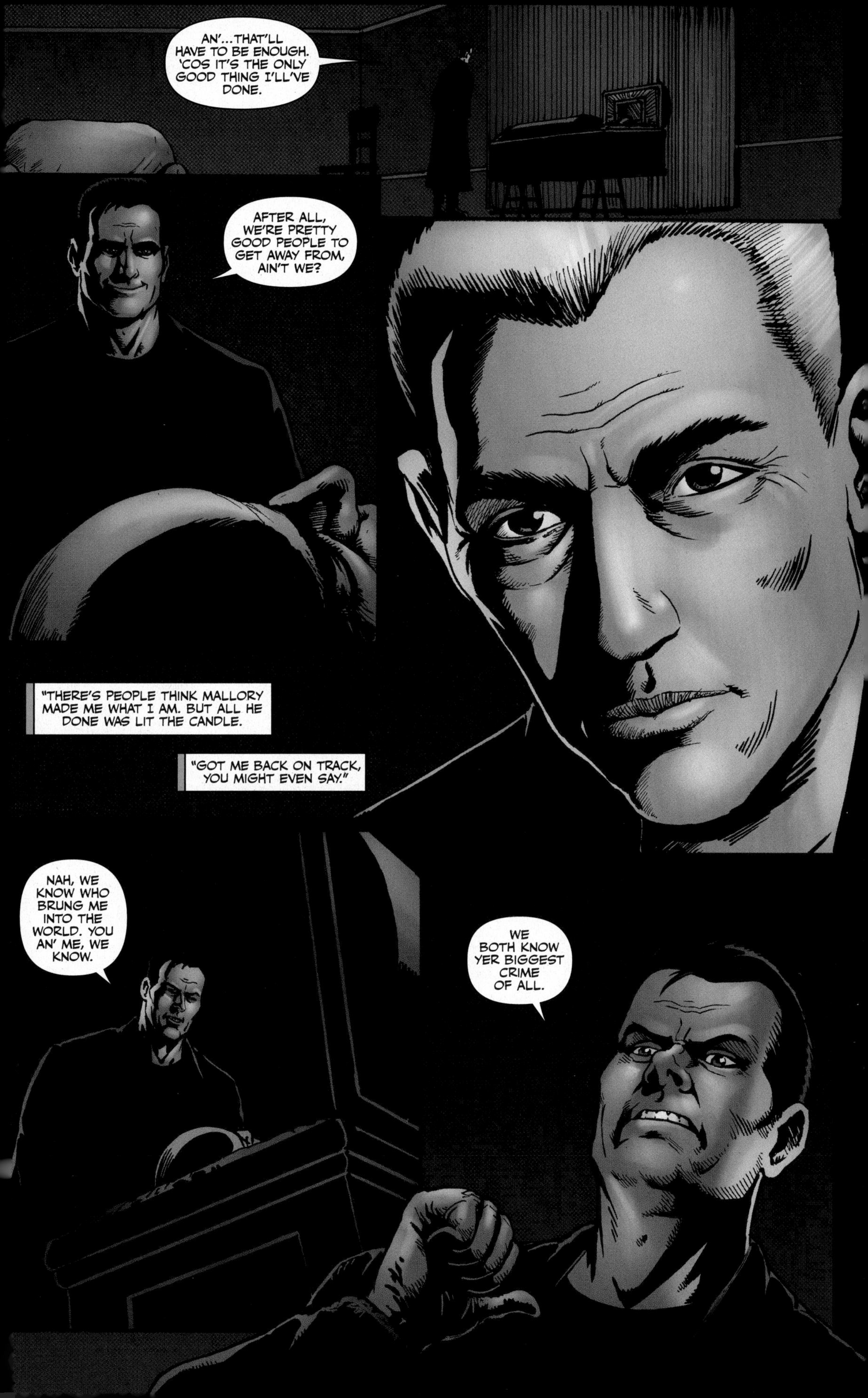
AN'...THAT'LL HAVE TO BE ENOUGH. 'COS IT'S THE ONLY GOOD THING I'LL'VE DONE.
AFTER ALL, WE'RE PRETTY GOOD PEOPLE TO GET AWAY FROM, AIN'T WE?
"THERE'S PEOPLE THINK MALLORY MADE ME WHAT I AM. BUT ALL HE DONE WAS LIT THE CANDLE.
"GOT ME BACK ON TRACK, YOU MIGHT EVEN SAY."
NAH, WE KNOW WHO BRUNG ME INTO THE WORLD. YOU AN' ME, WE KNOW.
WE BOTH KNOW YER BIGGEST CRIME OF ALL.

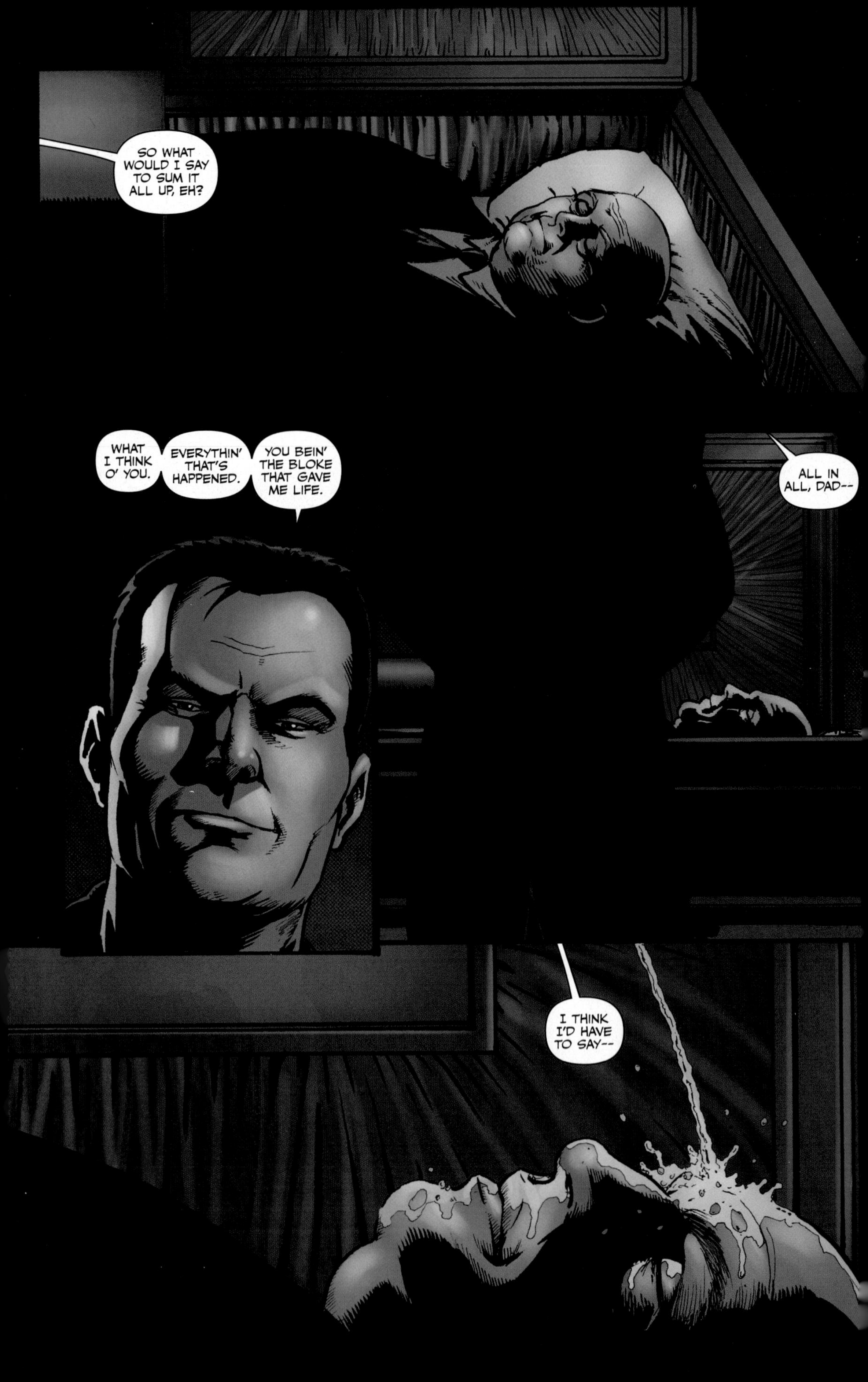
SO WHAT WOULD I SAY TO SUM IT ALL UP, EH?
ALL IN ALL, DAD--
WHAT I THINK O' YOU.
EVERYTHIN' THAT'S HAPPENED.
YOU BEIN' THE BLOKE THAT GAVE ME LIFE.
I THINK I'D HAVE TO SAY--

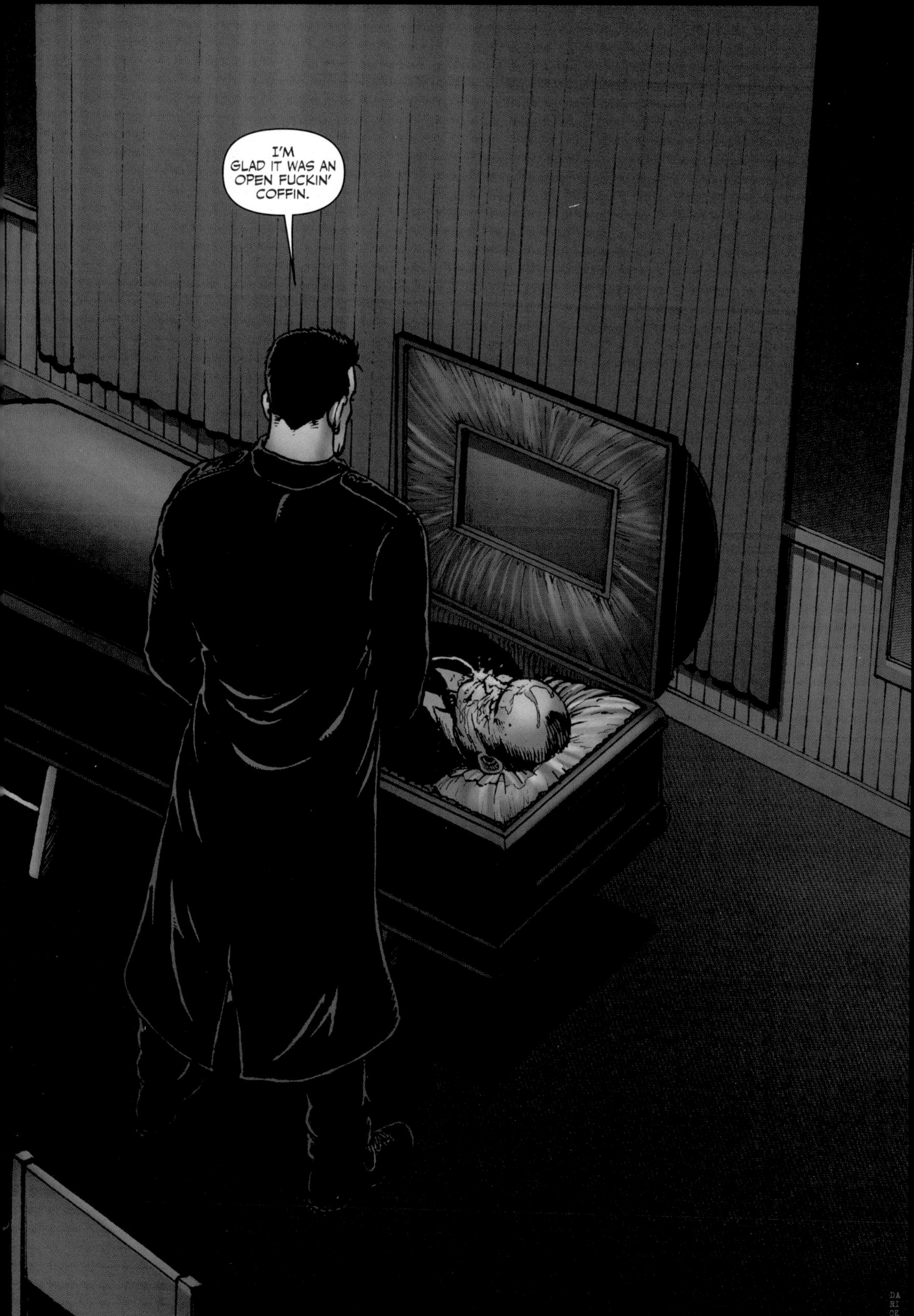
I'M GLAD IT WAS AN OPEN FUCKIN' COFFIN.

END

And there was nothing on the marker to explain to Mrs. Feathers
why her only daughter had married a known thief and murderer,
a man of notoriously violent and intemperate disposition.

-- *Unforgiven,* screenplay by David Webb Peoples

DON'T MISS THESE GREAT COLLECTIONS FROM *NEW YORK TIMES* BEST-SELLING AUTHOR

GARTH ENNIS & DYNAMITE

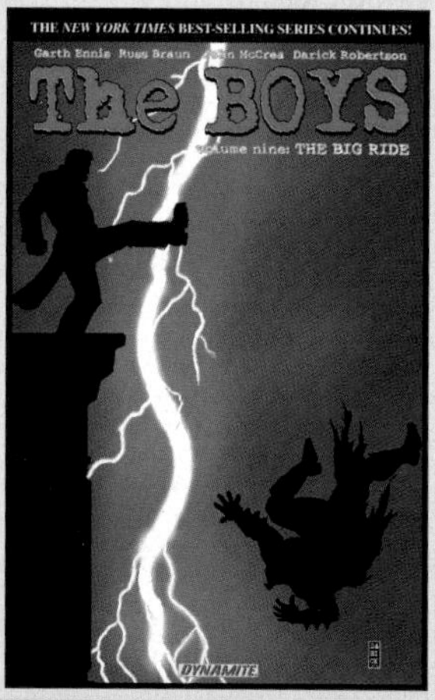

THE NEW YORK TIMES BEST-SELLING SERIES CONTINUES!
Garth Ennis Russ Braun John McCrea Darick Robertson
The BOYS
volume nine: THE BIG RIDE
DYNAMITE

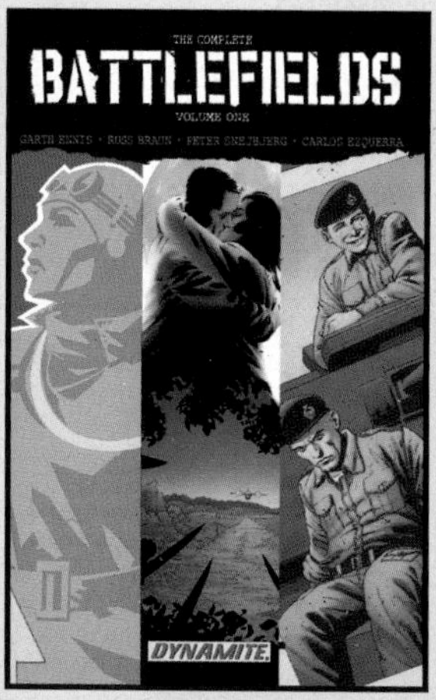

THE COMPLETE
BATTLEFIELDS
VOLUME ONE
GARTH ENNIS • RUSS BRAUN • PETER SNEJBJERG • CARLOS EZQUERRA
DYNAMITE

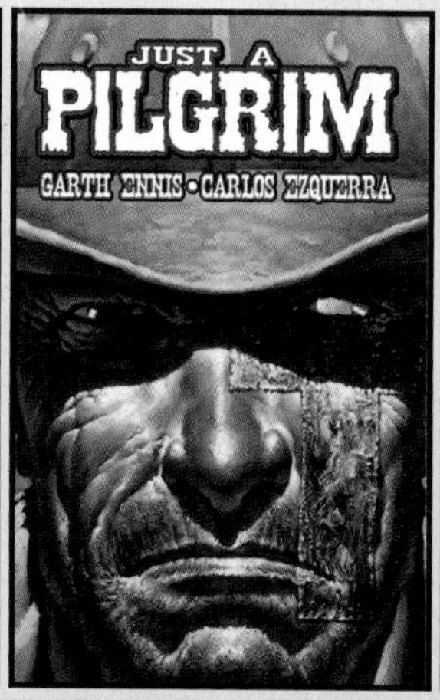

JUST A
PILGRIM
GARTH ENNIS • CARLOS EZQUERRA

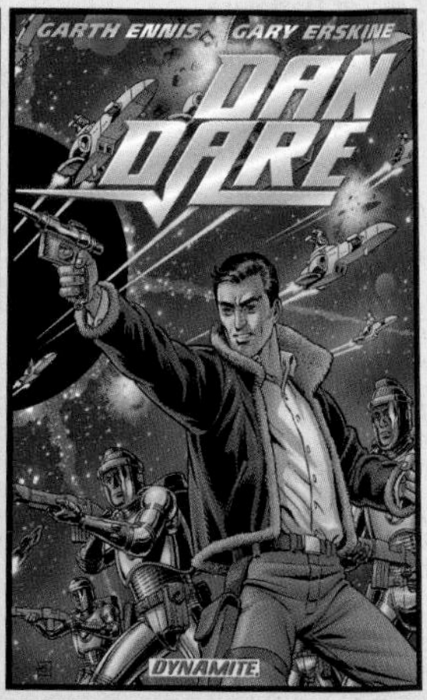

GARTH ENNIS GARY ERSKINE
DAN DARE
DYNAMITE

THE BOYS DEFINITIVE EDITION VOL. 1 HARDCOVER...........(SOLD OUT!).............**1933305800**
- Collecting issues 1-14 of the hit series by Ennis and Robertson

THE BOYS DEFINITIVE EDITION VOL. 2 HARDCOVER...........**1606900730**
- Collecting issues 15-30 of the hit series by Ennis and Robertson

THE BOYS DEFINITIVE EDITION VOL. 3 HARDCOVER...........**1606901656**
- Collecting issues 31-38 plus the 6-issue Herogasm mini-series

THE BOYS VOL. 1: THE NAME OF THE GAME...........**1933305738**
- Collects issues 1-6 by Ennis & Robertson

THE BOYS VOL. 2: GET SOME...........**1933305681**
- Collects issues 7-14 by Ennis, Robertson and Snejbjerg

THE BOYS VOL. 3: GOOD FOR THE SOUL...........**1933305924**
- Collects issues 15-22 by Ennis & Robertson

THE BOYS VOL. 4: WE GOTTA GO NOW...........**1606900358**
- Collects issues 23-30 by Ennis, Robertson and Higgins

THE BOYS VOL. 5: HEROGASM...........**160690082X**
- Collects issues 1-6 of the hit mini-series by Ennis and McCrea

THE BOYS VOL. 6: THE SELF-PRESERVATION SOCIETY...........**1606901257**
- Collects issues 31-38 by Ennis, Robertson and Ezquerra

THE BOYS VOL. 7: THE INNOCENTS...........**1606901508**
- Collects issues 39-47 by Ennis, Robertson, Braun & McCrea

THE BOYS VOL. 8: HIGHLAND LADDIE...........**1606902075**
- Collects issues 1-6 by Ennis & McCrea

THE BOYS VOL. 9: THE BIG RIDE...........**1606902202**
- Collects issues 48-59 by Ennis, Braun & McCrea

THE COMPLETE BATTLEFIELDS VOL. 1 HARDCOVER...........(SOLD OUT!)...........**160690079X**

THE COMPLETE BATTLEFIELDS VOL. 1 TRADE PAPERBACK...........**1606902555**
- Collecting the first 3 Battlefields mini-series by Ennis, Braun, Snejbjerg and Ezquerra

THE COMPLETE BATTLEFIELDS VOL. 2 HARDCOVER...........**1606902229**
- Collecting the final 3 Battlefields mini-series by Ennis, Braun, Holden and Ezquerra

BATTLEFIELDS VOL. 1: THE NIGHT WITCHES...........**1606900285**
- Collects issues 1-3 by Ennis and Braun

BATTLEFIELDS VOL. 2: DEAR BILLY...........**1606900579**
- Collects issues 1-3 by Ennis and Snejbjerg

BATTLEFIELDS VOL. 3: THE TANKIES...........**1606900757**
- Collects issues 1-3 by Ennis and Ezquerra

BATTLEFIELDS VOL. 4: HAPPY VALLEY...........**1606901281**
- Collects issues 1-3 by Ennis and Holden

BATTLEFIELDS VOL. 5: THE FIREFLY AND HIS MAJESTY...........**1606901451**
- Collects issues 4-6 by Ennis and Ezquerra

BATTLEFIELDS VOL. 6: MOTHERLAND...........**1606902210**
- Collects issues 7-9 by Ennis and Braun

THE COMPLETE JUST A PILGRIM HARDCOVER...........**160690003X**

THE COMPLETE JUST A PILGRIM TRADE PAPERBACK...........**1606900072**
- Both mini-series by Ennis and Ezquerra collected together for the first time

DAN DARE OMNIBUS HARDCOVER...........**1606900277**

DAN DARE OMNIBUS TRADE PAPERBACK...........**1606900404**
- Collecting issues 1-7 by Ennis and Erskine

DYNAMITE ENTERTAINMENT **WWW.DYNAMITEENTERTAINMENT.COM** Newsletters • Contests • Downloads • Forums • More